Undercover Muslim

Undercover Muslim

A JOURNEY INTO YEMEN

THEO PADNOS

THE BODLEY HEAD
LONDON

Published by The Bodley Head 2011

2 4 6 8 10 9 7 5 3 1

Copyright © Theo Padnos 2011

Theo Padnos has asserted his right under the Copyright, Designs
and Patents Act 1988 to be identified as the author of this work

First published in Great Britain in 2011 by
The Bodley Head
Random House, 20 Vauxhall Bridge Road,
London SW1V 2SA

www.bodleyhead.co.uk
www.randomhouse.co.uk

Addresses for companies within The Random House Group Limited can be found at:
www.randomhouse.co.uk/offices.htm

The Random House Group Limited Reg. No. 954009

A CIP catalogue record for this book
is available from the British Library

ISBN 9781847920843

The Random House Group Limited supports The Forest
Stewardship Council® (FSC®), the leading international forest
certification organisation. All our titles that are printed on
Greenpeace approved FSC® certified paper carry the FSC® logo.
Our paper procurement policy can be found at
www.randomhouse.co.uk/environment

MIX
Paper from
responsible sources
FSC® C016897
FSC
www.fsc.org

Typeset by Palimpsest Book Production Limited, Falkirk, Stirlingshire
Printed and bound in Great Britain by CPI Group PLC

I dedicate this book to everyone who taught me about Islam, to everyone who fixed my bike when it was really broken, and to everyone who gave me money when I really needed it (thanks, Mom).

Contents

Introduction

The Yemeni American internet imam, Anwar Awlaki, came into his own in the summer of 2008. He had previously been known to a small collection of admirers mostly through cassettes and pamphlets but now, leveraging the power of the internet, his popularity grew. That summer, as wider audiences tuned in, he often wrote about reading. 'Thrice,' he said, he read *Hard Times*; he also read *Oliver Twist, A Tale of Two Cities* and *David Copperfield* (twice). He concluded that Uriah Heep was 'similar to some pitiful Muslims today', that 'the thick and boastful Mr Josiah Bounderby of Coketown was similar to George W. Bush' and that he did not like Shakespeare: 'Probably the only reason he became so famous is because he was English.'

In general, Awlaki felt that books written by unbelievers were a kind of weak medicine which one could administer to oneself or not, whereas books by and for Muslims affected the soul. The best literature of this kind brought the reader into proximity with God.

Such books were not to be read as, say, one might read *Hard Times*. Instead Muslims were to position themselves within the range of these books, and then to allow the power of the text to consume the reader. In describing his encounter with *In the Shade of the Koran*, a twelve-volume commentary on the Koran by Sayyid Qutb, the Egyptian radical, Awlaki described what a reading experience of this order was like:

> Because of the flowing style of Sayyid I would read between 100-150 pages a day. In fact I would read until my eyes got tired. My left eye would get exhausted before the right eye so I would close it with my hand and carry on reading with my right eye until it can handle it no more and would just shut down. My vision started deteriorating especially in my left eye. Was it because of too much reading, or was it because of poor lighting? Allah knows best.

For the fans who read this essay where it was originally published, at anwar-awlaki.com, Sayyid Qutb, and Dickens and Shakespeare, for that matter, were beside the point. Occasionally, readers used to write in to the website to enquire if the Islamic histories and commentaries Awlaki wrote about were available in translation. Sometimes the fans asked Awlaki if Sayyid Qutb was upon the *haq*(the truth) or if he had strayed from it. The great majority of Awlaki's admirers, however, skipped over Sayyid Qutb – and the older, greater philosophers the blogger wrote about – entirely.

The fans were rather interested in the writing of one person in particular: Anwar Awlaki.

'Sheikh,' wrote a blog fan, Abu Dharrar after Anwar had posted his *In the Shade of the Koran* review: 'We need to know more about a scholar from whom we take these precious pearls of knowledge. Please write your biography.'

'i was thinking,' wrote another fan,

> why not know more about the one [sheikh] we listen [to] the most. For the ones that havent met you but InshAllah we will
> If its possible:

Your daily life?
Your Profession?
your hobbies if you have any?
are you married if so do you have children?
Imam Malik liked Bananas haha what foods do you enjoy?
Who were your teachers?

Anwar Awlaki's pronouncements hadn't always generated such enthusiasm but the summer of 2008 was a turning point in his career. In the spring of that year, Yemeni police released him from eighteen months of detention in Sana'a, without a trial.

Shortly thereafter, a group of fans in England set up anwar-awlaki.com. Now for the first time in his career, the itinerant preacher was in minute-to-minute contact with a world of blog fans. He opened a Facebook page.

'Alhamdulillah that you are online Sheikh!' wrote an Abdallah. 'You have benefited the Ummah greatly (already) but we want more! :)'

'I make dua [prayer] that i meet you in person, pray behind you and learn under you,' wrote a correspondent from Australia. He signed himself, 'Your brother on the other side of the earth, Muhammad Hassan.'

'Every person that I have come across who has already listened to the talk of Imam Anwar,' wrote another admirer, 'would like to be close to him and ask more questions or learn more about Islam. Is this not a spirit of Muslim brotherhood?'

That summer, as Anwar wrote abut his reading, his eating habits in prison, and the advisability of Muslims playing guitar (not advisable) the level of fan admiration kept ratcheting upwards. The fans wrote in to say that they loved their 'beloved brother, Sheikh Anwar', that they missed him, needed immediate advice and were wondering why he wrote private emails so rarely.

Others, fearing that Yemeni and American intelligence officials might harm Awlaki, wrote to supply spiritual support: 'Fear ye not!' assured one fan, Muslimah314, quoting from the Koran, 'we are your protectors in this life and in the hereafter. Therein shall ye have all that ye desire.'

Many of these fans had resigned themselves to lives in the West. They spoke of settled families and commitments. But many other fans were not tied down at all; instead they were in a mood to travel. On 14 July, jihad4life wrote with a query about travel study:

> Asalam alikum brother Anwar
> Since you live in Yemen. I was wondering if you can tell
> me if Yemen is [a] good place to seek knowledge.

Other fans like this one, Abdullah ibn Umm Maktum, were more direct:

> Dear Shaykh . . . I have a very short question and that is;
> Do you accept students in Jemen? Please answer it dear
> shaykh, as it is very important for me.

Over time during the summer of 2008, anwar-awlaki.com became an unsettling place to hang out online. The site, which has since been removed from the internet, plied its visitors with news of upcoming Paltalk lectures and links to lectures already delivered. The speeches themselves were learned but often wool-gathered or quoted at too conspicuous length from the scriptures, or combined these oratorical flaws somehow into fifty-megabyte blocks of speechifying. Nevertheless the ardour of the fans knew no bounds. There they were on page after page of anwar-awlaki. com, down in the comments section, declaring themselves prepared to do 'whatever you think best', 'to study with you one day as well as join you on any front', and to 'go and study overseas inshaAllah'. Many of the fans said they couldn't speak Arabic. Many others were still having issues with English. Now, it seemed, they were ready to pick up sticks, to move to Yemen, and to plunge into the study of the early medieval Arabic in which the Koran was written.

It would have been entirely reasonable for an outsider, happening by for the first time, to wonder: *what on earth is going on here?*

Because I was imprisoned in Yemen myself, and because, in other respects, I have followed Awlaki's footsteps – the travel to Yemen, the settling into a mosque there, the years of Koranic study – the atmosphere at Awlaki's website has always been a relatively familiar thing to me. Though I never recognised any of the fans personally, I've studied with this demographic for years, in Yemen and Syria, and by now I know enough about its enthusiasms to know that the excitement has almost nothing to do with Awlaki's preaching and still less to do with his writing. Awlaki's extraordinary accomplishment is his life.

It's no less extraordinary for its familiar opening chapters. Awlaki's story begins where the stories of his fans begin: in suburban tranquillity in the West. In his case, it was Albuquerque, New Mexico, in the heart of a middle-class family, the elder generation of which had recently arrived from Yemen. For Awlaki, there was normal schooling in America followed by a standard university degree (BS Civil Engineering, Colorado State, 1994). Later, there was an abandoned attempt at an advanced degree (Human Resource Development, George Washington University, 2001—) and a period of drifting between his parents' homeland and American Muslim communities in San Diego and Falls Church, Virginia.

The story picks up momentum after 2001 when 'a climate of fear and oppression' (the phrase belongs to a fellow imam in Falls Church) caused him to flee, first to London, and from there to Yemen.

In Yemen, Awlaki returned to his parents' native village, an ancient incense capital, now called Shabwa. He established a household here with a local wife, and a string of children.

It's worth pausing at this point in the story to mention an important sub-theme in Awlaki's blog and lectures: the slightly unbelievable piety and silence with which he discusses women. As an American imam, Awlaki was arrested for soliciting prostitutes three times, twice in San Diego and once in Virginia.

Many of the young Westerners who've been turning up in Yemen over the past ten years have also left behind a history of troubled – in some cases anguished – relations with women. Many of them have likewise arrived in Yemen with visions of a local bride – the deep, submissive eyes, the black clothing – dancing in their heads. Some of these young men marry once. Many marry several women.

Awlaki doesn't allow a trace of his former ambivalence to enter his blog. Where women are mentioned – and they are not mentioned much – a spirit of paternal protectiveness hovers over the writing. He is magnanimous. He is wise. The women are grateful and dignified but much too modest to speak.

One reads a lot about this particular model of male–female togetherness in the Koran and in the record of the Prophet Muhammad's deeds and sayings, the hadith. Since women scarcely speak in public in Yemen and rarely reveal details of their domestic lives to anyone under any circumstances, it would be difficult to maintain that such harmony doesn't exist. Perhaps it does. Perhaps in Yemen it is widespread. In any case, to the young men who read Awlaki's blog in the partner-swapping suburbs of the West, the Yemeni model presents a fantasy of love and stability. Sex may be out of control in the West, Awlaki's blog hinted, but out here in Yemen it is not. On the contrary, in a believing society, all is domestic harmony and fruitfulness in the desert.

Awlaki's domestic harmony was interrupted in August 2006, when the Yemeni government arrested him as he was trying to mediate a tribal dispute. It's unlikely that he was doing anything criminal. He was never charged. Still, the local authorities have never looked kindly on self-styled Americo-Yemeni religious figures who turn up in Yemen, particularly when they meddle in local affairs. He was sent off to a basement cell in the political security prison in Sana'a.

For the young sheikh with the international blog audience, the prison spell was a gift from Allah. It bound him much more tightly to his fans and generated writing that is by far his greatest accomplishment as a preacher. It's much better than anything he's done before or since:

> I was in an underground solitary cell made up of four concrete walls, with an iron gate on one side and on the opposite side a small window – rather a hole – covered with iron mesh to allow for some fresh air to come in . . . Then there was the roof with a bulb hanging from it which was on continuously day and night. Then the floor with a mattress 2-3 inches thick, a blanket, a worn off pillow, a plastic plate, a bottle for water . . .
>
> And then there was a Quran. In this environment there is nothing to do and nothing to read but the Quran, and that is when the Quran reveals its secrets. When the hearts are clean; when there is nothing clouding the spirit, the Quran literally overwhelms the heart.

This is Awlaki at his best. The writing works because it discovers the oldest, most heroic Islamic themes – the striving towards virtue, to transcendence of one's oppressors, the communion with the Koran, the cleanliness of the heart – in a crappy Yemeni jail cell.

The fans in cyberspace responded predictably: 'Subhanallah! – With tears i read the last few lines of your post,' wrote Naeem from . . . he doesn't say where. 'Allahu akbar!' exclaimed Muhammad Hassan from Australia.

Zachir (from America?) was also impressed but drew a conclusion that Awlaki probably did not intend: 'Maybe I should go Prison, coz whenever i read the Quran it dont hit me as it used to, my heart has gone too hard.'

This of course is the real source of Awlaki's power and it has nothing to do with his theology or his fluency in Arabic (or English for that matter), as some of the terrorism experts seem to believe. Awlaki has had a deeper experience of the Koran than most of the other young men, and he's had it in Arabic, and he's had it under extreme conditions. In short, he has taken a voyage of the spirit, as all heroes must.

His was as classical as any: when his conventional schooling had run its course, he left home. Finding himself on the far side of the earth, in a land both dangerous and magical, he faced his enemies. The battle in which he then engaged was a physical one that had a powerful spiritual dimension. It purified his soul, and opened up the mysteries of the sacred writings to him. The ordeal, as several of his fans pointed out on the website, could well have killed him. But instead because he relied on his faith in God – never wavering, never losing an iota of dignity – his inner powers were strengthened.

Luke Skywalker has lived out a similar tale, as did Jesus, Jason of the Argonauts, Joseph and the other figures discussed in Joseph Campbell's study, *The Hero with a Thousand Faces* – including, by the way, the Prophet Muhammad. In Awlaki's case, the story is true. He lived it, and wrote it up himself, day by day, and published it on his blog.

To paraphrase another spiritual voyager, Walt Whitman, there is miracle enough in this to stagger sextillions of infidels.

Nowadays, young Muslims are unlikely to invoke the myth of the hero when they speak of leaving the West. They're likely to say, 'In my religion, I'm required to seek beneficial knowledge. It happens to be in Yemen', or simply, 'I left England because the country is spiritually dead.' Nevertheless, the Awlaki model, his voyage to the Koran, is the dream that hovers over the lives of ambitious young Muslims in the West.

One of Awlaki's most popular internet lectures is called 'Allah is Preparing us for Victory'. If I were one of the investigators charged with discovering how middle-class kids are turning into terrorists, I would pay special attention to this theme – the triumph to come – on anwar-awlaki.com. Better yet, I would spend a few hours people-watching in one of the mosques in

Yemen where foreign students are welcomed. To do so is to undergo a speedy but deep education in what victory means to this particular class of young men.

These are not the lucky golden children of life. Not one of them has the winning good looks of the star athlete on the football team; not one of them knows how to charm a room with his smile. Many have the mousy air of people who've been overlooked in life. Which doesn't mean they intend to renounce popularity. They do want it. Most of all, they want women.

Islam in Yemen makes a promise to these – and to all – young male believers. The *ummah*, the global family of believers, will smooth away problems concerning the female sex, it says. We will bring you your helpmeet, it promises. She will have been raised on the Koran. She will love you for your Islamic learning, and for your dedication to the *deen*, or religion.

Westerners who come to Yemen in search of brides believe this – and with good reason. Many of their older friends have asked the local imam for a wife, have paid the bride price, have gone through an Islamically proper engagement, and have married. The bride is now the property of the groom. He will decide if she will study, or work outside the home – and where and when and with whom. It has always been thus in Yemen.

Often, these arrangements work. Anyway, when you bring up the subject of marriage with young men in the mosque, the unions they discuss certainly seem promising. There is trust. There is a religious law. There is the backing of the community and 1,400 years of local tradition supporting the couple. Now the young men can stop worrying about how to get along with women. What does this species really want? No one in Yemen asks this question. The sheikhs and the students already know: they want to become mothers in pious, Koran-reading families.

To have reached this level of certainty is in itself a major victory for many young men. With proper prayer, say the mosque authorities, there will be other, greater victories to come.

No verse in the Koran reinforces this teaching as well as the Sura An Nasr (Chapter of Victory), which is thought to have been delivered to the Prophet hours before his death, when his thoughts were on his imminent ascension. Every student of Islam in Yemen who doesn't know this vaguely eschatological sura will memorise it in his first days in the country, not because it is a creed, but because it is simple and beautiful:

> When the assistance of God shall come and the victory;
> And thou shalt see the people enter into the religion of God
>   by troops:
> Celebrate the praise of thy lord and ask pardon of Him;
> For He is inclined to forgive.

The excitement surrounding Anwar Awlaki's release from prison eventually died down, but he returned to prominence in a much bigger way towards the end of 2009. On 5 November, Nidal Hassan, a sometime email correspondent of Awlaki's who lived alone in a rented flat near Killeen, Texas, murdered thirteen US soldiers at the Soldier Readiness Center at Fort Hood. Two days later, a notice of approval appeared on Awlaki's blog.

Nidal is a hero, Awlaki wrote.

> He opened fire on soldiers who were on their way to be
> deployed to Iraq and Afghanistan . . . How can there be
> any dispute about the virtue of what he has done? . . .
> May Allah grant our brother Nidal patience, perseverance,
> and steadfastness, and we ask Allah to accept from him
> his great heroic act. Ameen.

US officials have since said that Awlaki had no direct 'operational' role in the Fort Hood attack. He was, however, in contact with Hassan via email, and this correspondence, it seems, was enough. Three weeks after the attack, American counter-terrorism strategists were huddling in the White House, where, according to WikiLeaks documents, they were devising a strategy, approved by the Yemeni president Ali Abdullah Saleh, to launch missiles at Awlaki's house in the Yemeni village of Shabwa.

The rest of the story is familiar enough. A twenty-three-year-old Nigerian blog fan, Umar Abdul Mutallab, had been having depression issues of his own. When he was living in London in 2005, he used to fantasise that jihad would deliver him from his problems: 'all right I wont go into too much detail about my fantasies,' he wrote to the Islamic Forum website, 'but basically they are jihad fantasies. I imagine how the great jihad will take place, how the muslims will win, and, inshallaha, rule the world, and establish the greatest empire once again!!!'

This happiness, however, seems to have given way to moments of acute self-doubt. Clearly he hoped that someone would rescue him from the emptiness. What else could he have meant when he posted this message, also in 2005, to the same chat room: 'i am in a situation where i do not have a friend, i have no one to speak too, no one to consult, no one to support me and i feel depressed and lonely. i do not know what to do'?

By the autumn of 2009, Mutallab had found his way to Yemen. At first he studied in the capital, Sana'a, but he disappeared in September. He probably made his way into the Yemeni mountains which is where all the most dedicated voyagers of the spirit eventually go. He seems to have established contact with Awlaki at some point though where and when we do not know.

In any case, Mutallab was soon sending startling text messages back to his father in Nigeria. According to a cousin who saw them, they said that in Yemen, Mutallab 'had found a new religion, the real Islam'. Another text, whose contents have appeared in the press, said: 'Please forgive me. I will no longer be in touch with you.'

To me, these sound like the words of a young man in the throes of religious excitement. He's discovered a new religion. The new religion has given him a new family. He can now tell his oldest adversaries (so often, it seems, this person is Dad) to fuck off.

Young men who begin to feel these sensations in Yemen can easily find themselves in a dangerous spot. If they have suffered from depression in the past, and have access to weaponry now, anything can happen.

The first strike landed on the village of al-Majalah, 300 kilometres to the east of Sana'a on 17 December 2009. The Yemeni government later said that it killed twelve villagers. The second one, which targeted Awlaki's house and killed about twenty people, occurred on 24 December. Awlaki was not in the vicinity.

It's not clear that the strikes advanced any of the US military's strategic goals but they did provide Awlaki's fans with exactly those ingredients required for a new round of spiritual excitement. A Muslim hero was once again set upon by a merciless force. What did he do wrong? He was never charged and no evidence against him was brought forth. Nevertheless, innocent Muslims were killed. Awlaki himself emerged without a scratch, which is exactly what one would expect of a spiritual hero. One would also expect him to take revenge.

Within twenty-four hours of the second strike, Mutallab turned up in Amsterdam with a ticket, paid for in cash, for Northwest Airlines Flight 253 to Detroit. He was wearing his explosive-lined underpants and carrying a cigarette lighter. I suspect he was in a pleasant, victorious frame of mind.

I happened to be in Aleppo, Syria, when these events occurred but my thoughts were focused on Yemen. In the back of my mind, I had known that my hitherto self-contained world of religious students in Yemen, Islamic study, and anwar-awlaki.com would one day turn up on the front pages of the world's newspapers. Now it was happening, more or less as I feared it would, with instant analysis on CNN, statements from the White House, and reporters doing live stand-ups from the terrace of the Mövenpick hotel in Sana'a.

One thing I didn't anticipate: I would begin to worry myself. I did worry, however, because I could see that neither the reporters nor the Western intelligence authorities had any idea how many Western kids were studying in Yemen. I could see they didn't know much about what these students were learning, how long they stayed in Yemen, how they changed over the years, and what might make them go, as the specialists say, 'operational'.

I also fretted for this reason: I knew the teachers and students with whom I had lived in Yemen were against book writing. I knew my account of my experience in Yemen would seem to them, a priori, the account of an enemy of Islam, a spy-apostate. These people knew me well. Now it seemed clear that if I were to publish my book, they reserved the option to take revenge in any of a variety of unfathomable ways.

Of course, they don't read secular books, I told myself. A voice in my head replied: This isn't necessarily good.

At the time, in January 2010, there was no immediate need to worry about the situation. I went to Russia to think things over.

One of the best things about getting to know the Western religious students in Yemen is that eventually they will tell you the story of their travels. Sometimes, it's boredom that makes the young people light out for the territory ahead and sometimes it's a spur of the moment decision, made in a mosque, or in front of a computer, or during a late night rap session. Once the students arrive in the Arab world, however, the narratives coalesce. Everyone lives through the same stages of the same voyage, more or less, and so everyone tells a similar story.

The tale below, which follows the conventional pattern, was posted by an Abu Suleyman to a popular internet forum in 2009. It describes the experience of a family of Muslims from Sweden at large in Egypt: 'Our childrens ages are 10, 8, 6 yrs old,' wrote Abu Suleyman (in English):

We have almost lost hope in this country and thinking of going to Yemen. Anyone who could give us naseeha [advice] in this regard, Yemen vs Egypt with regard to being able to raise God fearing children!!! That is, a good islamic environment for children to be in.

Sometimes you feel that you made hijrah [immigration] from dar ul Kufr [domain of unbelievers] and all the bad things there but here in Egypt you found liers, muslims are using drugs in the streets, most of the people are very far away from the religion they are even going to graves to worship, superstition, uttering things of kufr and so on.

In some versions of this tale, the narrators locate the site of Arab dissolution in an unhappy city or neighbourhood within Yemen; often the young men travel alone, and often they have in mind proper Islamic schools for themselves rather than for their kids. The basic pattern of the story, however, does not change: it is always a quest narrative whose object is a wiser, ancient, truly Islamic place. Perhaps it will be a village or a region or an entire society – anyway, Muslims will practise their religion proudly there, in peace, as one. The action of the story gets under way in Mansoura or Cairo, or Damascus or wherever the seekers happen to alight. Here they discover that the business tycoons who rule Middle Eastern countries revere Islamic law even less than Western governments do. Nor do the tycoons have any special fondness for secular, civil law. Students are thrown in jail at the drop of a hat, without even the pretence of an accusation.

Meanwhile, the travellers wander around their new neighbourhoods. They usually live in low-rent districts since they will now be living, for an indefinite period, off their savings. The Prophet counselled careful husbandry in all financial matters. So they rent cheap apartments in cheap areas and thus discover, right away, the social problems of the Arab street – the unemployment, the aimless young men, the boredom that afflicts them, their jealousy of the ruling class, their incomplete education, their longing to flee. Many of these young Arabs turn to petty crime, hashish and alcohol.

Is this what Islam has come to? wonder the Abu Suleimans of the world. The local religious authorities nod their heads.

Don't take your children into the public schools at all, they say. Stay away from the official, state-run mosques, since they've all been taken over by government agents. Perhaps you should consider going back home, say the religious teachers. Is there not more freedom there?

Eventually of course the students find what they're looking for: in Yemen it's not so hard to find villages dominated by the fear of God, in which every citizen lives under the law spelt out in the ancient texts.

The communities where this kind of Islam is still alive are almost always far away – up in the mountains or by the edge of the desert or in some rarely visited but storied village like Tarim or Dammaj in Yemen; anyway, they are in places not frequented by reporters or embassy officials or unbelievers of any kind. It's often dangerous to get to them, and the trip almost always involves secret drivers, disregarded roads, and several vehicle changes.

They are always in spectacular, Koran-redolent settings, in other words, but they are always, also, troubled.

Many of the Western students and not a few of the Middle Eastern ones have been in jail in the past or close to it. Many of the Westerners have had attention deficit disorder problems or depression or drug issues or all of these things. Now they've fled their native countries, and have given themselves new Islamic names. The night-time prayers are playing with their sleep rhythms, and the new clothing, the new friends and the new language are playing with the very nature of personal identity.

Add to this a further interesting factor: personal identity is not built from the same components in the Arab world as it is in the West. Among Muslims, especially in Yemen, you are who you pray with; that circle of beings with whom you break your fast, memorise the Koran, and travel around the countryside is you in a way no concept of the self in Western life comprehends. Whenever this collectivity is threatened, it is as if the organs of the self (in the Western sense) are threatened. Action must be taken.

In response to this new world, almost all students, at least at first, go through a period of depression – although they are surrounded by friends, although they are living in the cradle of Islam, although they are doing what they always dreamed of doing.

When they emerge from their dark moods, the students are transformed. Now, at last, they are surrounded by friends and family. Here is Islam as it should be: the orderly, barefoot rows of believers, every forehead glistening, everyone equal before God, every prayer spoken as if it emanated from a single body.

When I was in Russia recently the atmosphere of the religious schools I had attended in Yemen and Syria came back to me. The education had given me a healthy disregard for material things, to say nothing of a solid understanding of the Koran, but even as I was memorising, I knew that this education had a harmful side. In two and a half years of study, I had attended three schools and had visited friends in several more. Without exception, these academies taught that evolution is a fable, that Islam is the wisest solution for life's problems and that the Hebrew bible is a fraud, forced on the world's Jewish population by elders who wish to hide references to Muhammad. In none of these academies were students asked to read widely. In no schools were students directed to use their reading to construct a modern, self-supporting, nuanced system of ethics. In religious schools in the Middle East if you don't know what to do, you ask the sheikh. He has memorised much more than you. He knows what the Prophet would do and understands the Golden Time of Islam. Whatever the problem is, the sheikh, not the student, knows the answer.

As I walked around in the mountains of southern Russia, it also occurred to me that Anwar Awlaki's internet presence has, over the years, made him the owner of an important topic: young people's personal transformations through Islam. He speaks about this more persuasively, and more frequently, than anyone. Why should he, I thought, have this field to himself?

In a notebook, I drew up a CV for a rival teacher of Islam. Such a person, I thought, ought to begin as Awlaki had begun: he ought to leave the US for Yemen. *Al fiqh Yemeni, al iman Yemeni.* (Faith is of the Yemen; jurisprudence is of the Yemen.) So the Prophet is reported to have said when he stood on a bluff in Medina, looking south. Muslims often take this hadith to mean that essential Islamic properties inhere in the Yemeni landscape itself. It's an interesting idea, and it's made an impact in the housing developments and first floor walk-up mosques of the West.

Once the teacher-to-be gets to Yemen, it hardly matters which school he chooses or which strain of Islam he apprentices himself to. If he's memorising the Koran, learning to speak the classical Arabic in which scholarly discourse is conducted, performing every one of the prayers, hewing close to that which is enjoined and avoiding that which is prohibited, he is on the path of God.

Perhaps, during his travels, he'll be arrested somewhere out on the highway; perhaps he'll spend some time in jail. I did. If he is arrested the resulting jail time will contribute to his education rather than delay it – but prison is not indispensable because sooner or later every religious student in Yemen will be persecuted by some government agency. Usually the experience will teach the student to stay as far away from official places and people as possible.

Above all, if you want to have authority with young Muslims from the West these days, you must not look for the easy way out. If you got your degree in Islam in a two-year programme at a university with a campus and quadrangle cafes, it will be meaningless – for you and for whatever audience you'd like to address. If you lived in a decrepit, overcrowded neighbourhood in Sana'a, owning a Koran and a bike and not much else, and did this in winter and summer, over and over through your thirties, you might be on to something.

What I want to say to the population of young men who educate themselves in this way, or would like to do so, is contained in the pages of this book. I address these questions: what happens when a well-meaning, curious, adventure-friendly Westerner enrols in a religious academy in Yemen? What happens as the years pass? Also: what is beautiful about an education in Islam these days and what is sick?

Your target audience will not read your book, my book-reading friends in the West tell me. Fine, I reply. I'll find that audience on YouTube, as Awlaki did, on Facebook and via Paltalk. Your former schoolmates and teachers will be angry with you, says my knowledge of their behaviour. Fine. I will do these people the courtesy of writing for them and to them. I will speak directly, not as an academic or a journalist or an expert of any kind but as someone with a story to tell.

Sana'a, Autumn 2006

1

THE ROAD TO DAMMAJ

The rule concerning who may study at the most famous Salafi academy in Yemen is as follows: anyone on earth of any stripe or kind or age is welcome. In theory, women should be accompanied by a guardian but this convention doesn't have the status of a law and anyway isn't enforced.

You have to say that you believe Allah to be the one and only God, and that you believe Muhammad to be his prophet. After this the success of the student depends entirely on how well he warms to what's happening around him: does he like memorising? If so, he can go far. Can he learn Arabic quickly? If so, he's likely to make friends quickly. Does he have a talent for fasting? Is his body changing as the fasts go on? The kids who pray so well that they grow little clots of hardened flesh on their foreheads, a sign of piety not just to one's teachers but also to the guardians at heaven's gate, are usually well loved in Yemen. But these bumps grow naturally. Everyone who sticks around long enough has one. Most students enjoy seeing these rashes emerge, and thus pray more – which leads to smiles from their teachers, and admiring glances from fellow students.

Once this feedback loop kicks in, anything in Islam is possible, especially in Yemen. In my case, the feedback loop hadn't always run smoothly. Still, eight months into my life as a Muslim, all was well. I was memorising Koran every day, doing the five prayers and making friends. I knew I was going to go deeper in, and was vaguely frightened by the prospect, but like the others around me, I felt I was learning things about Islam I could never learn elsewhere. Islam was changing me.

I didn't want to stop this from happening. On the contrary I wanted to see what would develop if I kept on going to my classes, and kept on praying and memorising and fasting.

So in the morning, when I'd finished my prayers, I used to lie in my bed, daydreaming and wondering about my future. Of course one day the call I'd been waiting for came.

It was Ramadan of 1427, year of the Hejira, or 2006 in the Gregorion calendar. A Nigerian brother, Abdul Gorfa, was knocking on my dorm room door. 'Thabit,' he whispered. 'Driver here! Driver waiting. Hurry!'

I sat up in my bed. A stream of multicoloured light was falling across my prayer rug, my sandals, and an English–Arabic Koran I had been given on the street.

'Thabit? Sleeping? No, please. Rush!'

When foreign religious students set out for Dammaj, they try to slip out of Sana'a in the early morning dusk, as the citizens of the nation sleep. If they don't, the police force will awaken, man the checkpoints on the highways, and peer into the recesses of the vans and taxis. They might ask for ID cards and passports.

The students, therefore, have to hurry.

Being a reader of American newspapers, I was especially alert to a further danger. At this time, back in 1427, Rumsfeld and Cheney were still in charge of the government back home. Those two had been known to send Hellfire missiles on to people who drove along the roads we drove, worshipped in our mosques, and believed as we believed. Then there was the problem of the Shia, who were hostile to our kind of Islam; they were inclined to ambush people they didn't like. Beyond this, there were restive tribes in the back country and, so the news media said, terrorists.

Abdul Gorfa wanted to know if I had a white, Saudi-style robe he could borrow. The driver told him that his African dishdasha would raise the suspicions of people we might encounter on the highway.

I ransacked my luggage. Yes, I had something suitable. Abdul Gorfa changed in front of the ablution sink in my room, then hurried away, down a flight of stairs, through the mosque and into the street. I folded my prayer rug into a square, and fetched my toothbrush. Five minutes later I was standing in front of a van in my robe and sandals.

'Passport?' the driver asked me.

'Left it with a friend,' I said.

He shrugged his shoulders.

'Do I need it?' I asked. He shrugged again.

This would have been a good time for my nervousness to kick in. I have a tendency to worry at the outset of important voyages. On this morning, however, I wasn't anxious or uptight in any way.

It happened to be the morning after the Laylat al-Qadr, the Night of Destiny, which is a pretty holy evening in Islam. It's the anniversary of the first time the angel Gabriel brought certain special words down to Muhammad. It was the birthday of the Koran, in a manner of speaking, and I was feeling lucky.

Actually, I was more than a bit surprised to be travelling into the back country at all. Though I was a fairly serious Muslim at this point, with a beard and a tiny abrasion on my forehead from the prostrations I had been doing on our mosque carpet, not every one of my fellow students had confidence in me. In fact, certain French brothers had doubted, even in front of our sheikh, the degree of my commitment. They thought I laughed in my heart at the Prophet, which I did not do, exactly, and that I underestimated the Book of Allah, which I also didn't do.

So, for eight months, they talked to this driver and that fixer and made sure that I stayed stuck in our mosque in the capital.

Being stuck, I memorised Koran. I went to my classes. I learned about the problems the *ummah* faces in this day and age, and I discovered the excitement of praying with people who will solve those problems. Of course, I learned to respect my teachers. I hope they learned to respect me.

As I was taking my seat in the van, the driver stood in the street, squinting at my pinkish American face. 'Thabit,' he muttered. 'Is that your real name?'

In Arabic, Thabit means 'immovable'. For me, it stood for Yemeni qualities I admired – steadfastness, unshakeable faith, rectitude – and this is why I had chosen it. But Thabit was a country boy, salt-of-the-Arabian-earth sort of name. Sometimes, people smiled at me, an American from a city, when I introduced myself.

'Thabit is my real name now,' I said, and gave the driver a blank look.

He wondered at this information for a moment but did not smile. He shrugged his shoulders, then looked away. In Yemen, no one questions anything. You can be whoever you'd like to be.

It took the driver only seconds to strap the overflow luggage on to the roof. It took us a few more seconds to roll out of the alley behind the mosque. Soon, we were doing 80 miles an hour through the Ramadan dawn. Every time we came to a boulevard intersection, the driver accelerated. He was a holy man, with a long beard who said prayers as he came into the intersections. The traffic lights blinked. The Koran played on the van sound system. Sunlight streamed into his eyes.

If there had been a pedestrian or bicyclist in one of those intersections we would have mowed him down like a melon. Pedestrians don't have many rights in Yemen. Drivers will swerve for them but they won't brake. Our guy didn't brake and he didn't swerve. He too was feeling lucky, it seemed. Or anyway, guided by Allah.

We passed a few policemen right in the centre of the city, in front of a big international bank. They nodded. Were they winking? Maybe so.

We flew by Yemeni hoboes slumbering in the central reservation. We careened past little flocks of goats.

I scarcely knew my fellow passengers. The Nigerian brother, a family of Algerians from France, two American converts on my bench and in front, a young computer science student who'd come from Birmingham in England just two weeks earlier and could not speak more than three words of Arabic – that was pretty much it. The men wore checked headscarves, red for some people, white for others, robes, sandals, and in our breast pockets we carried a tiny book of occasional prayers called *The Fortress of Islam*. The woman in the van – from somewhere near Paris, like her husband – was dressed as all women in Yemen dress: black across the face, black across the head, black dress, black shoes, black gloves – black and black and black. Personally, I didn't think she had a lot of choice when it came to colours. Maybe she would have disagreed. Her two daughters – silent, about the height of elves – also wore facial veils and black robes.

Anyone who drives north out of Sana'a probably knows that the Yemeni government has forbidden outsiders from entering the Governorate of Sa'ada in the north. An enclave of Shia has been making trouble up there for several years now and the government likes to bomb them in peace, without outsiders poking their noses into the business.

So on this morning our van was, technically speaking, taking us into illegal territory.

We didn't care much about the Yemeni government (we cared even less about the Shia) but still, whenever we came to a government checkpoint, all but the French family wrapped their faces in their scarves. 'Sleebing, sleebing,' the driver called out. He would slow. As he rolled up to the candy cane barrier with its little soldier hut and limp flag, the students would fold themselves on to the floor of the van. Limbs lay on top of limbs. Heads nestled between duffel bags: the smell of suitcases and floor sand. 'Na'eem – sleebing, sleebing ,' the driver would say again and wc would press ourselves down deeper under the benches.

In this way, anyone looking into the interior of our van in a casual, rubber-stamp sort of way would have seen: a chaste Muslim woman, face covered in Dacron, her offspring, similarly clad, and her long-bearded husband. A driver. On the rooftop: luggage. In other words: a family expedition into the countryside.

It was true in a way. Once you submit to Islam, you belong to the *ummah*. Our little branch of the *ummah* was making an excursion into the countryside, though a particular, sacred one where the Prophet of God is thought to have walked. In the physical sense our destination was an academy on the Saudi border called the Dar al-Hadith, or the House of Prophetic Tradition. In a spiritual sense we were heading backwards, through the centuries, into the golden time of Islam.

2

About 50 kilometres outside Sana'a, an overstaffed government checkpoint loomed ahead at a rise in the land. We had no choice but to give it the slip. We dropped off the lip of the tarmac, on to a sandy path. Soon we were lost in a little sea of vineyards. Then suddenly, two little boys stepped out of the vines. Their long shadows sloped across the pavement. The van slowed. 'Which way back to the main road?' asked the driver. Simultaneously, in slow motion, they lifted their left arms. Their stillness, their white gowns, the clusters of purple grapes in the fields behind them, and the way the sun backlit their hair made them seem like visitors from the Islamic afterlife.

'Allah be with you,' the kids said.

'May he make you strong,' said the driver.

'All of us together,' said the kids. They lowered their arms by imperceptible degrees, like boys in a trance. Then they turned their eyes on us, the passengers in the back of the van, and smiled shyly as if to say: *we know where you're going. May Allah open the way!*

In previous excursions around Yemen in my earlier, secular, touristic life, the drivers I'd been with had been working for money. They had been taxi drivers and tourist company jeep excursion drivers. I'd never submitted myself to a driver working on behalf of God. Things are different with the believers: easier, smoother, safer.

3

Out here in the vincyards, the weight of the fruit pulled the vines down on to the valley floor. Here and there, between plots of grapes stood patches of stunted corn that resembled parchment. On the fig trees, fruit hung. Millet, which looks like bulbs of cauliflower on a cornstalk, was ripe. I hadn't realised that autumn came to Arabia. But it does come. The cities have been denuded of greenery. The trees have been replaced by hideous cement towers. If you only live in the city, you don't see. If you only come to Yemen for a little while, say in the summer or winter, you also don't see. In those seasons, the landscape, even outside the cities, is the surface of a science fiction planet: red, barren, unchanging, murdered by the sun. But in the autumn – this was news to me – there was fertility. There was fruit and there were harvests.

Soon we were back out on the highway. Two crumbling twin towers of sandstone blocks rose up on the horizon, then loomed. I stared at them as they floated past the windows. They were conical piles of stone, derelict and staggering into one another, like minor ziggurats, too destitute to attract the interest of the outside world. They cast black shadows across the grapes. Then qat fields flew by the windows, and a parentless family of children rose up out of the sunlight. Each child held a translucent bag of qat gleanings into the air. 'For sale!' said the children's eyes. Their mouths said nothing. 'For shame!' said the driver. We sailed by. The entire nation was addicted to qat, a leafy plant similar in effect to amphetamines. But the sheikhs of Islam had forbidden it.

'What are these people doing to themselves?' Abdul Gorfa wondered. 'Why?'

'For shame,' the driver said again.

We sped on, into the north. We slowed for further checkpoints but only as a formality and when the guards were sleeping, as they sometimes were, we really didn't slow.

To have slipped through the security cordon around Sana'a so easily was a surprise to me. The president of Yemen, Ali Abdullah Saleh, doesn't want rural extremists traipsing into the city to blow up embassies. Nor does he want foreign religious enthusiasts falling into the hands of zealots in the countryside. The checkpoints outside the capital are thus, in principle, well staffed. But the president doesn't personally control the checkpoints. Really, he has no idea what's happening on his roads. Or perhaps he does, and doesn't care.

Of course, it matters not a whit what the president of Yemen cares about. In Yemen, the Prophet is just a little bigger than the president. Soldiers on the highway almost always defer to people who love his messenger.

Anyway, the soldiers know what's going on. They know that a sheikh up in the Yemeni highlands has taken over a village, and that under his guidance the village is bringing the ways of the Prophet back to life: the ancient justice system, the scholarship, the love of recitation, the harmony between man and wife, the terror in front of God. It's all coming back.

When news like this appears on the internet, Western kids who feel strongly enough will eventually find their way into those highlands. I did.

So one morning the travellers will be woken in their bedrooms. A tape of the Koran will be playing in a van outside. As they sail through the countryside, as the military men wave at them, they're likely to feel the strength that comes to travellers on the Path of Allah. It's a personal dignity, a sense of proximity to holy places, holy people, and it is a command of the landscape.

But these young men – and the occasional women who come along with them – are now in a strange situation.

Belief in Allah is under threat in Yemen. Islam is far from dead but it isn't the force it once was in this pious country and every day Western commercial culture and Western science conquer it a little more.

With the religion under threat, instability has spread across the land.

In Yemen's north, where Shia and Sunni have often been at one another's throats, the society has descended into something close to permanent warfare. There are suicide bombers in the mosques, attacks on government buildings, and Shia takeovers of remote villages. Most of the Jews who once lived in the region have been displaced or murdered.

Even if the young men in the van have brought maps with them, which none of them will have done, the maps are not likely to show what is happening here in the heart of Islam. Who is in danger? Who controls what? Why does a sheikh in a tiny village in the middle of the war zone welcome Western Muslims?

The internet will have had nothing to say about these topics. When it comes to Dammaj, the Muslim chat rooms and the popular websites usually say that the purest of the pure still hold sway in Yemen's north. 'Voyage should be made and Knowledge should be sought in Dammaj,' says Salafitalk.net. 'It is a lighthouse from all the lighthouses in the world.'

So as the van rolls northward, the young men are likely to feel that they are leaving the virtual reality of the web for a true, 3D, real-time Islamic utopia. Many of them will have been waiting for years for this crossing over to occur. It's an exciting moment. Now it is at hand.

4

I was unlike the typical religious pilgrim in that I had done some poking around on the net – particularly on LexisNexis, and in the archives of the *New York Times*. I had asked some questions in Sana'a. Some talibs in Dammaj keep blogs. I had reviewed these, had read up on local history in libraries in London, and connected some dots on my own. As a result, I understood the history of the Dar al-Hadith perhaps more completely than did my fellow passengers. This is what I understood: twenty-six years earlier, that is, in 1979, there had been no Dar al-Hadith at all but only a tiny village of Shia farmers: adobe huts, ziggurats in the fields, millet and grapes.

Of course, 1979 was an interesting year in Islam, particularly in Arabia. The date corresponds to 1400h in the Islamic calendar. This year, which some Islamic prophecies once heralded as the date on which a redeemer would arrive on earth to vanquish the enemies of God, saw a popular revolution in Iran. It also saw a strange and frightening event in the holiest of Islamic places – the Masjid al-Haram in Mecca. In November of that year, about 500 zealots, believing that they could hasten the Apocalypse, laid siege to this mosque. They were armed with AK-47s and hand grenades. They slaughtered an imam. They slaughtered the Saudi soldiers who were brought in to rout them. They slaughtered the pilgrims who'd come on the hajj.

Most of the 500 died in the initial onslaught but a core group held out for two weeks.

The attackers' agenda was simple enough: seize the holy site. Restore the ancient pure untrammelled Islam to the Believers. Next: kill the Arab plutocracies, especially the one in Riyadh. Next: kill the Shia, especially those in Arabia. Not one unbeliever of any kind was to remain living on the sacred Arabian peninsula. With the holy site under control, the oil would follow. With the oil, the holy site, and the *ummah* at last guided by a pure Islam, the Koranic apocalypse would be at hand. And thus only a single task would remain: the slaughter of the *kuffar*, or unbelievers. This was the attackers' agenda.

My research had told me a bit about the founder of the Dar al-Hadith: he had been a professor in the hothouse where the siege idea was dreamed up, the Islamic University of Medina, but had avoided being gassed or beheaded as the other followers of this movement had been. He was only jailed. On his release, he promptly fled, in the company of a handful of the survivors, to his native village in the mountains of northern Yemen. Here, beyond the writ of any government or police force, in a halcyon valley, in the midst of the penniless Shia, he opened his academy.

Until the year 2000, this mosque attracted little attention from the outside world. It did a quiet business ministering to 3,000 or so rather extreme, very pious, often (but not always) poor talibs from Yemen and Saudi Arabia. Occasionally the odd questing youth from the mountains of Morocco or Afghanistan found his way to the academy. It did, after all, teach exquisite Koranic pronunciation (*tajwid*), and an inimitable kind of Wahabi serenity that made graduates known in mosques around the Middle East – as students, as teachers, as fighters.

Still, it was a highly obscure little academy. Its students learned to pray in the proper Salafi way, to memorise the sacred texts, to imitate the Prophet in all things, to turn their backs on representations of reality, and to regard the world of *this* life, the *dunia*, as a passing shadow. In short, the core of its curriculum was not really such a remarkable departure from standard Islam.

If it weren't for the intense godliness of the graduates, and the fact that they tended to find their way, in the 1980s, to Afghanistan, the place would almost certainly not have turned up on the radar screens of the Western intelligence agencies.

But the agencies did know about it, and therefore, when the USS *Cole* blew up in Aden harbour in south Yemen in the autumn of 2000, life in Dammaj changed. The intelligence agencies, eyeing the recent explosions in Dar es Salaam and Nairobi, and noting that Yemenis had been involved in both of them, began to focus on the sheikh of Dammaj. They knew that one of his most ambitious, best-loved early students had been a well-heeled Saudi talib, since vanished into Afghanistan, called Osama bin Laden.

So the Yemeni government came. They shut down the school for two weeks. When the government came, reporters came. One of the reporters was the *New York Times* correspondent, John Burns, whose article about Dammaj was entitled, 'One Sheikh's Mission: To Teach Students to Hate the West'. When he visited in November 2000, he did an interview or two outside the mosque. The village guards came immediately, and pointed their guns. He left right away.

And that, pretty much, was that. The school resumed its classes. The government, which is never welcome in these parts, went away. The reporters went away. Whatever window the outside world had on goings on in Dammaj closed.

Then came September 11. Slowly but surely, it changed everything. It brought heavy surveillance in the European and American mosques. To Muslim youths in Europe, it brought condescension in the press, bullying from the police, and annoying stares from fellow passengers on subways and aeroplanes. Then came wars in Iraq and Afghanistan. Then came an awakening of identity politics among young European Muslims. 'Where is Islam resurgent?' asked the young men in the exurban mosques of Europe.

'Where is it powerful and pure and ancient?' The answer filtered back to them: 'In the mountains of Yemen.'

Soon social networking sites were flourishing on the internet. Then cellphone service came to Dammaj. The Western students started coming. At first they trickled in. They kept trickling. They built huts from mud bricks next to the mosque. They called their friends back home and wrote text messages. They opened up an internet cafe. Sheikh Muqbel, who had always been well known in the Arab world, was, by 2002, becoming famous in Walthamstow, Roubaix, Grozny, and the jails of South Philly. More students came – also from Libya, Afghanistan and Pakistan – and in 2005 the mosque was rebuilt to twice its original size.

When Burns was in Dammaj in 2000, he wrote of a population of several dozen Westerners – strays, misfits, one-offs. I knew the population had expanded since then but by how much and who exactly was living in the village and under what conditions I didn't know. I was looking forward to finding out.

5

On my first night in Dammaj, I ate in the moonlight, on the mosque terrace, in a circle of impoverished brothers. Most of them had come over on rafts from Somalia. They were too poor to buy their own food. The mosque fed them.

Only a single Yemeni ate with us that night. He was incredibly gracious to me. He saw me ambling across the mosque terrace, saw me eyeing the circles of men sitting cross-legged in robes, and watched me wonder which cluster I might join.

'*Hiya la man jah!*' he called, which is an old-fashioned, Arabic way of welcoming a traveller. It has died out now in other, more contemporary nations. It means: *Greetings to the one who has come. Alive!* 'Eat with us please,' said the Yemeni. He smiled. He opened the palm of his right hand on a spot of empty terrace next to his knee. 'How was the voyage? How is your health? What is your news?'

'Praise Allah,' I said.

He asked after the health of my family, and how the world of this life was sitting with me.

'The world of this life is good with me,' I said. 'Praise God.'

He offered me bread from a stack of steaming flatbreads that the Somalis had been too polite to touch. As we chewed on the bread, he smiled at me.

*   *   *

When we had had our fill of rice and bread, he introduced himself properly. His name was Abdul Wahab. His parents had died five years earlier, when he was fourteen. Back then he had lived in a teeming Yemeni city, out in the east, called Mukalla. Every day he worried that without parents, and without money, his two younger sisters would turn into degenerates. He worried that the degeneracy of the city would affect his own mind.

'Mukalla?' I said. 'Not a believing place? I thought it was one of the most pious of the pious cities in Yemen.'

He shrugged. 'Not really. Anyway, God protected my family by bringing us here, praise him.' He turned his palms to the moon.

'The will of God,' I murmured.

For a few seconds our circle of diners sat in silence, smiling to ourselves, and marvelling at the workings of providence: it had rescued Abdul Wahab. It had rescued the Somalians. It had brought me, an American ex-poetry teacher, ex-bike mechanic to the House of Prophetic Tradition.

In the silence, I watched the East Africans staring at their dates, then pressing the tips of their fingers over the sticky clusters, then raising their fingers to their mouths. They sucked on the pits carefully as if they were filled with nutrients that had to be pulled out with the tongue and the teeth. Their enormous eyes sparkled in the moonlight.

After a while, Abdul Wahab, the Yemeni, nudged me in the ribs, and murmuring softly, told me that he knew why I had come to Dammaj. He grinned.

I grinned back at him. 'You do?' I said.

'Yes.'

'Really?'

'Yes. Allah – he has brought you here.'

'Exactly,' I said.

'Maybe there are people who know very little about Islam in your country.'

'Yes,' I said.

'Their ignorance is very great. Even the Muslims there. Especially the Muslims there. Perhaps they themselves know very little. Perhaps in some cases they know only a single prayer. And that they are Muslims. Is that right?'

I thought about this suggestion for a moment. 'In some cases, yes,' I said, 'certainly.'

'You already speak Arabic well, praise God.'

'Praise God,' I said.

'So you will learn more here and spread knowledge of Islam when you return, in your own country and wherever you go. Around the world. Allah has brought you here and this is the reason.'

I didn't say anything.

'Learn well so that you can teach well,' he said. 'Memorise Koran. Seek advice from the sheikh. When you return, you will help them understand. Islam is a complete and true religion and Muhammad, peace be upon him, is the final prophet.'

I nodded. 'Yes,' I said.

'Allah bless you,' he said.

'Allah bless you,' murmured the Somalians.

Soon it was time to pray the evening prayer, the *isha*. Abdul Wahab kissed me on my cheek as he stood up. 'Concentrate, study, memorise,' he said. 'You'll learn very quickly. This is the best place in the world to gain knowledge and science.' *Al ilm wa'l hikma.*

'That's why I've come,' I said.

'And write as you memorise because writing stabilises the memory.'

'Of course,' I said.

After the prayer I sat under a column in the mosque and scribbled the conversation I had just had with Abdul Wahab into a notebook.

Some of the brothers in the mosque cast funny looks at me as I wrote. I was a new brother. Maybe this was normal. A village guard ambled by with his machine gun. He didn't say anything.

He gave a half-smile. I half smiled back. If he had lingered, I would have folded up my notebook and taken out a Koran or something. I might have risen and thrown down a prostration or two. When you don't know what else to do, and the communal prayer has yet to come, it's usually not a bad idea to put down a private, solo prostration. You can pretty much never go wrong doing that.

If the guard had squinted at me, or wondered at all, I probably would have smiled right back at him and ambled away to an open stretch of carpet, suitable for prostrations and for contemplating Mecca.

That would have been my habit – a learned reflex. But there were times when I didn't follow my learned reflexes. There were times when I did what I felt like doing, habits be damned. On this occasion, I had had an interesting day. It had been filled with interesting events, highways, and interesting new people. I felt like writing it all down, everything that had happened to me, including the toothless checkpoints, the van driver's prayers, and the God-saturated dialogues.

So instead of wandering away to an open spot on the carpet, I remained in the shadows of the mosque, scribbling and stabilising my memory.

6

I chose an auspicious place for a spiritual adventure. Even though Nintendo and satellite TV are making headway in Yemen, the country remains, at the end of the first decade of the twenty-first century, an excellent place to discover what life feels like under the rule of a conservative, unreconstructed version of Islam.

Its mountains have kept it apart from the world, as has the poverty of the people, as have the country's imams and presidents, who've tended to govern the country, as the Yemenis say, with the windows shuttered. Apart from a small community of Jews, most of whom fled in a 1949 airlift called Operation Magic Carpet, Yemen has never had a significant non-Muslim minority. In this respect it is unlike the broad sweep of other Middle Eastern countries: Iran, Egypt, Syria and Iraq.

Women still move about Sana'a as little towers of black rayon. They are not addressed in public, except when absolutely necessary, and are not expected to speak. They never enter restaurants, do not sit next to men on public buses, and hurry home before dark. 'Human wolves,' say the religious authorities from their minarets, will prey on them if they don't.

Perhaps because he doesn't care, or perhaps because everyone is entitled to something in Yemen, the president has given control of the education ministry to the Islamist party. The results are not entirely unpredictable: most young people who would like to be educated in technical matters leave the country. At home, a class of young people have been brought up to understand the worst about non-Muslims. When young cab drivers find themselves in a confrontation with Westerners, they scoff, 'Nazarene!' or sometimes simply, 'Jew!' (or, more recently, for any foreigner, 'American!').

During Ramadan, the society comes close to shutting down entirely, since most people try to sleep through the daytime fast. At night, there is feasting, then prayers, then qat chewing. In the early morning, an army detachment fires a cannon from a precipice above Sana'a to wake the populace for the pre-dawn meal. 'Come to the prayer!' say the minarets which are scattered across the valley floor like poppy stalks. 'Prayer is better than sleep! Prayer is better than sleep!' cries the morning muezzin, at 4.30 a.m. No other Islamic country turns up the minaret volume quite this loud. 'God is great! God is great!' cry the many dozens of muezzins. 'Come to the prayer, come to the flourishing, prayer is better than sleep!'

If you're not awake by then, you might well be awakened by the sound of car horns in the street and door knockers, clanging away in the alley beneath your bedroom. At last, you'll get up. During Ramadan, an hour or so before dawn, the city streets bustle. The restaurants overflow. But you don't need to go to a restaurant because people will be happy to feed you at the mosque.

Predictable as this routine is, Yemen is in the process of a slow-motion disintegration. Desertification in the countryside, floods of migrants pouring into the cities, rising food prices, indices for life expectancy and maternal mortality far below the already lagging standards of the region, and teeming, understaffed maternity hospitals: this is Yemen today. Women have an average of six babies. When you enter the private houses, especially in the Old City, where people are poor, you can almost smell the approaching collapse: it is sewage overflow, qat on the breath of the men who've given up on work, warm, humid baby clothing, and big stews, boiling away in hidden kitchens.

The burgeoning population is draining away Yemen's fresh water. This is especially problematic in the capital, at 8,000 feet, which has to draw its water from a series of high altitude aquifers. They're drying up. Some enterprising property owners in Sana'a now sink their wells 900 metres below the surface. In theory, you're not allowed to drill without a government permit, but for every law in Yemen there is a sum that can be proffered to make it go away. If the bribes don't work, there is always the umbilical network of family connections, and if that fails, which it rarely does, there is always the Kalashnikov.

People avoid the courts because the judicial system is a joke. In theory some combination of Egyptian, Yemeni and sharia law apply but in reality, whenever an important case is pending, the president weighs in or the person with the most money weighs in, and the matter is disposed of. Usually people know what the judge will say long before he says it.

The government of President Ali Abdullah Saleh asserts a kind of authority but it is an intermittent one, more like trying to keep a violent dream under control than like governing power as we know it in the West. Anyway, the status quo – chaos burbling but not overflowing – seems okay with him. Meanwhile, the rebellious Shia continue to cause problems in the north, along the Saudi border. Al-Qaeda-style groups flourish in the country-side and fractious tribes, anxious for respect, kidnap tourists, blow up oil pipelines and periodically ambush units of the Yemeni army.

Some day, most observers agree, the fractiousness of the tribes and the religious groups will combine with the environmental problems, and this aggregate power will then confront the president's army. It's not hard to guess what will happen next. The army will fade away, more or less as Saddam's army did.

The poor will huddle in the mosques. Those without a tribe or a powerful family will pay for protection. There might be an ominous silence for a little while as the citizens of the nation load their guns. There are said to be some sixty million Kalashnikovs in Yemen, which translates to about three for every man, woman and child. During this silence the surrounding countries will probably fret. Then a new episode of Arab bloodletting, of IEDs, mutilated children, and blood-spattered hospital corridors will splash across the pages of the world's newspapers.

None of this does anything to diminish the excitement of a young man in search of spiritual experience. If anything, the instability heightens the excitement.

With its bribable officials and innumerable religious academies, Yemen is a friendly, pliant destination. Everyone will tell you that the national drug, qat, can make you hallucinate. People you meet on the street want to give you handfuls of it. At the same time, they want to instruct you in Islam.

So you take an apartment in the Old City. Within a few days, there will be such kisses on the cheek from your language teachers, and such delight in the eyes of the young men when you emit your first sentences in Arabic. You will smile back at your new friends. The tottering old men on the street, with their canes and their Kashmiri shawls, will stop in their tracks to stare. 'May Allah open the Way for you,' they will say, assuming that you've come, like most of the other Westerners in the neighbourhood, for spiritual comfort.

In fact, spiritual comfort is the one thing they do extraordinarily well. Five times a day you are reminded that the world is a Wilderness and that through it runs a broad, Straight Path, the *sirat al-mustaqim*. Five times a day you are reminded that the rest is a cursed emptiness. By and by, this prayer becomes familiar. By and by, the local dialect of Arabic becomes intelligible, and with it, a string of lovely phrases: *Morning of the Light! Morning of the Good, peace be upon you! Lead us on the Straight Path, Merciful Allah, King of all the Worlds.* At this point, the dilapidated state of the government here, or any government for that matter, hardly seems a shame. It seems a propitious thing, in fact; an opportunity.

Then one day, perhaps, you will find yourself sitting in the top room in one of the gorgeous tower houses of Sana'a. In the *mafraj*, or place of seeing, you are way up in the air – far above the city, far beyond the reach of women, who are in any case not permitted in such rooms. Your friends will be offering you sprigs of qat, which has a bitter, tart flavour, not unlike maple leaves. It rots your teeth but it does stimulate unusual thought.

The longer you sit among these new friends, the more likely it is that you will feel you have come to a place where your life can change at last. You will survey the mountainscape outside and contemplate the men around you: they live by a code of justice that hasn't varied much in 1,400 years. They are kind but severe. On occasions like this, it can feel as though the entire early part of your life, in which you laboured to bring things and girls into your orbit, has amounted to precious little. Where are the girls and the things now? The answer: far away and indifferent. If the frivolity of this programme of acquisition and loss never struck you before, it might well strike you now.

In such rooms, at such times, it would be altogether reasonable if a smart young man from the West, attached to no special life plan or place, should happen to fall under the spell of an immensely powerful vision. Naturally, that vision would be built on the idea of the journey, which is an overarching notion in this part of the world, among this formerly nomadic people. *Haraqa fiha baraqa*, says the Prophet: 'in onward movement there are blessings'.

In Islam in general, the voyage is not just a metaphor by which to understand our fits and starts as we pass through the terrestrial world, though it is that. It is also a physical obligation, a *wajib*, incumbent on each worshipper, meant to spread the religion, to teach the seeker, and to bring him closer to God.

The young man in the qat-chewing suite reflects. What form will the voyage take? It could be a scholarly voyage, through Arabian history, through the Koran, the hadith (the Traditions of the Prophet) and the *sira* (the biographies of the Prophet). It could also be a physical journey, to various schools, perhaps in Yemen, perhaps elsewhere.

In Yemen, a Western Muslim is a figure to be admired: he tends to have a better education than the locals, can sail through the airports of the world, can speak the European languages, and tends to have more personal money at his disposal. In Yemen, these qualities are not the lucky accidents we take them for in the West but are thought to be signs of leadership. They hint at a figure with a special destiny.

So what should this young man do?

If he likes, he can devote his otherwise blank future to the *sirat-al-mustaqim*, that ever-present Straight Path, and to serving the intrepid millions who adhere to it. Nothing specific will be asked of him, just spiritual struggle, on his own behalf and perhaps later, if things go well, on behalf of the people. They do need it, as every nightly newscast – from Iraq, from Palestine, from Yemen itself – shows. If he does commit, he will have a mission – a beloved one in this part of the world. Every child in the street, every veiled woman lurking in a doorway, every wise man in a qat-chewing hall will admire and celebrate him for it. Why should he not?

7

Before I left for Yemen, I had a job teaching poetry in a prison in Vermont. During my last years there, in 2002 and 2003, Bush and Cheney were rolling out their adventure-in-Iraq programme. Most of the prisoners in jail, and all of those who came to my classes, knew it was a reckless, stupid idea. Nevertheless we were jealous of the people who were in a position to set out into the wide world and probably would have traded places with them if we could have. Instead of setting out, we daydreamed about travel, and of new lives as explorers of faraway, crazy countries.

One day, one of my students brought a news article to class that described the Afghan life of the so-called American Taliban, John Walker Lindh. Before he turned to jihad, Lindh had apparently scoured the internet for information about Islam. 'I have never seen happiness myself,' he wrote to a chat room friend, allegedly an authority on Islam. 'Perhaps you can enlighten me . . . Where can I go to sneak a peek at it?' When the CIA arrived in Mazar-i-Sharif, they found him inside a cave with his Taliban regiment.

This story fascinated my students, as it did me. A few days later, I found a video of Lindh on the internet which showed him being removed from his cave. I brought this to class, and watched it with the students. That autumn, this was the only certain, unimpeachable method I discovered to calm my students down.

The tape showed a California kid at the culmination of a long journey. His eyes had sunk into the depths of his head. His chest and shoulders had been racked by starvation. He spoke in a poetical Arabic accent, though of course he had grown up in Marin County and had come to Islam three years earlier through the Alex Haley book, *The Autobiography of Malcolm X.*

In the video, he looks like he might be about to die. A week earlier, he and his Taliban brothers had bungled their attempt to surrender to the American army. In panic, they took refuge in the basement of a fortress at Mazar-i-Sharif. In order to dislodge them, American planes bombed the fortress. When the bombs failed to kill Lindh's Taliban regiment, soldiers on the ground poured diesel fuel into the fort and set the fuel on fire. A few days after that, they dropped grenades down the air shafts and several days after that, having determined that some of the holdouts had yet to die, the Americans decided that the best thing for it was to drown whoever remained. In came the water. 'We were crying out to Allah,' said an American-Saudi survivor who was interviewed later. 'Men who were wounded, men who were sick, men who were dying: the Koran tells you how to pray in all situations. People there who couldn't move and couldn't turn to face Mecca still prayed. They prayed in one position until they died.'

Now, in the video, Lindh is in the custody of the US Special Forces. Could you explain, wonders the CNN cameraman, how you found your way to Afghanistan? 'I started reading the literature of the scholars of the Taliban,' says Lindh. 'My heart became attached to them.' He was sorry about the bungled surrender. He was tired, he said, and had been travelling for nearly two years. Most recently, he and his Taliban brothers had marched a hundred miles across the high altitude steppes in order to surrender to the American army.

Every time I replayed that video, and I replayed it a lot, the students in the class sat quietly, as if entranced. The kid had clearly been lost in Arabia – but he had also found himself in some important way.

Anyway, the Marin County chat room surfer had died. In his place there was Suleyman, a soldier scholar with a love of Taliban religious writing, a new native language, namely Arabic, and new friends.

At the end of the video, the cameraman asks Lindh-Suleyman if, in retrospect, he thinks the jihad has been worth it. Suleyman pauses. He wants to give an honest response and searches his mind for the right English word. 'Definitely,' he says, thoughtfully. His head rolls on the gurney. *'Definitely.'*

By this point in my life behind bars, I was beginning to wonder what exactly the purpose of a poetry teacher in prison should be. In theory, studying poetry and short stories can help prepare young people for life. But many of my students were going to be spending the next twenty years locked up in maximum security. They were frightened and needy but they didn't exactly need preparation for life. They needed preparation for life in prison. It is similar but not quite the same thing.

I did want to help my students. They liked me and took my advice seriously. But they had needed my advice when they were alone and driving their cars 90 miles an hour down the icy back roads of Vermont, with guns in their cars and plans to kill someone.

So that autumn, a new career idea came to me. Instead of bidding young men goodbye as they disappeared into the correctional system, I would find young men out in the world, now, on the road. They would be Muslim searchers like John Walker Lindh, and their roads would be the high altitude footpaths of the Islamic world. I would meet them before they had committed any crimes, when they were just mulling things over in their minds. How best to live? Should I kill? Why? Whom? I would listen to their discussions, take notes and if they asked for my advice, I would give it.

Even at this time, before I left for Yemen, I was aware that Americans wandering around in the Arab world often wandered into trouble. Later on, when I got to Sana'a, I bought home-made DVDs in the marketplace of the old city which depicted the kind of trouble to which adventurous travellers are sometimes subject in Yemen. This is what the DVDs showed: a group of tourists is driving down a desert road in a Toyota Land Cruiser. A second Land Cruiser signals for them to pull over. The tourists emerge. The men with the machine guns utter a word of prayer. Then the tourists kneel in the roadside sand. Then the Protectors of the Faith, or the Soldiers of Yemen Brigades or whatever they happen to be calling themselves of late, empty their magazines into the tourists.

In the videos I watched, the tourists were killed near Marib, a site tourists like because it is the location of the biblical capital, Sabea. Local Islamists dislike it for this reason. Or maybe they don't. Who knows? In general, in Yemen, when tourists die no one explains anything. At the same time, most people there understand that militants kill tourists, especially when they go to Marib or Shibam, or any other spot far away in the desert, because they – the outsiders – have ventured too far, into territory they do not fathom, which happens to be under the sway of a steadfast, ultra-serious kind of belief.

As the Iraq war moved towards a disaster in the making at the beginning of 2004, I taught my poetry classes in jail. The students were fascinated by the violence on TV and laughed and chatted about this in class, just as they laughed and chatted about the violent things they had done.

They asked me to bring in YouTube clips of the war, which, obliging teacher that I was, I did. At home, I entered 'war Iraq death video headshot' into Google, then saved the videos, then brought them into class. The students were pleased. Together we watched videos which depicted US soldiers standing in the turrets of their tanks, then dying as snipers shot them in the neck. A particular sub-genre within this category of

YouTube video attracted my attention: the insurgent-filmed IED video. Generally what happens is this: a Hummer is lumbering down a Baghdad highway. Religious chanting rolls in the background. In the next instant, it is aloft and disintegrating. The bits and soldiers tumble through the sky. Here is an excellent way to offer yourself the sensation of Westerners adrift in the land of Islam, of the wrong road taken, of the irretrievable error, and of the ground that seems, to a foreigner, stable, negotiable. But it is not. The locals are watching. They've prepared the way. They've even prepared the video camera. Careful.

As I watched these videos in jail, I thought to myself, I can do better than this. I would study Arabic. Instead of wandering around amidst religious feelings I couldn't understand, I would try to understand them. Naturally this would involve a deep study of the religion, the history and the culture.

I might be disoriented for a little while, I told myself, but eventually, like Lindh, I would find my way.

It was certainly a naïve idea, and as it turned out, I was a naïve traveller for many years but it did have an outstanding virtue: it was safe. To travel about Yemen in Islamic dress, as I have done, in the company of one's brothers and teachers, is to feel a pleasant invulnerability and a belonging that no Western tourist and certainly no Western soldier can feel. As a proper Muslim in Yemen, you can drive back and forth through Marib all day long if you like. Your skin can be pink and your beard blond. When you stop your van, you'll emerge to shake a lot of hands. You'll smile into the watering eyes of old gentlemen, who will wish the mercy of Allah on you, and will praise him for having given you Islam, and praise him again for having given you the wisdom to leave the land of unbelief.

As it turned out, no one – not my mum, or my girlfriend at the time or anyone else I spoke with – was enthusiastic about my adventure. I hung around in Vermont for another two years. Then George W. Bush was re-elected. I couldn't take more prison and I couldn't bear even a few more minutes of George Bush, not even on the radio.

I went back to the internet to read about the specifics of John Walker Lindh's voyage. I discovered that he had begun his excursion into Islam in the Yemeni capital, Sana'a. The school had a telephone number and a website.

When I got to Yemen, it took me about two weeks to discover that language academies in the Middle East teach an entirely notional language, which they call 'Arabic' but which no one, not a soul, not a single Yemeni or Palestinian or Iraqi or anyone else in the street, actually speaks. This version of the Arabic language, sometimes called classical Arabic and sometimes called by its Arabic name, *fossha*, is a Platonic ideal: it's what the Arabs would speak if they were all one, all educated, despised short cuts, loved complicated grammar and never felt the need to adapt a tongue to a specific geography and time.

As I was studying this formal language, I went looking for the kids on the road in need of help. I looked at the entrances to the local mosques and in the corridors of the language academy where I was studying. I asked my tutor if he had known John Walker Lindh. 'Yes,' he said. 'A sweet boy.'

'Where did he go?' I asked. The teacher, Adel, didn't know. He suggested I ask around at the other institutes in Sana'a which catered to Westerners studying Arabic. There were three such academies at the time. I soon discovered that every institute claimed John Walker Lindh as a graduate. None of the teachers knew how he had passed from Yemen to jihad in Afghanistan.

I asked Adel: 'Do you know other Western Muslims in Sana'a, and if so where are they?'

'Um, in their mosques?' he answered. Mosques were of course off limits to unbelievers. Tourists and students like me were allowed to use the urinals in the basements of Yemen's mosques. Setting foot inside the actual sacred space as an unbeliever was by consensus, and by law, forbidden.

Which left my 'discover young believers at risk' plan in the lurch.

In truth, it had been in the lurch from the very beginning. From the moment the airport taxi driver dropped me at my school, I could feel my plans being broken apart by an unyielding force, namely reality. The laughing, barefoot, homeless kids in the alleys wanted to play football with me. A grandfather who sat on a bench near my school wept when I gave him coins. My teachers at the school hinted to me that I might buy them qat, and when I did, we sat in the late afternoons in a room high above the Old City discussing how they could emigrate to America. They wished for new, better-paying jobs. Could I help them with their résumés? I could. With visas? I could not.

Neither in that school, nor in any of the marketplaces or rice and bean restaurants I frequented did I find the young men I had imagined I might find. Instead I found dutiful, pious Yemeni men who prayed a lot. 'We're poor,' said the young men, and: 'Islam is a religion of peace. Terrorism, no! My friend, no!' My new friends, the teachers, said, 'We have democracy in Yemen but no opportunity.' The teenagers in my neighbourhood spent their days and nights sitting on the steps of the mosque in front of my house. They seemed like unlikely terrorism candidates to me. 'Can we ride your bicycle?' they used to ask me. 'Can we buy it?'

One month to the day after I arrived in Yemen, I sat in a top floor tower-house chewing room by myself, as a hundred minarets issued the evening call to prayer. I could see with my own eyes that I had arrived in a gorgeous, other-worldly, heartbreaking, deeply pious, almost medieval country. It was medieval but for the cellphones and the traffic from hell. Why inflict one's fantasies on such a place? I thought. Isn't the country interesting enough? It seemed to me that Muslims in the Middle East had been putting up with their share of Quiet Americans, of cowboy fantasists, over the past six years. My language teachers suggested to me that this country needed, above all, rural health care and a more equitable system of distributing the oil and gas revenue.

I couldn't help with this.

I was at a loose end.

When a fellow student mentioned he was interested in working at a local newspaper, I went along with him to his interview. We were both hired on the spot. Within minutes, we were put to work.

8

I started as a copy-editor and moved up in a few weeks to serve as sort of all-purpose assistant to the newspaper's publisher, Faris Sanabani. The publisher was himself an all-purpose assistant to the president of Yemen, Ali Abdullah Saleh.

Faris's job, among other things, was to receive journalists from the West. So in the evenings, when the newspaper work was done, he and I used to take the correspondents from *Die Zeit* and the *Washington Post* to his favourite restaurant. We would fill them in on the problems facing the administration of President Saleh: fundamentalists in the opposition parties, restive tribes in the hinterlands, terrorists, and a weak sense of democratic norms in certain cities, particularly in the south, where the communists ruled until 1990. All of this, we would say, is compounded by other well documented problems: the surging population, the national addiction to qat, the drying up of the aquifers, and the absence of any real natural resources besides oil and gas.

The journalists would listen politely. 'We're doing what we can,' Faris would say. 'We're among the poorest countries on the face of the earth. Better to change slowly than to knock the entire house down.' We would eat our fish. There were usually sceptics among the journalists and some probably doubted the degree of Saleh's commitment to solving certain problems but when we read their articles on the internet we could see that they had accepted the general picture: Yemen was a struggling democracy. The reformers were in charge. We were moving in the right direction.

After dinner, the journalists would return to their hotels. Faris and I would return to the office to chat, chew qat and to assist in putting the newspaper together.

This is where the real fun was to be had. The *Yemen Observer* came together like this: every Wednesday night, at around sunset, in a neighbourhood less crowded than the Old City, less raffish and filthy, but still raffish and filthy in its own way, four or five local reporters and a Canadian editor began to filter into an office suite on the first floor of a rented villa. The Canadian guy, Gabriel, checked his email. The locals exchanged gossip, argued, smoked cigarettes, cursed each other, then retreated to the courtyard to pray.

At ten, other less resolute journalists arrived. More arguments erupted, and a news story or two, lifted from one of the Arabic papers in town or the state news agency, was typed, in broken English, into a computer. At midnight, graphic designers arrived and at nearly one in the morning the staff spilled out into the courtyard again. A table laden with blackened fish and gummy, steaming hot Yemeni flatbread stood waiting.

Now the fun began. The staff set on the fish like wolves. The journalists had to be aggressive while dining. Everyone wanted his fair share and Yemeni fish came out of the oven like incinerated toast. There wasn't much flesh left over after the cooking. If you didn't hurry, you could fill your mouth only with bits of seared bone and woody, dried out flesh.

When the journalists were finished eating, they threw the heads of the fish out into the darkness for the cats. Sometimes a journalist accidentally or on purpose threw a bone at someone else, and then a round of filthy cursing and laughter began. Then came the qat.

Out in the privacy of the guardhouse or sometimes in the open, in front of the computers, the journalists began feeding their cheeks. At first, nothing much happened. Then beads of sweat appeared on their brows. Then the veins in their eyes filled with blood, and as this was happening, their breathing quickened. 'Can you see New York?' they said, laughing. 'Wow! Take some!' One of them would pluck the most succulent, tiniest leaves from the qat branches and arrange them in his fingertips in the shape of a rose. Then he would present the rose to his poorer friends, who couldn't afford daily qat or to a foreigner looking on in bemusement. If the foreigner refused he would drop the bouquet into his own mouth as if it were a fancy sort of chocolate made in the shape of a flower.

Within the hour, the qat chewers' patience with the outside world would have faded a bit, and after the first hour, the patience and the chewers themselves were gone. If a foreigner or a non-qat-chewer approached to ask a question, the journalist would open his mouth and stare, like someone on the verge of a seizure.

There wasn't much you could do then except breathe in the odour of mown grass and silage that poured from the mouth of the chewer, and repeat your question.

Probably, on balance, qat did help produce the newspaper. It brought on bouts of sustained concentration. From time to time, it brought the journalists out of the newsroom to spit, to drink water and to curse the gatekeeper, Obadi, who was a good-hearted countryman whom everyone loved. Out in the cool of the evening air, the reporters collected their thoughts, chatted with each other, refuelled on qat, and smoked. When they returned to their computers, they focused like fiercely bright graduate students sitting an exam. This drug-induced concentration was the only way anything ever got done.

By three in the morning, news was being written. If the president had addressed a military college – and usually he had – a gloss of his remarks appeared on the front page. Everything the fisheries minister had announced, and some parts of some of the announcements that had been made by the planning ministry, appeared on the inside pages. A handful of college students from America and the UK, under Gabriel's supervision, tried to clean up the inscrutable Arab bureaucratese in which the Yemeni journalists – who were really not journalists, but ex-English-language students from the local university – wrote.

Usually by dawn, though sometimes not until twelve the next day, the staff had produced an object that bore a physical resemblance to a conventional Western newspaper. It didn't at all read like one, but legible or not, every production felt like – and in some ways really was – a triumph of the human spirit. Hours before there had been qat. And fish bones in the courtyard and cursing. Now black marks – not quite news, not quite English – had appeared on white newsprint. Plus photographs. A rough kind of justice had been done to the president's speech, the fisheries minister, and to the planners at their ministry. Probably, they had got what they deserved.

When the disks had been dispatched to the printers, the staff spilled outside, into the bright sunshine of Thursday morning. They blinked and yawned. On their way out of the gate, they bid the security guard good morning and he returned their greeting. Their voices had the thickened, swaggering tone of athletes who'd pulled off yet another unlikely victory.

9

It was a stroke of luck for an ex-English-teacher like me to happen on an institution like this. Technically, the journalists wrote in English but often their sentences were so long, so arabesque and so filled with ten-part terms translated directly from the Arabic that the sentences were, to all intents, still in Arabic. The bigger, underlying problem of our newspaper was that the sentences hadn't meant much in their original language. When they were rendered into English, they meant less. Native English speakers stared at the major stories of the week as if the journalists had produced a cubist word collage. *The point? The point?* they wondered. My instinct was to help. But every sentence had been written in the same mood of vagueness, passivity, and zero information content. How to help with that?

I found out later that all Arab newspapers read this way, even when they're written in Arabic – especially when they're written in Arabic – and that this is because journalism in the Middle East is a low-status profession, whose employees are too little equipped (poor education, no budgets, no institutional and little popular support) to confront the always multifaceted, always shifting facts on the ground. But I didn't know this then. I knew – because I was an overconfident American ex-teacher of people with drug problems – that I could offer some well-meaning words of advice. I decided that I would follow the twelve steps. First, the people would have to admit that they had a problem. After that, they would have to acknowledge a superior power, namely intelligible writing, after which they would have to renounce ongoing mistakes and correct those that could be corrected and so on, and so on, through to the final stage of adapting a new code of conduct.

One evening, I took a walk with the most fluent, confident English speaker at the newspaper. I meant to kick this 'twelve steps to better journalism' programme into high gear.

'Look, Zaid,' I said when we were out in the street, by ourselves. 'We're friends, right?'

'Right,' he said.

'So I can offer some constructive criticism?'

'You are welcome,' he said.

'Those first five or six sentences in your article this week – they're too long – they're like mazes, Zaid. They mess with the reader's head.' He stared at me. 'Go easy on this reader, man,' I said. 'Give the poor guy a break. Put the most important stuff first. Start with a bold statement. Then use examples. Example, example, example. New statement.' We were standing beneath a street light. His eyes darkened. The glow of the lamp made his skin look yellow.

'Look,' I said. 'In journalism, they value directness. No ceremonies. Just give the customer the goods. It doesn't mean you can't be poetical, Zaid. You can be, my brother.' I told him that the best writers in America had been journalists first, before they were anything else: Mark Twain, Stephen Crane, Walt Whitman. 'Whitman was very direct and yet poetical as hell: "Stop this day and night with me and you shall possess the origin of all poems." What could be more direct and poetical than that?' My lecture was carrying me away a bit. 'If I stop ten seconds with you, I'm in ten mazes. Every sentence leads nowhere. Every sentence leads everywhere. Why do you do this?'

I paused. I smiled. 'I'm sorry,' I said. His eyes glinted. 'You know what I'm talking about, right?' He craned his neck and squinted at me out of the corner of his eye as if I were a stranger.

'What the fuck *are* you talking about?' he said. 'Are you laughing at me? Why are you laughing?'

'I'm just trying to help,' I said. 'Constructive criticism.'

He thought about that for a moment. 'What the fuck?' he said. 'Can you write in Arabic? Can you come close in Arabic language on your best day to what I do from myself in English language on my worst?'

'No, Zaid,' I said.

'No, of course no,' he said. 'So you should . . . quiet your mouth.'

'Okay,' I said.

'Piss off,' he said. 'You don't need to come to the store with me. I can buy cigarettes on my own.' Without smiling, or even looking at me, he hailed a cab, climbed in, and was gone.

In my cab on my way home, I thought about the incident. I had ruined things with Zaid – maybe not for ever, but for now. The argument had flared up from nowhere, over nothing. I hadn't even broached the bigger issue, which was that there was no news, not a hint, but rather drivel from the information ministry, in his article. How to bring that up? I didn't know.

I did know, and this episode confirmed, that collaborating with Zaid – and with the other journalists, too, for that matter – was going to require a delicate touch. Perhaps, I thought, the journalists were not as eager to be enlisted in my twelve-step programme as I'd imagined. It also occurred to me that the difficulties I was having winning over my colleagues were nothing in comparison to the real goal: influencing Yemeni public opinion. The Yemeni public didn't read English, nor, for that matter, did it go in much for newspapers at all.

The next morning Zaid greeted me in the newspaper court-yard. His attitude towards me made me wonder, at first, if I had arrived in the right courtyard. Was this the right Zaid?

'Theo, the American,' he exclaimed. 'From my eyes,' he said, 'if there's anything I can do for you, I will do it.' He touched the fingertips of his right hand against his right eyelid and then pulled them away as if he was plucking a flower of truth from the inner regions of his brain. 'From my eyes and from the top of my head, from my legs and my hands – anything. I will do it. I love you! I'm going to try riding your bike,' he announced, and pulled it from my hands.

He pedalled around the courtyard to the amusement of Obadi, the guard. He got off. He kissed me on the cheek. 'You're the best American we've ever had,' he said. 'Best foreigner, period.' He turned to Obadi and, gesturing at me with his elbow, announced: 'What a teacher this man is! He can teach me anything, any time he likes. A poet! That's what he is. An American poet! Were you really a teacher in America? Would you do a class for us? Walt Whitman! Dead Poets Society! Anything you like you can teach. We will learn. In exchange, I'll teach you Arabic. Deal? Okay?'

'Okay,' I said, slightly dazed, but happy.

From this episode I concluded that, as a teacher, I was mixing around in a cocktail of volatile emotions: love and hate, envy and admiration, curiosity and contempt. I concluded that it was an unexamined, occasionally dangerous mixture and that it did not want my interference. Zaid was charming and he wanted to do well in my eyes. That's why he had come on the walk with me in the first place. That's why he wanted me to teach him about Walt Whitman.

One thing neither Zaid nor anyone else at the newspaper, for that matter, wanted from me was deeper expertise in journalism. Their work was good as it was: they were being paid. They were employed. They were improving their English. Perhaps, in due course, they could move to a better-paying job at a cellphone company, an embassy or an oil company. The well-born children of Yemen never bothered with a newspaper. They went straight to where the money and the connections were.

In the wake of this incident, I thought to myself: perhaps I can allow Zaid to continue teaching me. The reverse arrangement, which had seemed like an urgent idea once, was now less urgent. Furthermore, it wasn't working. Furthermore, it was endangering the little influence I had over my colleagues, which came entirely from their affection for me.

Later on that day, to cement our newfound fraternal feelings, Zaid gave me a CD on which a Sana'a oud player sang songs about love. 'This is the best way to learn Arabic,' he said. 'Listen every day. Learn to sing these songs and you will become Yemeni. This singer' – he tapped the CD case – 'is our teacher, too.'

I put the CD tracks on my iPod. It turned out that Abdul Rahman al-Akhfash sang about temptresses, about men being tortured by love, forbidden love, and the way the wind in Sana'a whispered to lovers, confusing them, inspiring them, and seducing them. I tried to memorise the lyrics.

Random people helped me. The taxi drivers, qat sellers and waiters knew the lyrics well and prompted me when I forgot.

Sometimes, when I found myself in a convivial place – a friendly restaurant or qat market – I repeated what I had learned out loud, and as I did, bystanders crowded round. 'A wind is rattling the door of my house. The rattling makes me think my lover has come,' I sang to them and immediately everyone knew who I was quoting, and burst into laughter. 'Who is rattling really?' they asked me. 'Is it Abdul Rahman al-Akhfash?'

'Maybe,' I said. 'I don't know. Should I check?'

'Yes! Check!' they said, slapping their thighs and burying their faces in the backs of their friends to hide their mirth.

'More! *Bravo aleyk!*' they called out. 'More! What else does Abdul Rahman al-Akhfash say? Sing!' I produced more lyrics. Often I had only the vaguest idea of what I was saying, but at this time I was delighted to be saying anything in Arabic.

Of all the songs on that album, the one about the wind battering the door of a mountain cabin seemed to have the most resonance with my audience of waiters, cab drivers, and bored newspaper journalists. I couldn't quite understand what the song was about – something to do with a man listening to the wind while waiting for his lover – but it had a pretty melody and was therefore easy to learn. Bringing out lines from the song in conversation was like bringing out a secret password that opened the hearts of the meanest taxi drivers and the most sour qat sellers. Suddenly the fare cost nothing; suddenly people were trying to give me bags of their expensive drugs.

10

In my first months as an employee of the newspaper, I felt I had stumbled into an Arabian *Alice in Wonderland*. All the employees were minor variations on the theme of Zaid: they were all loving, brotherly and, as journalists, indifferent to Western standards. Maybe they were wise to be so. Anyway, they were intensely proud of themselves. Most of them had bad drug habits. They were proud of this, too, but not in front of the boss. If Faris turned up as they were chewing qat – and he did turn up every day as they were chewing qat – a look of shame and panic passed through their eyes. 'Still chewing qat!' Faris would shout. 'Donkeys!' He would turn to a secretary. 'Bring me tea!' A black form with a slit over her eyes would rise to fetch tea.

When he had ensconced himself in his office, the reporters would pull their qat from their pockets and devour more leaves, in a quicker, more desperate rhythm as if only additional quantities of stimulant could make them feel better again. 'Qat makes you strong,' they would say. 'Hiya! Chew!' Then, later in the evening as the sadness that qat brings on hit them, they would murmur to each other and to me, 'It's too expensive these days. Everyone is addicted. Qat is ruining Yemen. We are already bankrupt. Now things are getting worse.'

* * *

As an employee of the government newspaper, I did want to fight for the country. If I squinted at the crowds in the streets, and tried to focus on the big picture, which I often did, I could see things in a sunnier light. Yes, there were farm animals marching down the pavements, even in the diplomatic neighbourhood, and sewage coursing through the lanes in the poorer ones, and rednecks from the countryside crowding the banks and the restaurants. Preachers, not a few of whom were charlatans, bellowed from the minarets.

And so? In the 1840s, when democracy was taking root in America, we had had similar problems: a sea of faith, unscrupulous politicians, and sewage – which led to cholera epidemics – in the streets. Our pavements too had been crowded by farm animals.

In America, at that time, a grand, forward-looking political movement, namely democracy, had risen from this chaos. It grew strong partly because every city had a scrappy newspaper, filled with scrappy journalists who worked for nothing but had good intentions and probably also had a wonderful time writing up the news.

With thoughts of the fledgling American democracy in mind, I threw myself into the work. I went to meetings, press conferences and rallies at the journalist union for oppressed journalists. I wrote articles about everything that seemed urgent: street children, micro-finance projects, disease outbreaks, fires, and new forms of cooperation between the Yemeni government and Western NGOs.

I paid special attention to the American ambassador since his words carried a lot of weight with the Yemeni government officials who were our bosses.

I did not mention that most American diplomats were too frightened to leave the embassy compound. I did write what the ambassador said to me in our interview: that while Washington was committed to helping the reformers in Yemen, Washington also felt that there was much work to be done in Yemen. The American government, he said, would be a lender, a donor and a partner, especially in the war on terrorism, provided Yemen helped itself.

Faris noticed that I liked my work. He allowed me to write whatever I liked. To pass the time he put me in charge of the tourist magazine. I went on trips around the countryside and wrote cheerful articles about tourists, castles and the undiscovered island of Socotra, where the inhabitants lived in caves and hunted for honey in the forests.

As I wrote, I felt good about my work, though there were signs that the reality of the newspaper was not as I supposed it to be. Many of the signs were easy to ignore but some were not.

For instance, I found it odd that in a newspaper whose purpose was to push for a fairer, more modern, more Western society, the journalists, most of whom were young men, were not paid enough to accomplish the one thing they really longed for in life, namely marriage. They made about $200 a month – enough to keep them in a state of dependence and sexual blockage.

Other things were odd. I found it strange that no one was really in charge of editorial content. Every week, each one of five full-time journalists pulled the paper in a different editorial direction. When the Canadian editor asserted his will, he pulled or tried to pull the paper in a sixth. Employees came and went, not really hired, never fired. Mistakes were made. No one was held accountable. Everyone knew that Faris was the real boss but he preferred to let the institution drift like a ghost ship. Why?

It also seemed strange to me that our newspaper was printed in English. The illiteracy rate *in Arabic* in Yemen was about 50 per cent, and higher among the women. Only a tiny fraction of the population could read English. The newspaper did appear at the kiosks but I never once saw an actual Yemeni reading it.

One evening as Faris and I were rolling through the streets in his Mercedes sedan, he happened to mention that he was spending $80,000 a month to produce the newspaper. This can't be, I thought. The brideless reporters, their $200 a month salaries, the hungry street children tapping on the windows of the car whenever it slowed – and we were spending $80,000 a month for a newspaper no one read? What was the point? Why?

By far the most important monthly event that occurred at our newspaper was the unveiling of our tourism articles. In our glossy magazine supplement, French, Italian and German tourists trekked through faraway mountain villages. They admired precipices and waterfalls. When the articles were ready to be published, Faris's friends from the presidential palace came to review them. They arrived in BMWs and Lexuses, often with armed guards following in jeeps and Land Cruisers. As the VIPs filed into our office, the guards milled about in the courtyard, saying nothing but keeping a close eye on their Kalashnikovs.

On afternoons like this, all business in the newsroom stopped. Clouds of airport duty-free perfume lay over the computers. The visitors murmured politely to each other as the graphic designers escorted them through images of Yemeni mountains and islands. It was nice to have the attention but it seemed strange to have so many big shots so focused on such trivia. One would have thought that big shots would have been interested in the news. In fact, they handed the copies of the newspapers we gave them to their guards or deposited their copies on messy countertops when no one was looking. They coveted only the tourist magazine. Why?

11

I had been working at the newspaper for about five months when an insurrection broke out in the streets. The ostensible cause was that the president, following suggestions from the World Bank, had ordered the lifting of a fuel subsidy. There had been rumours that he would do this and then one day, quite suddenly, he did. Overnight, petrol prices rose by a third. The next morning, citizens armed with shovels and with lengths of steel rods pulled from construction sites poured on to the boulevards. They tipped over police cars and littered the streets with flaming tyres. The better-armed citizens shot out the windows of the oil ministry. As chaos spread out of the capital, Yemen held its breath for two days. Then the president's son's Republican Guard, an elite troop that trains in the mountains above Sana'a, was called in. Tanks rolled down the streets. Helicopter gunships hovered over the dirtier neighbourhoods. A peace that felt – and continues to feel – rather temporary descended on Sana'a.

When calm had been restored, Faris called me into his office. He wanted our forthcoming editorial to suggest that the disturbances had been the work of directionless teenagers. I mentioned that they had looked like normal citizens to me – not just teenage ones or poor ones, but the inhabitants of the city – grocery store workers, clerks, neighbours, bus drivers. 'No, they were teenagers,' he said. They had been out for a thrill. 'Write that.' I wrote that. 'Say that complete order has been restored.' I wrote that order had been restored to the streets. 'Say that Iran has been known to stir up trouble in Yemen.' I wrote, 'Iran has been known to stir up trouble in the Arabian peninsula.'

But as I was writing, a frightening possibility lingered in the streets. It was that there had been a religious element to the violence, that it had been hatched in the mosques of the people (not by foreign agents) and loosed at an auspicious moment by local religious figures. The further possibility which seemed, at least, worth enquiring into was that the people had lived for a little too long under their petrol-obsessed ex-tank-commander-turned-president, Ali Abdullah Saleh, and were interested now in a new dispensation. We didn't know much about the motivations of the rioters because we didn't interview them. But, even without interviews, it didn't require much imagination to suppose that under a new dispensation, the old tank commander would find his way into a spider hole somewhere and from there to a gallows, a chopping block, or the bloodstained wall at the back of a prison yard.

Now that tanks were in the streets, the newspaper went into shutdown mode. Faris saw to it that the reporters filled the paper with the news that fills other Arab papers: the president's five-year plan for agriculture, the arrival of a delegation of ministers from Malaysia. The reporters wrote straight from the scripts supplied by Saba News, Yemen's bedraggled Minitruth. They never left the office. Neither did the photographer. Why should he? He had been prohibited from photographing.

In the privacy of his office, I asked Faris if he thought there had really been an organising force behind the violence. He shrugged his shoulders. He didn't know.

'How deep is the frustration?' I asked. He waved off the question.

'Not deep,' he said. He looked out the window: 'I don't know,' he admitted. After that conversation it was clear to me that whatever was occurring out in the streets, he didn't want to know. My job that summer was to photograph a French beekeeper as he ambled across the beaches of a Yemeni island. Above all, Faris wanted to know, and wanted everyone else to know, that there was delicious honey to be eaten in Yemen.

Now, in the wake of the violence, a new theory concerning the workings of our paper occurred to me: Faris, the counsellor, exercised control over the office grounds, when he wanted to, and over his employees. Outside of this, he didn't control much. Neither were the VIPs from the palace particularly in control. That's what the retinues of armed guards were for. Faris – or really the office of the president – was paying $80,000 a month to publish the *Observer* because the president and his aides wanted to see pretty pictures more than they wanted to see reality. The president loved illusions. And bling. So did the apparatchiks.

I had thought that $80,000 a month was a kingly sum for a nation of street children and qat addicts. But it wasn't really. The office of the president made few domestic investments and drew profits on 350,000 barrels of oil a day. In that sphere, $80,000 a month was petty cash.

As for my role: I had been assigned to tourist articles because they actually were important. The tourists were proxies for the Western embassies and the oil companies. Just like the tourists, who wandered about, being welcomed into humble dwellings, drinking tea and scattering their money across the landscape, the other foreign guests in Yemen (that is, the oil companies and the diplomats) were expected to behave. Were the tourists sometimes kidnapped? Yes, they were. The embassies and oil companies were to take the appropriate cue. *We can do this the nice way or the brutal way*, my articles had said, between the lines, though I had been too naïve to guess. The Yemeni government officers much preferred to divorce Westerners from their money by means of a show: the magical kingdom, the pliant natives, the cascading waterfalls, and the admiring tourists. That's what the cabinet officers came to the newspaper to see, and when they did see it, they smiled and afterwards filled their mouths with qat. In the end, the qat and the tourist articles accomplished the same thing: they offered soothing illusions – in other words, lies.

It seemed to me that there might also have been a purpose behind the rudderless management style, which was not at all an uncommon technique in Yemen. As long as the employees were squabbling among themselves over who was in control, nobody was in control. With no one in control, the squabbles worsened into rivalries and the rivalries hardened into factions. As long as the factions disliked each other, they were not uniting to demand higher wages, education and opportunities for career advancement. They made no such demands.

As I was putting the pieces of the newspaper puzzle together, I thought a lot, during my workdays, about Zaid, and the other reporters who had welcomed me to the newspaper. Their lot was to be frustrated. They couldn't marry because they didn't have enough money, and had difficulty advancing as journalists because they had had only inadequate, on-the-job training.

They lived in a state of state of sexual, financial and professional blockage.

But this system worked. As long as the blockages were relieved intermittently – and they were – the journalists remained hopeful. As long as they were hopeful, they were easy to control. They were exceptionally easy to control.

12

Before I moved into the mosque dorm, I lived on the sixth floor
of a tower house in the old city of Sana'a. In the early mornings,
a gritty hot wind picked up and banged against the windowpanes.
It blew all day, flinging a fine red silt, like tennis court clay, against
the glass. In the summer, when the monsoon rains came to
Sana'a, the wind had real destructive power. By midday plastic
bags and little bits of hay and sweet wrapper were being carried
aloft by updraughts. They swirled round outside my sixth floor
windows, then drifted away, over the tops of the other tower
houses. In the late afternoon, heavy globules of rain like pebbles
began to pelt the windows.

But the wind was strange. Often in the monsoon season, it
would rage at midday, promising a typhoon-like deluge, and then
subside in the afternoon into a soft gentle wind that the locals
called a *nasseem* – a cat's paw. For the rest of the day, the doors
and windows of the tower houses would tinkle in a gentle,
musical way as if they had been made rickety on purpose to
murmur to the inhabitants.

In Sana'a, the wind had worn its way into the habits of the
people. You could see it in the black acrylic gowns of the women
and the silken shawls the men wore around their shoulders.
Everyone loved breeze-responsive material. The wind also turned

up in the poetry, in tall tales, and in the songs of the oud player, Abdul Rahman al-Akhfash.

A week after the riots, I rode my bike out to a village on the outskirts of Sana'a to confer with the newspaper's oldest reporter, Muhammad al-Kibsi. He had a veteran reporter's intuition about the direction of public events, and was a subtle interpreter of all those things in the local landscape, like the mood of the crowds and changing winds, that confounded me. I was hoping that Muhammad would help me understand more about the violence that had recently swept through the streets of the capital. What was really behind this anger, I wanted to know, and was he at all worried about what would come next? The riots had made me believe that the citizenry was concealing a dangerous outrage beneath its solemn, pious outward aspect. What, I wanted to know, were the people really feeling?

At first, Muhammad spoke to me about the news business as it had been in Yemen when he was a young man. Back then, in the early sixties, the Imam of Sana'a had been the country's spiritual and temporal ruler. His news had been boring but it had been honest. Every few months he met a foreign leader. Several days after the colloquy, he issued a statement to the effect that there had been a colloquy and that it had been productive. To be a newsman in this environment was to be like a messenger working on behalf of the king. There was a status and a dignity attached to delivering pronouncements. Furthermore, a new awareness of modern statehood and nationalism was rising throughout the Arab world. To serve the imam had been to participate in the Yemeni awakening of these sentiments.

At that time, news from the outside world was not a big factor in the job of a Yemeni journalist. Regular flights to Yemen didn't begin until the 1970s. Until then, working in the Yemeni media had been like working in the last telegraph station in the longest, most distant telegraph line in the Arab world. The bulletins came at irregular intervals, and described a world so far away, in which so few Yemenis held a stake, that few people actually understood – or cared, for that matter, to read – the bulletins.

Back then, Muhammad said, when Yemenis wanted direct information about the world around them, they went to their imams, whom they trusted to have a comprehensive knowledge of the Koran and the hadith. This was where practical news you could use was to be found.

Nowadays, with 300,000 barrels of oil being pumped from the Yemeni ground, day in and day out, plus terrorism, plus nascent democracy, there was news everywhere. There were press conferences, speeches, bulletins from the Saba News agency, and events that were not quite news and not quite advertisements staged by the cellphone companies and car dealerships. A veritable storm of news swirled over Sana'a all day and all night. It huffed and puffed but one thing it did not do, Muhammad felt, was supply the people of the nation with information about changes in the world around them. Where did the oil money go? How much of the national wealth was being spent on weapons? Why exactly were the Shia in the north being bombed and how many of them had been killed to date? No one knew the answers to these questions, nor was anyone going to know, because when the news mattered, the office of the president preferred to keep it secret. The task of the journalist at that point, like that of the citizen, was to shut up.

There was almost no light at all left in the room by the time I got around to asking Muhammad about the riots. Soon there would be none, because the electricity had been cut: a consequence of too much demand, and too little government capacity to plan, build and pay. In other words, to govern.

'Nobody knows how widespread that violence really was, right?' I asked. 'Or exactly how many people died.' Some reports had said eighteen people had been killed across the country, but reports tended to pull random figures from the air. I wondered what the real number was.

He shrugged his shoulders. 'Only God knows.'

'And does anybody really know whether this violence was organised? And if it was organised, by whom? And how and to what end?'

'How would we know?' he said.

'Good point,' I said. 'We'd have to trust the newspapers for that sort of thing.'

A boy (a servant? a son?) brought a candle. Muhammad lit it and nibbled at his qat. There wasn't much more to talk about after that. I had my iPod with me. In Yemen, the iPod is still a miraculous invention. Yemenis are delighted by how clear the sound is, and how much musical junk it can hold. I plugged the headphones into his ears and turned on the worried lament about the man, alone in his mountain house, whose door was being battered by the Sana'ani wind.

Every time the wind knocks at my door, it tells me that my lover has come. But the wind and the door are liars, liars. They have come to test me, to test me.

I had heard the song hundreds of times by then and had understood little but that afternoon, for the first time, the lyrics produced a picture I could read. The man in the song was at his wits' end. The lover he was waiting for wasn't coming. But why not? Did she have another man? Had wagging tongues lied to her about him? Maybe she had forgotten that he was alone and waiting for him. But that couldn't be. She loved him. Did she not? Why was the wind making such an incredible racket at his windows?

The religious term for this state of internal division and self-doubt is 'fitna'. In the presence of fitna, Muslims, it is thought, become befuddled, and their commitment to the Straight Path disintegrates. Satan takes the upper hand.

Towards the end of the song, the singer concludes that wind itself is made of lies: 'the air around me, you are fitna,' he sings, 'and life is a lie into which one falls.'

The meaning of the song, Muhammad said softly as he took the iPod headphones from his ears, is that this is how we live now. The public side of life in Yemen, in his view, was a whirlwind of lies. We don't trust one another. We have no one to trust. The nation was now a collection of mutually suspicious individuals who lied to one another and were lied to by their government. In such an environment, he felt, there wasn't much left for someone to whom faith mattered. You could lie in Yemen nowadays and you could be paid for this but one thing you could not do, he felt, was trust.

Now he wanted to move to America. He believed that the job of journalists in America also involved lying but at least they were well compensated, drove expensive cars, and travelled the world. Some time in the future, perhaps soon, he hoped to apply for a Green Card.

13

A week later, on returning from a lunch with European journalists, Faris summoned me to his office.

He picked up a telephone. 'Two coffees, quickly,' he said in Arabic.

When the servant woman had come and gone, he lowered his eyes to me. He spoke in a solemn voice in English. 'I'd like you to write a letter for me.'

'Okay,' I said.

'Now, I want you to be in the picture.'

'Okay,' I said. The picture was that the chancellor of Germany was arriving by plane that afternoon at the Sana'a International Airport. We were going to meet him. When we got there, we would deliver a letter to him.

'Now, just because you're in the picture, this doesn't mean that anybody else is, right?'

'Right,' I said. It was a rare privilege to be invited into the picture in Yemen. From a distance, decisions often seemed random, or counter-productive, and to try to understand was to stare at a collage of seeming facts and shadows. Now I was going to be in the picture.

'What we're trying to do here,' Faris said, 'what we're going to be doing is asking for some equipment.'

'Okay,' I said.

'Why don't you write this: "Dear Gerhard."'

'Dear Gerhard,' I wrote.

Faris continued: '"As you know, we – Yemen – our government of Yemen . . ."' He paused. 'No. "*The* government of Yemen has, over the past five years . . ."' He stopped again. 'No, "*My* government of Yemen has, over the . . ." no – make that ten, "for ten years been a big partner in the war on terrorism."'

He stopped. I rewrote his line a bit and read it back to him. He focused on it. His brow furrowed. 'Okay, good. But now . . . I don't know,' he said. 'What next?'

This was where my job kicked in. It wasn't such a hard job, really. It involved a few sentences in plain English, plus typing. It was the sort of job that ought to have gone to the foreign ministry but the president didn't trust it. Or he did trust it, but not all the time. No one knew.

The situation was this: the Yemeni president, Saleh, needed the German chancellor, Schröder, to facilitate the sale of a batch of high tech eavesdropping equipment. Religious extremists out in the Yemeni deserts were ramping up their operations. How could he fight the war on terror with RadioShack walkie-talkies? He couldn't. The Republic of Yemen needed a certain kind of high grade sonic hardware manufactured in Germany. The Yemenis would pay. But they needed the red tape on sales of this equipment to go away. In a hurry. A letter to this effect had to be drafted. Now.

'Write. You're in the picture now?'

I nodded.

'Write something. Anything. You got the idea?'

I nodded. 'Go ahead then and write.'

I listed instances of progress Yemen had made in the war on terror: no major attacks in Yemen since the one on the USS *Cole* in 2000. Terrorist cells had been disrupted. Kidnappings had been almost eliminated. Then I wrote:

Despite our success, our government is still facing difficulties. The technological capacity of some rogue elements in Yemen is keeping pace with the latest industrial innovations. We, as a government, must surpass this considerable rate of innovation. We have no choice but to move faster than our foes.

When I got to 'foes', Faris stood up from his desk. He was a tall, well-groomed, good-looking former athlete. He put on his jacket and dropped his pistol into its holster. 'What have you got for me? Read it to me.'

I read him the note from beginning to end, without pausing or looking at him.

'That's perfect,' he said. 'Keep that.'

'Okay,' I said. 'Now what? We ask for the equipment?'

'Yes,' he said. 'Put it nicely.'

'Okay,' I said. 'I think we should be direct. Let's just say what's on our mind. No beating around the bush.'

He nodded.

'So we should write this: "Give us the goods now, you German assholes. Or the terrorists will kick you in the ass." Okay?'

He smiled. 'No,' he said. 'Settle down.'

I did settle down. I finished writing the letter. This was my job.

The chancellor was due at Sana'a airport within the half-hour. We printed out our letter, then piled into the boss's Mercedes sedan. It had been a gift from President Saleh, a reward for loyalty.

The airport was forty minutes away, so we were late. But this was normal. We were late for everything, every day. We dashed to the car, then tore through the streets, barely braking at the red lights, and nodding at the policemen as we flew by. In the straight stretches, we picked up so much speed that we couldn't read the billboards, and when we hit the turns, they came at us like bends on a racetrack.

As we got closer to the airport we had to slow to pick our way through traffic accidents and crowds milling at the entrances to mosques.

Two miles from the airport tarmac, we had to stop altogether because an impromptu qat market had spilled into a part of the street normally used as a bus depot. Dozens of robed men swarmed around the qat sellers and the minibuses, pushing and yelling and raising their cash in the air. As they crowded around the qat booths, they tugged at one another's headscarves, dropped them on to the pavement, laughed and picked up their fallen turbans, then piled them on their heads again like disorderly salads.

Yemenis loved silliness. They loved pretending they were living in a wide rocky loony bin of zaniness. Zaniness, insouciance, roughhousing: this is what they had instead of a future.

At one point two tribesmen wearing more dignified, tightly wrapped silken bandannas approached the car. The sight of such a new, gleaming, black Mercedes froze them in their tracks. They stared at it with their bloodshot eyes as if it might be a newfangled sort of animal, something they could devour later on, in the privacy of their huts. As they stared, an odour of freshly butchered sheep, urine and minibus exhaust filtered into the car.

Faris nudged the car forward. A moment later, we came across the aftermath of a scuffle. Two men were clutching each other; each held a handful of robe. They yelled and spat at each other, their faces flushed, the fronts of their white gowns spattered with blood. The crowd itself was making a low, slightly ominous rumble.

One of the combatants turned to us as we nudged forward. From his mouth he let loose a red bubble of blood and spit. It landed on the windshield of the Mercedes.

Did he mean to do that? I wondered. Certainly not, I thought. Surely he could see from the licence plates, if not from the car itself, that we were government officials.

'Yeah, look at this,' Faris said, as the car idled, more to himself than to me. 'Chaos. Mess. It's because of the qat. They're all addicted. They just want to chew. All day, every day. It's not like we haven't given them opportunities. The army, schools, universities. We're a poor country, okay. But look.'

Far away, across the road from the crowd, which was about

a hundred strong now and growing, a sprinkling of black robes pushed at brooms. The women kept their distance – from the horde and from one another. They were wearing the full veil, and gowns so long the hems trailed in the dust. Of course they knew that no gowns and no veils would have protected them in an emergency. And they knew that any little thing – the passing whim of a passing addict, for instance – could put them in physical danger. That's why they kept their distance.

Finally the police did clear a lane for us. Within seconds, the Mercedes was back up to speed. It sailed past more billboards, more butchers' shops, and roadside sentries standing in the setting sun like statues in a ruin. We rolled up the car windows. We checked our mobile phones for messages and fiddled with the stereo until it found a pop music station. For the rest of the ride to the airport, we listened to Supertramp and Cat Stevens. Cat Stevens was singing a happy, mystico-Islamico 1970s song:

> Now I've been happy lately, thinking about the good things to
> come
> And I believe it could be. Something good has begun.

At the airport, the generals and ministers milled about on the tarmac. A banana-republic military band assembled itself on a magenta carpet. I listened for a bit as they tooted into their instruments. The generals scanned the sky for Schröder's plane.

As I watched the apparatchiks chatting with one another, then gazing at the sky, then gazing at one another again, I realised that I probably did know the truth about the Schröder letter. I had known it for some time, but I had not wanted to confront the implications.

In Yemen, governing is the art of dividing, then befuddling, then presiding over the low-level anarchy that results. Even in his own palace, in the security of his private suite, perhaps especially there, the president must be busy at this task. The reason is simple: the last three rulers of Yemen were assassinated in palace coups. Now, thirty years into the Saleh regime, the atmosphere among the ruling junta remains tense. The president would like his son to succeed him. Others feel the presidency should be put to a vote. Those who would like the vote are thought to dislike the son, but how deep their dislike is and what they are willing to do to advance their aims no one knows.

Now the president trusted in military hardware. The Germans had invented special code-decrypting radios. If he could get hold of one of these, he and perhaps a few of his closest friends – those without loyal armies behind them (maybe Faris?) – could listen in on the generals who did control the armies. I doubted that the high tech sonic equipment would be put to use surveilling terrorists in the back-country hills. The terrorists were too primitive and too uninteresting to the ruling clique. It would have required too much effort to get to them, and there were better ways of approaching them, such as calling their imams on the telephone.

Anyway, if the terrorists did do something, whatever they did wasn't going to touch the president and his friends, who had excellent security. It would, however, prove to the West that Yemen really did need greater quantities of military equipment.

Though we were not telling the Germans this, the high tech equipment, I guessed, was probably more for domestic, palace use. The innermost clique wished to have a high-resolution, computer-based system for monitoring the activities of the next most inner clique.

The more my thoughts moved in this direction, the more working in the government didn't seem like such an interesting idea. The government, such as it was, was a closed circle. It spent its days staring at its cynosure, the president, who was in reality a minor Wizard of Oz. His apparatchiks were puffed-up stagehands. Their job, which they didn't do all that well, was to erect complicated stages on which Yemeni VIPS, visitors from Europe and Saudi Arabia, could strut. Why did I want to contribute to the success of such an enterprise? I didn't.

*   *   *

I did know that beyond the set designers and their props an actual nation of believers, tribes and dwindling natural resources was working out its own purposes. I didn't know much about those purposes but now, for the first time in my life in Yemen, I wanted to.

I undid my tie and deposited it on the tarmac. By the time Schröder and Saleh passed in their limousines, it had been trampled many times by running journalists and caught up in the wheels of a military jeep. I was happy to see it go.

In theory, the *Yemen Observer* staff was meant to go back to the office after this airport reception. I had been asked to write an editorial about Yemen making common cause with Germany to defeat the two scourges of the Middle East: poverty and terrorism. Now it seemed to me that I was being paid $200 a month to write propaganda which few people read and fewer people believed. At that rate, I had to be in love with the work. I had to believe it was worth dedicating my life to. Now I felt it wasn't worth even a twenty-minute detour to the office, so I went home, opened a bottle of black market Djibouti vodka, and watched the celebratory Yemen–Germany friendship fireworks sparkle over the city.

14

In the late afternoons, just before six, in the courtyard of the villa we used as an office, the staff would line up before a spouting garden hose. At that hour, the opening lines of the call to prayer were tumbling out of the sky. 'Allahu akbar,' the muezzin would call and then 'Allahu akbar,' again. Then silence.

After the Schröder visit, I felt there was nothing more for me to do at the newspaper. I came only in the evening to hang out with the reporters and to watch them go through the rituals of the sunset prayer.

Sometimes someone would turn the garden hose on Obadi, the gatekeeper, who, at almost forty, was more desperate than anyone else to get married. He had a beautiful smile.

For the most part, though, people carried themselves with dignity before the prayer. The reporters rolled their trousers up over their knees. They turned back their sleeves. They clamped the garden hose between their shins and filled their palms with water. It splashed down over shaved heads. It doused their faces and trickled through their toes.

The newspaper owned a mat of imitation bamboo. Usually someone who was eager to get on with the prayer would roll the thing out across the polished marble of the courtyard. One or two reporters would step out on to the mat and perform two optional, extracurricular prostrations.

I never knew this until I converted to Islam, but when the muezzin calls the faithful to prayer, he's meant to weave a note of sadness – in Arabic this note is called *huzn* – into the melody of the call. *Huzn* reminds the faithful of the vastness extending between humankind and God, and appeals to the conscience of the Believer: *abstract yourself from workaday life for a moment. Return to the house of God. Come home.* The local muezzin seemed to know that in this day and age, with all the fitna about, the Muslims of Sana'a were going to need a fair amount of *huzn* in order for the call to accomplish its magic. So he took long pauses between every line, and allowed the echo to roll through the streets. 'Come to the flourishing,' he sang. 'Come to the flourishing,' he sang again, and waited while the idea of flourishing on the Straight Path of Allah reached into the minds of the believers.

The men on the mat concentrated their brows.

After these words fell from the sky, sometimes right away, sometimes as much as a quarter of an hour later, the rest of the employees would line up on the plastic bamboo. Standing out there, barefoot, shoulder to shoulder, glistening in the last light of the day, they looked like a troop of Huck Finns, ready to alight on a current, ready to slip away into the river of life. One of them – it didn't matter who – stood at the head of the raft. He was their pilot, their rough and ready seer. The doormen, the guards, the delivery drivers, the hangers-on and the reporters lined up in rows behind this temporary imam.

You're not supposed to stare at your work colleagues when they're lowering their faces to God, but I did. I liked watching their routine: so brotherly, so out of synch with the world of computers and phoney news from which they had just withdrawn, so ancient.

How strange, I thought, as I watched them.

I hadn't seen sincerity like that in six months inside the offices of the newspaper. But then maybe I hadn't been looking in the right place.

*   *   *

Afterwards, when the last of the prostrations had been performed, my colleagues would roll off their haunches and lounge on the mat, and speak in quiet voices as darkness swept down out of the sky. Often, they would wave me over and urge me to learn to pray.

These were friendly moments. They made me think that submitting to Islam might not be a huge deal, that it was another step into the culture, that I had already taken some and might as well take more. I would have more friends, learn the language more thoroughly and live in a world where words actually meant something. Here, in this domain, I would discover Arabia itself – how have the people lived these many centuries? What do they know? What do they love? What do they read and how? The artificial version of Yemen wasn't bringing me news like that.

At that time, when I was considering a submission to Islam, I had Huckleberry Finn in mind a lot: the way he committed himself to the wild, lovely, unfathomable current of the river. Anyone who admires such a person wouldn't dream of sitting on the banks of the great gushing, ever-flowing spirit of the nation all his life. Not when it was so close, not when it had so much to teach, not when the people he liked most were urging him to take a little step forward, just enough to feel the power of the current.

15

My guide to living, during those first few weeks of unemployment, was Charles Nicholl's book, *Somebody Else*, about the poet Arthur Rimbaud's experience in Yemen and Africa. As an adolescent, he had dazzled Parisian literary circles though he had been, at the time, a troubled teenager, driven by a powerful urge towards self-destruction. The longer he stayed in France, the more trouble he caused: there were fights, scenes, and there was the famous episode in which Verlaine, driven to distraction by his bratty lover, shot Rimbaud in the wrist.

When Rimbaud turned up in Aden in 1880, at the age of twenty-six, he was a broken man. He had repudiated poetry as an occupation, had little money and had broken off communication with his former acquaintances in Parisian literary circles.

To judge by the poetry he wrote as an adolescent, this was a consummation he had been wishing for for some time.

> The marine air will burn my lungs. Unknown climates will tan my skin. To swim, trample grass, and above all smoke, to drink liquors as strong as molten metal . . . I'll have gold: be lazy and merciless.

According to Charles Nicholl, he had been neither lazy nor merciless in Yemen but instead scholarly. He had learned Arabic. He had made money: by trading in coffee, then in guns, and perhaps, here and there, in African slaves. He translated the Koran into French. In Abyssinia, he married a local woman, and may have fathered a child. By 1883 he had taken a new name, Abdo [Abdullah] Rimbo. Local Muslims came to him when they wished to discuss abstruse matters of Islamic theology.

Actually, this transformation into Abdo Rimbo, I learned, was the result of a programme Rimbaud had invented, as a teenager. What can you do to write something interesting? To outdo your peers? To bring something new to the table? '[The poet] must make himself a seer,' he had written.

He makes himself a seer by long, immense and systematic derangement of the senses. All forms of love, of suffering, of madness. He searches himself, he drains down all the poisons so that only the quintessences are left.

All right, I thought, when I read this passage, I can see how deranging the senses might be fun. So I experimented: chewing the local narcotic did not give me visions as the sellers promised but it did kill my appetite. Being without appetite made me wonder how much food I really needed per day. Maybe an egg in the morning? Yes, okay. And a bowl of watery rice at lunch? Quite enough, really. Sometimes, I added a slab of roasted chicken to the rice. The Yemeni chicken tended to make me sick. So I went home from the tin-plate restaurant in which I usually ate, vomited, then chewed qat leaves through the afternoon. I started to lose weight. I'd never really lost weight before. Now I could watch my body change under the influence of a strange climate, strange diet and strange people.

In the evening I couldn't sleep because of the amphetamine in the qat, so I had to settle down with the Djibouti vodka. I woke in the early dawn, just when the morning call to prayer was ringing out over the city and streaks of blue sky were appearing on the horizon to the east. That was a beautiful hour in which to read: 'My daytime is done; I am leaving Europe. . . . quick. Are there new lives?' So Rimbaud had written at the age of seventeen.

*　*　*

After a few weeks of this routine, I noticed that I had stumbled across an incredibly cheap way to live. My rent was costing me $200 a month. My food was costing me about $2 a day, and the vodka and qat cost another $5. Since I had $30,000 in savings in the bank, I calculated that I was a minor Bill Gates, at least in relation to my neighbours and that I could probably live on this budget, barring boredom or a tropical disease, counting in a freelance newspaper article or two, until the Day of the Dead. But I had no intention of sticking around for even twelve more months and still less intention of counting out my pennies so I started to live like a king.

I looked at the Yemeni currency which came out of the ATM machine smelling like so much pawed-over, foul, Third-World monopoly money, as a joke. No currency I'd ever seen left me this estranged from it, and this uninterested in its value as money.

I paid much too much for my qat and for cab fares and told myself that I was evening out global injustice by doing so. But when I was honest with myself I knew I wasn't accomplishing anything at all, and since giving away money wasn't accomplishing anything, and holding on to it wasn't accomplishing anything, I started to think that it just didn't matter what I did with it.

The local kids quickly picked up on this truth about me. They cheated me at the corner store. Sometimes I made a fuss. Sometimes, I didn't. Often, they hung on my sleeves the moment I set foot in the little alleyway in front of my house.

When they were too insistent, when they were hanging on my arms or reaching their hands into my pockets, or standing on the pavement before me, shrieking into my face, I seized them by the front of their robes. 'Shut up!' I told them. 'If you want to talk to me, talk quietly,' I told them, yelling. This frightened them. But there were times when so many kids were clustering around me, and so many shrieking faces were yelling at me, that I wanted to do more than frighten them. I pushed the most aggressive kids to the ground, and when they fell, I held their throats to the pavement and ground their tiny wrists into the cobbles.

Before my first such episode, I had been under the impression that I was turning myself into an altruistic, feed-the-poor, Bob Geldof person. But one afternoon, after I had had a proper battle with a pesty kid I had to wonder: where did this violent streak come from? Is this really within me? I didn't give it too much thought, though, because I was glad of it. I needed it in those swarms of pushing and tugging children.

16

The website for the Mahad Medina, a religious school in Sana'a, said that new students had to be 'Salafi Muslims in good standing with strict observation' but I just walked in off the street. An American friend I met in a fast-food restaurant accompanied me. Together we climbed to the fourth floor of an apartment building in a newer, disregarded section of Sana'a. I stood in front of a door and knocked.

When it opened, my friend, Muhammad from Maryland, introduced me as Thabit. 'He's looking for knowledge,' Muhammad said. 'I thought you could help him.'

A heavyset American who introduced himself as Omar shook my hand. He pointed to a spare foam-rubber mattress in a corner. 'Have a seat,' he said. When I sat, he introduced the other students in the room: a British Pakistani named Abdul Majid, and Ibrahim, a Bosnian, who had recently been a computer-science student in Denmark.

Introducing myself, I said, 'I'm interested in what you guys are doing here. I've been in Yemen for a year now. I have a pretty strong feeling that I'm missing something.'

The students wanted to know if I believed in God at all. I temporised. 'I don't know,' I said. 'I'm sort of interested in what you guys believe about God.'

*   *   *

Omar yawned. I asked him why he had left Philadelphia. 'America is jess a big ol' Seven-Eleven,' he said. 'Jess people buying up stuff they don't need, you know. Shampoos and shoes, drugs and sweets. Here in Yemen we got Science,' he said. 'Here we don't buy nothing.' He was twenty-eight years old and had been living in Yemen for six months. Abdul Majid was twenty-three. He had come to Yemen so that he could teach his Pakistani parents, his English sisters and his Canadian wife what Islam really was. Ibrahim had come because Islam in Bosnia had been massacred by the Serbs. 'No Islam in Bosnia, no. Some Muslims live there, yes,' he said, 'but they are afraid.'

On this, my first afternoon in the Mahad Medina dormitory, we perused some of the easiest, most self-explanatory chapters of the Koran. The passage we talked about more than any other had to do with wasted lives, and the dumb, profitless passage of time.

'By [the passage of] time, mankind is in loss,' said the Sura al-Asr, the Chapter of Time. 'It is in loss except for those who truly believe and worship Allah alone, and do righteous deeds, performing that which is obligatory upon them and avoiding that which they are forbidden.'

Ibrahim had memorised these words in their mellifluous Arabic. He was the most learned of the students and therefore the leader of the discussion. His part as leader was to mumble the passage to himself on his mattress. When he was finished, Omar, a giant, oval man with an enormous oval face, turned to me. 'Your lord, he *created* you,' he said. 'He *created* Ibrahim. He created you all for a purpose. If you don't find out what it is, you just wasting your life. You might as *well* be dead.'

Such was the verdict of the students and I could see it immediately in the saddened faces of Abdul Majid and Ibrahim. The conversation continued for a few more minutes but it didn't need to because I had understood the point well enough. Without Islam, the passage of time was merely stupid. Without knowledge of what was obligatory and what forbidden to men, life was an aimless and profoundly selfish thing. It might drag on at great length – or it might not. In either case, without God it had no meaning. Ibrahim made this point sternly and slowly in rumbling, Slavic-inflected English. 'If knowledge is available, we as Muslims – we believe it is death if you do not seek it. Even life is death.'

Just before he rose to do his ablutions, he reached into a plastic bag by his pillow. He withdrew several pamphlets, examined them, and then passed me one: *The Way of the Salaf.*

Then, without ceremony or smiles, he asked me to leave. Prayer time had come. At that hour, I had no business in this room, in the dorm, or in the neighbourhood at all, really. Ibrahim showed me the door.

17

You don't have to be a Muslim to feel that a simpler, truer way of life endures in the East.

When Gertrude Bell first arrived in Syria, in 1909, she wrote home from Damascus: 'Existence suddenly seems to be a very simple matter, and one wonders why we plan and scheme . . . when all we need to do is to live and to make sure of a succeeding generation.'

I had similar feelings when I first arrived in Sana'a, but not knowing what to do, I busied myself in a life of planning and scheming.

My discussion with Ibrahim, Omar and Abdul Majid suggested to me that these were three kids who knew enough not to do what I had done. Now they would focus on the important things: God, Knowledge, Koran.

'I'm here to learn my religion,' Abdul Majid, the Mancunian, told me when I asked him why he had come to Yemen.

But what did he mean to do once he had learned his religion?

He shrugged. 'You never finish,' he said. 'But when I advance, maybe in five years, maybe in ten – whenever my knowledge is strong – I could teach. Only Allah knows.'

'Teach who?' I asked.

His mother and father. Beyond that, he didn't know. Anyway,

he wasn't worried. Things would take care of themselves. In the meantime, he would study.

Later on that evening, at home, in my apartment in the Old City, I leafed through *The Way*. It was unexceptional. All Islamic pamphlets in Yemen recommended following the ways of the Prophet, as this one did. All of them were written in badly translated English-Arabic, with spelling mistakes, and quotations from the Koran. 'Stick to the Sunnah,' the quotations in *The Way* said, and 'Muhammad is not the father of any amongst your men but [the] Messenger of Allah and the seal of the Prophets.'

On Wikipedia, I looked around for context about *The Way*. I discovered that the term *salaf* referred to the community of disciples and warriors who surrounded the Prophet at the dawn of Islam (*salaf* = ancestor). I also discovered that Salafism and Wahabism were essentially the same. Muslims preferred the former term to the latter.

The Salafis abjured politics, idealised family order, and loved the Prophet above all things. Salafism honoured scholarship and scholars. Millions of Saudis and millions of Yemenis were leading pious, ordered lives by revering these precepts.

Despite these virtues, sects within this strain of Islam were causing trouble. Its military wing had swept Osama bin Laden from his family of plutocrats, and had brought him to a life of caves and jihad. For fifty years, I read, the angry side of Salafi Islam had been guiding the most important names in jihadism: Sayyid Qutb and Ayman al-Zawahiri and the Palestinian theorist, Abdullah Azzam. It had inspired the London bombers, and was calming the suicide soldiers of Baghdad as they strapped themselves into their bombs.

The kids in the dorm, however, didn't belong to anything angry. If anything, they were escaping earlier, angrier lives. In Yemen they were perhaps getting themselves in slightly over their heads. And so? That didn't bother me, nor apparently did it bother them. This is what we were there for: immersion, deeper Islam, a radical change in our lives.

Since I had no job then and not much to do, I sat every night in the place of seeing, or *mafraj*, in my apartment in the Old City.

Every evening at around 6.30, a muezzin whose voiced cracked and sometimes cut out altogether clicked on his microphone. He coughed and sputtered for a moment. Then all was quiet. Then he took a deep breath and called out to the heavens: 'God is great, God is great.' Before he could get through the second *akbar*, he was joined by another bellowing voice and then instants later by another and another until the whole valley rang with echoing, overlapping cries: every voice said that God was great. Every voice said that he witnessed there was no God but God. *Except Allahhhh, except Allahhhhh, except Allahhhh.*

For me, this time of day was always a little nerve-racking. But the storm of cries over the city also reassured me. It made the single human voice, particularly the one inside one's head, sound petty and unimportant. Meanwhile, the universal, stereophonic sound, bouncing from one side of the valley to the other, constricted space. It made the towering escarpments that surrounded the city seem to loom and drape, as if they had picked up and advanced a little bit during the day while the citizens napped and chewed their qat. These could be ecstatic moments for the tourist because the late afternoon sun turned the cliffs the colour of whiskey and the muezzins' voices really did bang and ricochet between the brick tower houses. But it wasn't a great time to be an unbelieving resident. The streets emptied. The darkness fell at that middle of the world latitude like a cellar door collapsing. One minute it was dusk and the sky was a storm of cries. The next minute a wall of black air had fallen over the minarets, the moon sat on top of the tallest spire, and the mountain ridges, overlapping and chaotic during the day, melted into a single dark velvet curtain surrounding the city.

A week later I was standing in the courtyard parking lot of the Mahad Medina, fixing my bike to a mulberry tree. Ahmed, a director of the school was waddling towards me in his robe and sandals. He had a jolly smile in his eyes, and in his hands were the keys to the new Land Cruiser from which he had just emerged.

If I was to enrol in the school, I would need the permission of this eminent personage first.

I used to have the same conversation with Yemenis when I was interested in them being interested in me. It was a sort of comic routine – silly, but foolproof. It was odd how universally consistent the Yemeni reaction was, and how automatic the dialogue. The script worked because I loved what Yemenis loved: their sense of virtue, their drugs, and their dream of Yemen as a confederation of God-seeking mountain brothers, all loving, warm and prepared at a moment's notice to clash their sabres together in acknowledgement of God's supreme power. This, they believed, was their quirky place in the Arab world.

Often on the street, especially when I was riding my bike, passers-by would stop to stare at me. The starers were always men and were never shy. I would sometimes pull my bike over and introduce myself.

'My name is Thabit al-Mattari,' I would say, 'and I come from Beni Mattar.'

The starers would raise their eyebrows.

'*What* is your name?' they would say. 'Where did you say you were from?'

'Behind that mountain there,' I would say, and nod to the hills. 'I am from the land of the Beni Mattar.' *The land of the sons of the rain.* This was a village on the road to the Red Sea, famous in Yemen for its weapons trafficking and its opposition to the federal government. If other people on the street happened to hear the name of the village in my mouth, they would stop. They would rest their hands on the pommels of their waist daggers or lean on the shoulders of their neighbours.

'Beni Mattar?' someone would wonder. 'Really?' *Amana?*

'Yes, Beni Mattar,' I'd say.

This puzzled Yemenis. It especially puzzled the country folk from Beni Mattar who were everywhere in Sana'a. Someone in the group would reflect for a moment and then conclude, wisely: 'No, can't be.'

Heads would turn. I would stare into the crowd. I got some pretty blank, mystified looks. 'No, where are you *from*? Which *country*?' someone would correct. 'Which *nation*?' he would say. *Ayi bilad?* I would stare.

'Beni Mattar!' I would reply, pointing to the farthest and highest mountain summits. 'Behind that mountain, there!' I would say, feigning annoyance and indignation. 'What do you mean, No? Where are *you* from, my brother?' A few smiles would ripple through the group, and more people would stop to listen. My words were just vaguely plausible not because I could pass, in a physical sense, for a local but because I had learned Arabic almost entirely from the street. My Arabic then was straight imitation of Yemeni vowel sounds and rehearsed phrases. But I had no self-consciousness in the language. I plunged forward. 'I'm the mountain son of a mountain man, the tribal son of a tribesman (*qabili ibn qabili*)! I'm *made* in Beni Mattar. I live for the rich coffee of Beni Mattar and the green qat that grows on the hillsides. I chew only this qat! Everything else is for the dogs of the street – for the *sons* of the dogs of the street!'

Then I would stop. Actually, the qat from Beni Mattar was a cheap, low-grade affair. No one ever got excited over it. But excitement over Mattari qat was funny. More people would gather. Now there would be a dozen turbaned gentlemen staring at me in blank incomprehension. 'He tells you he's from Beni Mattar,' someone would murmur.

At this point, I used to find a person in the crowd whose eyes were boring into me. 'We've had quite a bit of rain up there,' I would say. People would blink. Others would scan the street nearby for policemen. In the silence of their unease, I would try to look a little sorry for myself. At last, I would say: 'Well, if you want to know the truth, I'm not a hundred per cent from Beni Mattar. My mother . . .' and then I'd look down at the ground. 'I mean my mother, may Allah protect her and guide her – she's not from there at all.'

Ah . . . a clarifying light would break across a dozen heads wrapped in turbans. *Faransah?* someone would suggest. *Almania? Amrika?*

'No, my brothers,' I'd say. 'My mum, she's from . . .' and I'd name the other village hidden away in backwardness and religious foment next door to Beni Mattar.

That was it. That's all it took. Yemenis have the most wonderful faculty for delight and wonder and laughter. They would bend over in hysterics. 'Ya Mattari!' they would exclaim. 'Welcome!' 'Who's your sheikh?' 'Where in Beni Mattar?' 'You are the son of which house?' I had answers for all these questions. They were all ridiculous. For instance, my sheikh was a bona fide sheikh, Ali Muhammad al-Mattari, but he'd been dead for ten years. I said that my house was in 'the valley', underneath the waterfall.

Irony isn't known in Yemen. It is too traditional and too sincere a society for irony to flourish and when Yemenis meet a little bit of it, they are often transported by delight. It can seem to them like an odd, delicious drug, dropping from the moon.

'Welcome! Welcome, ya Mattari!' the people around me would declare as I blathered about the rain and the waterfalls of Beni Mattar. Whenever there was a lull in the dialogue, someone would fill the quiet with the beautiful Arabic expression, *mashaallah*: Such is the will of God!

Outside in the courtyard, I undertook a version of this dialogue with Ahmed, the man with the Land Cruiser and the cheerful smile. I knew he didn't approve of qat – Salafists believe it will send you to hell – but I carried through with a muted, humbler qat paean anyway. As he listened, he smiled. When I got to the part about my mum, he opened his mouth. A full-throated fundamentalist laugh poured out. He called to some other Arabs milling before the door of the mosque. They had similarly round bellies and beards and came tottering over in their sandals. Ahmed nodded to me. 'This is Thabit al-Mattari,' he said gravely. 'He's from Beni Mattar but his mother's from al-Heima.' The other teachers and officials at the centre were educated, canny people and knew this was a joke right away. 'Inner or Outer Heima?' said one, smiling.

'Inner,' I said, 'of course. Much the better one.'

He smiled. 'May Allah receive you and welcome you,' said Ahmed's friends.

'He chews only Mattari qat and only on Fridays,' said Ahmed. The friends shifted in their sandals. They smiled shyly as if they knew they were in the presence of a joke but didn't want to laugh.

'Qat is *haram*', or forbidden, said Ahmed, but he didn't mean it, and as the words were leaving his lips a naughty look appeared on his face. 'Allah welcomes you. You like qat from your countryside?' That sounded suspiciously like an invitation to an afternoon qat-chewing session to me, but I said nothing. A lot of invitations came whizzing through the air in this country and extinguished themselves in the ether. They meant nothing.

'He's going to be taking classes with us,' said Ahmed to the other teachers.

'You are welcome,' they said.

'We are going to pray the *Maghrib* prayer now. Come with us to pray the *Maghrib*,' said Ahmed, looking at me.

This seemed too sudden to me.

'Come with us to pray the *Maghrib*.'

'I don't know how.'

'Come,' said Ahmed and he took me by the hand. Off we went to a sink. Ahmed asked me to say that there was no God but God and that Muhammad was his Prophet. I said these words in Arabic then performed the ablutions and when I was done with these, without shoes, without congratulations or ceremony or additional holy words of any kind, I walked upstairs, into the mosque, and joined a prayer row. I touched my feet to the feet of the men next to me. I raised my hands to my ears, then bowed from the waist, then stretched myself across the sandy carpet.

★   ★   ★

Among the believers, Islam remains an evangelising religion. Fourteen hundred years after its birth in the deserts to the north of Sana'a, it is still an expansionist, practical, muscular, intensely social force that eyes foreigners as so many twigs clinging to the bank of a river. They must be swept away into the swift mainstream of Islamic worship. You can become any kind of Muslim you want to be later on – stern, learned, evangelising, humble – but the sweeping itself is always simple. Say: 'There is no God but God and Muhammad is his Prophet'; say 'Muhammad is the Prophet of God', and you will have satisfied every immediate requirement.

After the prayers, I was directed to a circle of Americans sitting beneath a column. They were all in their thirties, all wearing glasses and all black men from the east coast. Their teacher wore a turban and a dress shirt with an Oxford collar. He was in his mid-twenties. 'Welcome, welcome,' he said to me and gestured for me to sit.

The Americans pulled lined notebooks, coloured pencils and Arabic alphabet primers from their briefcases. This was the kindergarten circle, it seemed. The teacher was not interested. He was tired. He hardly talked to his students but lectured them in a language they could not understand.

To me, he seemed to incarnate all the worst Yemeni qualities: shiftless, proud, racist, dismissive. He put us through ten minutes' worth of spelling exercises, then sent us on our way.

Outside, puffy clouds floated above the tabletop mountains on the western edge of town. Since it was a calm, pretty afternoon, I thought I'd roll through the streets a bit on my bike. I'll visit my old friends at the newspaper, I said to myself, and tell them what I've done.

As I pedalled up to the front of the gate, I could see that the official, government-run part of Yemen was boldly marching into trouble, as usual. It did have a planning ministry but one thing it hated to plan for was the disintegration of Somalia, just to the south, across the Bab el-Mandeb Straits. On this afternoon, about

200 Somalian refugees had gathered for a protest in front of the UNHCR, whose offices happened to be just across the street from the *Observer*.

Many of them were outraged: after ten years as refugees in Yemen, they were still homeless, still penniless and no one, apparently, was making efforts to resettle them. So they had come to the UNHCR to complain.

The real problem, as a lawyer who worked for the UNHCR explained to me, was that while Yemen, unlike other countries in the region, permitted automatic entry to Somali refugees, it did nothing for them once they arrived. Once the Somali men hit the shores of the Arabian peninsula, they scurried off to Qatar and Dubai and Jeddah in search of cash for their families. The women had to fend for themselves. In the absence of their men, the Somali women in Yemen were in deep trouble. Their belongings were plundered; they were beaten and often raped. Sometimes, said the lawyer, who interviewed the people in gravest need, the police took them to jail, then raped them.

So the Somali women had gathered in their colourful veils and abayas to demand sanctuary from the sanctuary Yemen was supposed to have been. Moments before I arrived, some fifty of their men – the sick, the elderly, those who refused to leave their wives – were carted away in a Yemeni army truck. To frighten away the women, who were apparently clutching at their departing husbands and brothers, soldiers fired a dozen AK-47 rounds into the air. This brought a crowd of Yemenis on to the street and sent a ripple of terror through the demonstrators. As I pulled up on my bike, a dozen women, seeing the colour of my skin, and taking me for a UNHCR official, leapt up from behind the blue plastic tarps where they had been sleeping and cooking in recent days. They scurried forward – a great flourishing of olive green abayas and flowing black skirts. With their arms in the air, their eyes outraged, and their wrists turning helplessly at the sky, they called out: Help us! Help Us! Then one of them yelled out in Yemeni Arabic : 'We want death!' Then many of them were shrieking: 'Give us death! Give us death! *Nishti al maut!*'

So it had been with the riots earlier in the summer: puffy clouds, soaring blue sky and that Sana'a sensation of things slipping into chaos, of locals asking soldiers to shoot them, of the whole city, even the women, especially the women, electrified by the prospect of death. The fundamentalists in town knew how to exploit these sensations of course but it could hardly be said that they had invented them.

18

The most famous Islamic university in Sana'a, the one known for its red-bearded, fiery-eyed cleric and leader, Abdul Majeed al-Zindani, sat on a north-facing hillside about 10 kilometres outside the city. The students here were the sons of Yemen's clerical class, along with a few sons of lawyers and judges. Their education was free, or mostly free. Its purpose was to supply the nation with the next generation of imams.

These students called themselves *tulab al ilm*, or students of knowledge. The *ilm* in this phrase referred to the various academic disciplines within Islam: *fiqh* (jurisprudence), *hadith* (prophetic tradition), *sharia* (law) and *tarikh*(Islamic history).

The Islamic Studies department at Sana'a University, in the middle of the city, enrolled an additional hundred or so *tulab al ilm*. The course here lasted four years, was open to women and was given on a cosmopolitan campus, where there were no fiery clerics, no mandatory prayers, and no suspicions of extremism.

Then there was our school, the Mahad Medina. We hardly were a school at all – just a few classrooms on the fourth floor of an apartment building in a disregarded neighbourhood to the north of the real university.

Our students had happened on the idea of a new life in Yemen while they were surfing the posts on Islamic bulletin boards, or they had heard about the Mahad Medina from friends in their local mosques back home, or they had travelled to Syria or Egypt and had decided to go one step further. They were usually in their teens and twenties, and poor. They scrimped on everything, including the 10-riyal bean and bread breakfasts which we ate in tea shops on the street below the dorm.

Classes in our school cost $80 a month. You could enrol at any time of the year except Ramadan, when classes were cancelled. In theory, Muslims of all stripes and colours from across the globe might have managed this. In practice, they tended to be the underfunded, jobless, occasionally frustrated, but accepting and hopeful children of the Western public education system. They were black men from Virginia, French Algerians from Lyon, British Pakistanis from Birmingham, Moroccan Dutch from Amsterdam, Yemeni Americans from New York, and, now and then, university-educated, pale-skinned converts from good schools and pretty suburbs in the West.

After my conversion, I rented a room on the fourth floor corridor, above the imam's apartment. It also cost $80 a month. It was equipped with a small bathroom, a foam rubber mattress, and a window that faced south-east, into a light shaft. Ibrahim and Omar lived across the hall from me. My friend Muhammad from Maryland lived two doors down and a physical fitness instructor from North Carolina named Broadway Bilal lived in a room to my left.

In theory, all the dorm room residents had come to Yemen to study Islamic science, but time and chance had distracted some of the students from their goals. Muhammad, who was dyslexic, had given up on his classes. He now taught English. Broadway Bilal had come to Yemen to study at the Dar al-Hadith, in the northern village of Dammaj, but had caught typhus, and had had to come back to Sana'a for medical treatment. Now he worked in a gym and did not take classes. One of the dorm rooms on our hallway seemed to operate like a youth hostel for travelling Nigerians. Young men in caps and gowns would come, smile at everyone on the hallway, stay a few days, then disappear.

The students here led city lives and had private, mysterious schedules. I had expected unity of purpose, and a militant schedule of prayer and study. In fact, students drifted through the dormitory as if they were passing through a bus station in a town they wanted to visit but did not want to inhabit. They came with plastic suitcases, and sleeping bags. They looked for work, but when they didn't find it, or when they discovered that work in Yemen paid little, they moved on. The ones who stayed, like Broadway Bilal and Muhammad from Maryland, were hoping not to stay for long.

From the pavement, our apartment building looked like most other piles of cement in Beirut, Cairo and Damascus. Our facade of air conditioners, business signs and dangling TV cables was marked with dark water stains as high as the building. A complicated filigree of piping and electrical wiring had been affixed to the rear facade.

In addition to the classrooms, the fourth floor housed the office of the school secretary, and about twelve dorm rooms. A lawyer's office occupied the third floor, along with an apartment for our imam and his family. The second floor had once upon a time been an office suite but it had been re-purposed in the eighties to serve the neighbourhood and the students of the Mahad Medina, who numbered, in total, about a hundred, as a mosque. A mattress store, a rice and beans restaurant, and a religious bookstore occupied the ground floor.

If a visitor were to stand in front of the mattress store and look up, he would see a small sign in Arabic indicating 'The Shariqain Mosque'. It pointed into a corridor beside the mattress store. At the end of the corridor was a flight of stairs. Here in the darkness at the bottom of the stairs women beggars sat in black robes with their little girls. They cradled their kids and held out their hands to the passing students of knowledge. Sometimes they held out a photograph which showed a frightening skin condition with which they or their children were afflicted.

★ ★ ★

The official part of the curriculum at the Mahad Medina offered students basic training in how to read and write in Arabic. Arabic was not only the language of the Koran but also the language of heaven.

These classes were given by the imam of the mosque, Sheikh Moamr, every morning on the fourth floor.

The rest of the Mahad Medina curriculum, which was the interesting part and the reason most of the students were there in the first place, was given downstairs in the mosque. Here, one could take part in ad hoc classes, offered by Yemeni university students or local men of learning or, sometimes, by the sheikh himself. These were roughly similar to book clubs: people sat on the floor and discussed *fiqh* or *sharia* or *hadiths* and practised their *tajwid* (pronunciation). This educational programme was supplemented every day at noon by a speech the sheikh would make from a chair at the front of the mosque. It was usually a homily about an incident in the life of the Prophet or a saying attributed to him. On Fridays he gave a longer speech, which usually lasted about forty minutes and tended to touch on events in the modern world.

It took a few months for the Westerners in our school to acquaint themselves with the vocabulary in which the speeches and classes were given. But this vocabulary was a relatively simple thing, describing a relatively simple world, and if one had a basic competence in Arabic, as several of the incoming students had, it didn't take longer than a few months to follow the drift of the speeches.

Ikhlas was sincerity; *iman* was faith, *al tawheed* was the unity of God, *shirk* was polytheism, the *dunia* was the world of this life and the *achira* was the world to come. If you could follow these words as they changed into adjectives, verbs and plural nouns according to their grammatical function, you were well on your way.

When the sheikh talked about people in the modern world, he classified them according to a series of oppositions which we also learned quickly: the *moomineen* were the people who believed in God; the *kuffar* denied God. Good students were energetic: *mooshtahideen*. Bad students were *kaslaneen*: lazy. Good women were *mootadeyniat*: religious. Bad women were *jahceliat*: ignorant. Young women who were suitable as brides were *moobtessimat*: smiling. The unsuitable ones were *wakia:* insolent. Good ones were shy (*moostahai*) rather than proud (*mootakebira*) and walked with their eyes on the ground rather than in other people's faces.

As soon as you understood that the daily prostrations were divided into two kinds, those which the Prophet required of all Muslims (*al fard*) and those which he did not require but recommended (*as sunnah*), you knew what a complete religious day felt like and what an incomplete one felt like.

If the Prophet did it and if he recommended it, that should be enough, the sheikh said. Why debate it? In our mosque, the same logic applied to the beard, which it was permissible to trim but not recommended to trim, the facial veil for women which was not required but recommended, and the robe (for both sexes) which was desirable but not mandatory.

Spending time with unbelievers was not recommended. You could do it, and in working environments you sometimes had to do it, but too much time among them led to imitation (*teldee*) of Western customs. As students of knowledge, we were trying to imitate the customs of the Prophet (*teldee an nebi*), as described in the hadith, or Traditions of the Prophet – and no other.

Anyone who understood this and was willing to study a bit to pick up the relevant vocabulary could make progress quickly in our mosque. The sheikh's speeches were never all that complicated anyway and on Fridays, when there could be as many as a hundred Western students in the Shariqain Mosque, he spoke especially simply.

On those days, the mosque in our apartment building filled with believers: about seven hundred or so waiters, lawyers, mattress store salesmen, university students, schoolboys and shop assistants.

They started turning up in the second floor prayer hall around eleven in the morning. By a quarter to twelve the prayer hall was full. The twenty or so dormitory residents had washed themselves and come down by that time, and the remaining seventy-odd Westerners filled out the hall.

To judge by his face, Sheikh Moamr lived in the sunny prime of life; he was in his mid-forties, with broad shoulders and youthful, beaming eyes. On all days of the week except Fridays, he frolicked with his toddlers on the floor of the mosque, smiled at the students of knowledge and bounded up and down the steps of the apartment house. But on Friday, in the role of pastor, he behaved like a much older man. He wore an expensive Kashmiri shawl as the old gentlemen of Sana'a did and carried a walking stick. He coughed into the microphone and smiled weakly.

The content of the speeches really wasn't so different from the mosque speeches that were broadcast over every minaret sound system in Sana'a. He spoke about Islamic hypocrites and sincere believers; he spoke of those who revered the traditions of the Prophet and those who betrayed them; there were those who insisted on living large in the world of this life and there were wiser Muslims who knew that the Straight Path of Allah would lead to eternal life.

If America was in the news, and it often was in the news, the sheikh spoke about cold-blooded technological prowess and heartlessness. If Israel was in the news, he spoke about Zionists and war crimes.

'Remember the Prophet, in everything you do,' he would say, 'and remember his family and his companions. The Prophet, peace be upon him, said "stick to my *Sunnah* and to the traditions of the rightly guided caliphs who come after me."'

When he was angry, he banged his cane on the plywood platform and spoke of bombings and invasions: 'the Jews are committing these crimes! The Jews! The Jews the Jews!' It was a common refrain in Sana'a. If he wanted to insult Western politicians he would call them 'the sons of pigs and monkeys!' And then lift the index finger of his right hand. 'Do not imitate the unbelievers.

Do not be near them in restaurants. Do not allow your family to be near them. Does a Muslim go to a restaurant in which there are alcohol and prostitutes? Muslims do but in this way they cease being Muslims. So do not go to such restaurants. Would you allow your daughters to pass their time in such places? Stick to the *Sunnah*,' he would say, sometimes yelling, sometimes only whispering. 'This Path and no other is the Path the Prophet has laid out for you, O Slaves of God. If you are Muslims, this is the Path you will follow from this moment, now, until the Day of Judgment.'

At the climax of these Friday lectures, there was often a minute or so of full-throated shouting. But this was an oratorical style more than actual outrage. Like the real thunderstorms that sometimes rumbled through Sana'a in the afternoons, the shouting made the windowpanes in the mosque rattle and the believers huddle together more closely in the prayer hall. But no matter how much fuss and bother the sheikh stirred up, the speeches always finished on time. The clouds of outrage dissipated. Long before sunset, all was finished.

19

Once upon a time, there had been cubicles in our prayer hall, and telephones and computers. Suited Arabs had walked across our carpet in dress shoes. But that had been back in the 1970s, in a more hopeful, outward-looking era in Yemen – a time of emerging nationhood and commerce.

The carpets remained, but the telephones, office dividers, secretaries and suits had gone away. Now the theme of the decor was emptiness.

There were bookshelves to hold sandals, butterfly-shaped Koran stands, and a single chair, at the front of the mosque, in which the imam sat as he delivered his sermons. The windows were small, transom windows, about the size of shoeboxes, that had been slotted in high on the walls, just beneath the fibreglass ceiling. Sometimes, on hot days, a mosque assistant or student would set up an orange water cooler such as are used on football fields, in the middle of the hall. Worshippers drank from a tin cup attached to the cooler by a tin chain.

There wasn't much more to the place than this. The word for mosque in Arabic, *masjid*, literally means 'place of prostration'. The literal meaning of the word Islam is 'submission'. Our mosque was a place for uniting the act and its meaning: here you performed prostrations in order to enact submission before God.

There were no fancy carpets, no marble, no gold fixtures in the bathrooms, no fountains of any kind, no domes, no gardens, no pulpits and special niches in the Mecca-facing wall. There was just a gritty carpet, and a microphone stand. There were copies of the Koran in sagging bookshelves. The rest was up to us.

The Westerners who had married Yemeni women were the aristocrats among the students of knowledge. They lived away from the school, in the hurly-burly of Sana'a commerce and family life. Some of them had proper jobs teaching English. Some worked for travel agencies, and some worked in the businesses of their wives' fathers. They all spoke excellent Arabic, quoted from the Koran in conversation, and dressed in robes with blue dress socks, sandals, and well-aged, oily turbans. They dressed as Yemeni tribesmen dressed, in other words, and spoke as if they had long ago discarded their Western heritage.

My first friends at the Mahad Medina occupied a lower rank in the hierarchy: the level of the greenhorn, the recent arrival. Often, they couldn't speak much Arabic. Occasionally, they were converts to Islam and had to be reminded about the most basic things: who was Khadija? (she was the Prophet's first wife and the first convert to Islam). When did the Prophet's early followers flee Mecca and why? (in AD 622, because they were oppressed in the land).

Some of them had turned up in Yemen without enough money to rent a dorm room. Others were not planning to be in Sana'a long enough to make it worthwhile, so they slept in darkened nooks and corners of the office suite. They kept their belongings in an alcove under the back stairs of the mosque, next to the toilets and the women's prayer room.

At night, when these mosque sleepers were preparing themselves for bed, they pulled the hoods of their Adidas sweatshirts over their head, or they wrapped their Kashmiri shawls over their faces and rested their head in the crux of the Koran stands. Some just dropped on to the carpet wherever they happened to feel drowsy, covered their eyes with a scarf, and dozed. At eleven o'clock in the evening, when these travellers were crashed out in odd angles and attitudes, a collective snoring and sighing rose from the floor of the former office suite.

Sometimes, when I was studying or chatting with acquaintances, a passed-out brother would stir on the carpet next to me, then sit up. He would unveil himself, and smile in the sleepy-headed way of someone napping in a youth hostel. 'Salaam alaikum,' he would say. 'Yeah – I'm Abderrahman, from Australia. How're you, mate?' Or sometimes: 'I'm originally Turkish but now I'm from Toronto. You?'

Often in our mosque, when the day's prayers had been prayed, and the fasts fasted, the brothers who were not sleeping spoke about what they really hoped for from Yemen. So often, their hopes were simple, and could be expressed in a word: *wives*.

In Yemen, one is allowed to be married to four women at once. This is uncommon because it requires resources most don't have but two wives are not uncommon, nor is polygamy looked down on as it is for instance in Syria and Egypt. To the outside world, wives are a sign of well-being, mastery of the world, prosperity and abundance. But our late-night conversations focused on what wives might mean for us, personally, in our private, as yet unlived lives.

Since we were all bachelors, we really didn't know much. Still, it wasn't hard to guess.

In the suqs in Yemen, one could ask the shopkeepers to display the *labes dakhlia eros* – the undergarments of the bride. These were often fantastic, unearthly creations: bras with flashing red lights over the nipples, or turning sunflowers, or strings of fake diamonds. There were exotic, sex-kitten suits made from red pleather strips and dangling glass jewels. There were panties with buzzers and massagers built into the crotches, which could be activated by remote control. There were edible panties and panties that weren't anything more than silk strings, which the salesman removed from an envelope, dangled briefly in the air, then, overcome by confusion and shame, crumpled into his palm.

Later on, when I discovered more about the Islamic marriage, I learned that wives sometimes danced for their husbands in these costumes. They themselves bought these bride undergarments – or their friends and family bought them for them.

Sex was hardly the only reason Yemeni brides haunted our mosque. When the Yemeni men in our mosque spoke of the wives they would marry next, they conjured a picture that was both other-worldly and believable. The next bride would be a religious girl, one who didn't come and go as she pleased but preferred staying in the house, preferred the Koran over TV, family over career, and Yemen over anywhere else on earth.

In conversation, such women kept their eyes on the ground, never took food when it was offered to them, and spoke in tiny voices about their faith in God. They smiled with their eyes when they mentioned 'our Prophet', and whispered as they quoted the Koran.

One might speak for an hour with such a woman without discovering any individuating characteristics. All young women in Yemen loved 'our Prophet'; all of them said that they never lied, kept the fasts, and prayed, but not often in a mosque because, in Yemen, women did not pray in mosques. Of course they would marry, but they would not search out husbands; rather they would allow their father and Allah himself to give them a husband.

A suitor in such a conversation would make eye contact only briefly. He would watch the bowed head of the girl for a while, and then watch the father nodding as she said the things young women are supposed to say. The father would be proud. The girl would be rigid with fear. For the suitor himself, the conversation would be like interviewing a blankness, a sheet of paper. This was something he could purchase. In Yemen, the cost was usually about $3,000.

For Western students interested in marriage, Yemen was an auspicious place. Their passports and the reputation of Westerners as people of means gave them incomparable advantages in the marriage market. Furthermore, because the population of eligible young people was ballooning, marriages were happening at a rate never before known in Yemen.

Every Thursday evening – the beginning of the weekend in Yemen – some street or alley near our mosque would be shut down, a tent erected, light bulbs strung over the alleyways, and loudspeakers latched to lamp posts and tent poles.

Crowds of cousins and neighbours would gather. At around nine o'clock, a man with a microphone would stride through the crowd singing traditional songs. The men would chew qat in a tent. The women would ululate from the rooftops. The sexes would not meet, and the bridegroom and bride would not appear in public together. The bride would appear inside, in some closed-off room or salon, before her female friends and relatives. The groom would sit in a high backed wicker chair in the street, while his neighbours sang and danced at his feet. Some time in the evening, the bride would be ushered in a veil and cloak to his house, where the marriage would be consummated.

Because of this boom in weddings, there were whole neighbourhoods in Sana'a in which nothing was sold but marriage regalia. The shop windows displayed the thrones, flowers, garlands, ceremonial swords, wedding dresses, sashes, ribbons and ouds. The shop clerks, all of whom were men, sat in folding chairs in front of their store windows beckoning to the passing women.

Religious students who wanted to marry Yemeni women were meant to ask the imam of the mosque to introduce them to a woman in need of a husband. The imam would then contact a father in the mosque, and the father would bring the daughter to a room with a partition. The interested male party would then interview the prospective bride as her father and the imam listened. If the interview was going well, the partition – but not the veil – might be removed. Later in the engagement if things were still going well, the groom might ask to see the bride's face.

Some brothers in our mosque did go through this process but after the unveiling came another stumbling block: the bride price.

Muhammad from Maryland badly wanted to marry and spoke every day about 'rolling out my game' – his personal flirtation strategy – but he didn't want the flirtation to end in his having to pay a fee.

One evening as the nappers were snoozing nearby on the prayer hall floor, I asked him if he was willing to pay the $3,000 a Yemeni bride might cost. 'Hell, no!' he said, laughing. 'Hell, no! I don't got that kinda money and if I did I wouldn't spend it on a wife. I would not do that!'

'This is the tradition here,' I replied. 'Why not respect it?'

'I just wouldn't do it,' he said, 'and I know a lot of brothers from America who wouldn't either. These Yemeni dads, they think they're running a business. Now, they're just plain greedy. They just want to see the green, you know? They have two daughters and they think they're gonna get rich. In the Koran it says you give the father a *consideration* for his daughter. It does not say you give him $3,000 and enough qat to get high on for the next twenty years.'

There were other brothers with different points of view: Bilal from Nantes had converted to Islam five years earlier. He had been a truck driver for DHL in Nantes but had to quit because an imam in Yemen, whom he had contacted on the internet, advised him that transporting wine, as he was obliged to do, was illegal in Islam. 'Many of the Moroccans in France,' he said, 'they go back to Morocco to find brides. What should I do? Go back to Nantes?'

No. He hoped to participate in the Yemeni bride purchasing system and he acknowledged that that would cost: the only problem was that his Arabic was poor, and he didn't want to pay a lot for a lifetime's worth of communication issues with his wife. He wondered if I had ever heard of a French-speaking observant, believing girl in Sana'a. 'There is a French school here,' I said. His eyes lit up, 'but many of the students are the children of embassy employees and French government officials. They are not Muslim.' He was disappointed. 'I want someone who is secure in the religion,' he said. 'Someone who prostrates herself before God. I can surely find a woman like that in Yemen? If not here, where can I find her?'

'Surely, you can,' I agreed.

In the months to come I learned how difficult these East–West marriages can be. I heard stories of Yemeni brides who fell out with their English husbands over what time the children should be put to bed, what the kids should eat, and at what age the girls should wear the hijab. In Yemen girls sometimes do not put on the hijab until the age of nine. Many Western Muslims felt that in order to exhibit respect for the Prophet's traditions, and to protect the child from unwanted attention, it was best to put on the hijab at the age of six.

There were other problems. Children don't necessarily have bedtimes in Yemen but rather fall asleep when their parents fall asleep. I met an Englishman who was surprised to discover that his Yemeni wife and her entire family lived in a two-room apartment and fell asleep at the same time, usually in front of the television, usually at some hour past midnight.

When he married the daughter, the Englishman, a convert, tried to bring some order to the situation by forbidding TV in his own house. But the bride liked to watch TV, particularly during the daytime, and anyway had grown up in a house in which everyone learned to fall asleep to the noise of the television. Now, without the TV, she had a hard time sleeping. She had a hard time putting her own children to sleep.

There was also the issue of whom the children might speak with. The English father felt that the local children used foul language, thus corrupting the morals of his daughters. He preferred that the children play inside and got angry if he saw the kids outside, sitting in the dust with the neighbours' kids.

But the mother needed to clean the house and it was a local habit to send the children, even toddlers, into the lanes and alleys during daylight hours.

Many of the arguments in this marriage apparently revolved around food and how it should be eaten. The father felt that

Islam prohibited junk food. The mother liked Nestlé baby formula and creamy, European-style desserts. The father managed to tolerate some junk food over time but believed that Islam prohibited people from speaking while taking food. The mother felt that there was no such rule in Islam and wanted to watch TV during dinner. Thus did the marriage dissolve.

Since most Yemeni brides abandoned school in order to be married, the husbands generally assumed responsibility for the remainder of their education. My friend Bilal from Nantes wanted to teach. Every day he memorised Koran, studied Arabic grammar, and discussed *fiqh* and *sharia* with friends in the mosque. An excess of learning bubbled in his head. On Fridays, he sat in the front row of worshippers and listened intently to the *chutba* or sermon. He was certainly accumulating a store of Islamic knowledge, and had the money to pay for a bride, but the French-speaking, observant one who did not cost too much and whose parents did not mind her marrying a foreigner refused to turn up. Bilal slept in a dorm room above the mosque for four weeks, then disappeared.

Perhaps the women the students at the Mahad Medina knew best were the beggars who sat in the stairwell that led from the street up into the mosque. They lifted their hands to us as we filed into prayers and touched the sleeves of our robes as we filed out. No one spoke to them but we could guess, from the way the black Dacron fell across their hips, what their bodies might look like. My friend Muhammad from Maryland told me that the idea of marriage to one of them had occurred to him – surely the bride price would have been negligible – but he had problems with their practice of Islam. 'They just sit around and wait for money,' he used to say. 'Without praying? What kind of a Muslim is that? They gotta pray and maybe then they'll get husbands.'

Sometimes, in the street, I bumped into a classmate from Canada or the UK or France who was followed not by one wife but by two. A trail of toddlers tottered along behind the two adult women. One hardly breathed a word to the fathers on those occasions because a conversation would require the father to stop in the middle of the pavement, shake hands and exchange greetings, thus causing a traffic jam. On those occasions the dads did not want to chat. They had brought their wives into the street with some specific purpose in view – a visit to a doctor's office or to wait in line in the immigration office or the post office – but not so that their wives could loaf about in the street while people stared.

Accordingly, whenever we saw a father with his family in tow we made silent eye contact only with him, and nodded and ceded the way. Nor did we ever ask the husbands about their wives. They didn't volunteer any info and the bachelor students didn't enquire.

Once in my first weeks as a talib, I went to a French brother's house for dinner. He had married a young woman from Sana'a. We never saw her, or heard her for that matter, but as he brought forth platter after platter of food from the kitchen, a sensation of pleasant domesticity filled the house. His dinner guests did not so much as mention the wife (we enquired after the health of his 'family') but the lightning speed with which the platters appeared in his hands, and the heaped piles of rice topped with parsley and orange slices seemed, to me anyway, very much like tokens of marital happiness. Ahmed, who had come to Yemen from Vénisseux, outside Lyon, said that he got along splendidly with his in-laws. They were hoping and praying that he would find a job and were prepared to take the wife back to their own house if need be and would look after the son until such time as he had enough money to do it himself. But no one had any money in Yemen and most young men were unemployed. Ahmed had a little money from the mosque, enough to buy baby food and rice, and was thus not under pressure to find a job, as he might have been in Europe.

I left his house that evening feeling that I had visited a happy and warm place. But a grammar class schoolmate of mine, Bilal from Bradford, painted a different picture of domestic life among the married students.

If his wife left the house, he said, it would be only with his permission, and usually only under his supervision. 'She wants it that way,' he said. 'She insists, not me.'

'Why?' I asked.

'Because she's a good Muslim,' he said. 'It comes naturally to her.'

Before coming to Yemen, he had divorced his English wife. Now he had a new English Muslim wife in Sana'a. In his house in Yemen, anything that reminded him of his previous life as an unbeliever was prohibited: there was no TV, there were no newspapers, and there were no images of animate beings.

'She's much happier than she ever was in England,' he said, 'I can tell you that, and she doesn't talk back.'

In Sana'a, the bachelor students of knowledge only really had an opportunity to get to know a single family: it belonged to the imam of our mosque, Sheikh Moamr.

He lived in an apartment just above the prayer hall. We saw his toddlers emerging from his front door in the mornings – son after son, barefoot, robed and joyous. They wrestled and pulled on one another's hair in the mosque. They played with their father's mosque microphone and brought books to his chair at the smallest sign from his right hand. In the mornings, as Moamr emerged from his apartment, he smiled. His beard glistened. In the evenings, when he stood in his doorway, we could smell dinner in the air behind him – cumin and lamb or rice and chicken or, during the holidays, beef. When he emerged into the hallway, it was obvious that he was coming from some sweeter, warmer region of our dorm building, a zone of indulgence and ease. In that place, there lived at least one and possibly several wives.

If I had not seen Moamr's children, I would never have imagined the existence of their mothers in one dorm. I would have guessed, on the evidence of his bare feet, his nightgown and his tranquil smile, that the sheikh lived in a monk's cell. During the day, he was clearly a scholar-monk. He read and prayed in the mosque. But he had a complete and absorbing second life to go home to at night. To most of the students, I think, this seemed an interesting lifestyle and if there had been any way to inspect it more closely, I'm sure someone would have. But the sheikh did not ask the students to eat with him and no one that I knew ever set foot in his apartment.

20

I met my closest friend in Yemen, Said, a twenty-four-year-old former auto body repairman from Roubaix, in April. I had been a Muslim for about three months by then.

By that time, Said's patience with Yemen was gone. His five months in the country had given him more than enough opportunity to issue his final verdict on the lazy officials, the idlers in the streets, the qat-strewn hallways of the ministries, the decrepit taxis and their not always scrupulous drivers: it was a *pays de clochards*, a nation of hoboes. It refused to leave the twelfth century. It had been a mistake for him to come at all. He only liked one thing about it, which was the chance it gave him to wear proper Islamic clothing.

Said slept in a corner of the prayer hall, and didn't have a private place to dress. But every morning around ten, he crept to a closet in the basement of the mosque in which he kept his suitcase, discarded his pyjamas, clad himself in a beautiful shining, silky robe, either of black or of powder blue, and then emerged, his beard fluffed out, his hair combed, in a little cloud of perfume. He admitted openly that he was a clothes-horse. This was not at all common in our mosque. 'Je suis un dandy, moi,' he liked to say, 'tu vois? Il faut savoir s'habiller correctement.' He felt that *les Salafistes* were the aristocrats of Islam and should also claim their heritage in their choice of clothing.

On Fridays, he wore a proper Yemeni dagger and scabbard.

If he was to attend a local wedding, or had been invited by friends to a private house, he would wear a smooth white cape made from Algerian lambswool over his robe and daub his eyes with kohl. Sometimes the French brothers wondered what on earth he was on about with his capes and his eye make-up. He would point to his robe, or to his waist dagger, and say, 'Ça? ça? Ça, mon ami, c'est la classe!' He knew that his lambswool cape didn't suit the Yemeni climate. He didn't care.

As a part-time auto body specialist in a suburb outside Roubaix, Said had sometimes worn his robes and capes to prayers in the local mosque. But the place, as I later discovered, wasn't much of a mosque. It was a retrofitted grocery store, whose coolers and shelves had been replaced by wall to wall carpeting. Most of the people who prayed there were Algerian grandfathers who'd spent their lives working in the textile mills of northern France. They wore jackets and slacks to prayer.

There was more to Islam, Said had felt, than praying with those fossils, in that mosque. When he was in his early twenties he visited other, more genuine, stricter mosques in the city of Roubaix which were frequented by young French Algerians who wore long beards and tracksuits. For a year, Said made friends among these Muslims. But the prayers at their mosques were often conducted in French, and afterwards the brothers in the tracksuits tended to lecture him, also in French, about what was forbidden in Islam and what was permissible.

When he turned twenty-three, he knew his faith in God was deepening and he knew that he would not spend his future wandering around a housing development outside Roubaix, while French-Algerian secondary school dropouts, who could barely speak Arabic, pontificated about the life of the scholar. 'I came to Yemen to put my faith in evidence,' he told me. When he left Roubaix, he said, his ignorance about Islam had been formidable: he had memorised only tiny bits of the Koran, and those bits were in French. About Yemen, everything he knew was contained in the hadith about jurisprudence (*fiqh*) and faith (*al iman*) being 'Yemeni'.

In Roubaix, Said had memorised this hadith. 'But how to trust yourself to God and to live like a Muslim – that I didn't know. I just believed in Allah,' he told me. 'So I wanted to prove my faith.' (*Je voulais mettre ma foi en evidence*.) 'Voilà tout.'

21

Our friendship began one cool, blustery morning in April. During the previous night, as he slept in his pyjamas in the mosque, a mosque bandit had made off with his robe. It had been made of a fine, expensive Egyptian cotton and was his favourite one. In the morning, he awoke, reached his fingers across the carpet near his head, and knew, even before he opened his eyes, that it was gone.

He went to complain to the school secretary, Ahmed, in his pyjamas. I bumped into him here, in Ahmed's office.

On that morning, as it happened, Ahmed wasn't interested in listening to Said's complaints. He was busy. Maybe he felt that Said ought to have taken better care of his robe. Maybe he felt that one lost robe wasn't such a big deal no matter what kind of cotton it was made of. Things do disappear in mosques, especially shoes, as every Muslim knows.

'Inshallah, it will be returned to you soon,' Ahmed was saying when I walked into the room.

Said couldn't believe what he was hearing. 'Inshallah?' he said. 'Inshallah? In the heart of a sacred space, in the house of God, while a brother sleeps, his own clothing, his best clothing, is taken from him? What is that? What on earth is that? *C'est un pays de clochards, mon ami!* And you say "inshallah"?'

Said's Arabic was a mixture of Berber, French and Algerian

Arabic. Ahmed smiled at me as Said ranted – a patient, tolerant, brotherly smile, as if Algerian gibberish were a kind of music that he enjoyed listening to in the mornings.

'I can help translate,' I suggested to no one in particular.

'Ah, the American,' Said said when he saw me standing at the office door.

'Can you believe this? Can you believe what has happened to me?'

I asked him what a new Egyptian cotton robe might cost. I said that I knew brothers in the mosque who would be willing to chip in to buy him a new robe. I myself would be willing.

'What I really need now is breakfast,' he said.

'No problem,' I said.

He flashed me a dubious look. 'Do you have enough?'

'Of course,' I said.

'I'd like to buy some olives and cheese at the supermarket. Is that okay?' Breakfast for two in our neighbourhood at a restaurant would have cost pennies – but Said didn't want to spend more cash than necessary, even if it wasn't his own, since the Prophet had counselled frugality in all things. So we went to the supermarket, bought provisions, and consumed them in a nearby tea shop.

As it turned out, we did not discuss the lost robe. We ate our olives and feta, drank our tea, then ignored the robe altogether. Instead, we discussed my own inability to perform a proper Islamic prayer. 'I've seen you many, many times, my brother the American,' he said. 'Do you know you hesitate as you pray? You don't know what to do with your hands. I've remarked on that, if you want me to be completely honest with you.'

'Never mind,' I said. I fingered the olives. Okay, I admitted. I had not had a proper lesson but had picked up the prayer by imitating the people next to me.

'Yes, you're lost,' he said. 'And what do you do if you miss a prayer and have to pray by yourself?'

Twenty minutes later, we were standing at the edge of a large piece of office carpeting in the basement of our mosque. Our Mecca-facing wall was the closet door behind which Said's suitcase lived. In an adjoining bathroom, old men with long white beards and canes were lost in their morning ablutions.

I slipped off my sandals. I stepped out on to the carpet. I turned to face the closet door. 'I'm waiting,' Said said. 'Any time now. Pray.'

At the time, I was under the impression that during prayers one communes a little bit with Allah, or the heavens or the angels, or in any case Mecca, and that this communion should somehow transport the worshipper. Accordingly, as I prayed I sometimes bobbed my head. Sometimes as I stood there waiting, I swayed imperceptibly.

On this morning, I listened to the old men washing their beards. They muttered and moaned to no one in particular. Then I did my normal thing: I raised my hands to my ears, lowered them to my chest, and recited the opening chapter of the Koran. Perhaps I did sway a bit as I recited. I might have bobbed once or twice. Anyway, Said interrupted.

'My friend the American,' he said, 'stop that. Stop it, now.'

'What?' I said.

'No, do it again,' he said. 'I want to see that again.'

'What?' I said. 'What? I'm not doing anything.'

'Do you think you're a jazz singer?' he said. 'Do you think this is a gospel chorus? There's no bobbing your head in Islam. There's no swaying. My friend the American, it's not a dance. You're not communing with the spirits, may Allah forgive you. You're not telephoning a friend in another galaxy. What on earth is going through your head?'

'I'm trying to pray,' I said. 'I'm trying to have a spiritual experience.'

'Who told you to dance as you pray?' he said. 'Who?' He said that if I persisted in this error, the prayer would stop being valid.

'This is not improvisational aerobics, you know. If that's what you want, you've come to the wrong place. Go elsewhere for that. Do you understand, my friend the American? A Muslim learns how the Prophet prayed and prays like that. Okay?'

He was right. The Sufi, a mystical, occasionally heretical branch of Islam, have their own way of going about things, as do the Shia, but in the world's most populous, common, international variety of Islam – namely Sunni Islam, which was the variety prevalent in Yemen, to which 99 per cent of the believers in our mosque subscribed – you were not supposed to express your feelings at prayer. You were meant to abstract yourself from your feelings while you stood before God.

Said made me stand aside while he demonstrated.

'Make sure that all your fingers on the carpet are pointing towards Mecca. The five toes of your right foot should point to Mecca at all times, even when you are kneeling in prostration. Touch your forehead to the carpet, not your lips and not your nose.'

I practised. The old men gazed. If Said had not lost the pocket booklet of invocations and instructions for prayer which in French is called *Le Citadel de l'islam*, I could also have learned, at this time, how to say the Arabic prayer liturgy.

Because we had no such booklet we had to rely on Said's memory of the French prayer. As I bowed I said, *'Gloire à mon Seigneur, le Très Grand.'* As I stood, I said, *'Allah écoute bien celui qui Le loue.'*

When I bowed a second time I said, *'Gloire à mon Seigneur.'*

'Remember this well,' Said said in French. The old men watching chattered among themselves. Perhaps they had not heard people praying in French in their mosque before. Perhaps they were just interested. Anyway, five Yemeni grandfathers and Said Chikouche from Hem outside Roubaix were the witnesses to my first correct Islamic prayer.

22

Prayer is the second pillar of Islam, after monotheism. It is indispensable to Muslims, as central to the life of the believer as food, friends and family.

Five times a day, the Muslim effaces the selfness of the self. He is meant to synchronise the movements of his body to the movements of the five or five hundred or five thousand people standing in rows in his mosque. In this way, the believer unites himself with the global body of believers – the *ummah*. He is larger than himself, and his personal idiosyncrasies will only throw the movement off course. Because in Yemen the entire city is praying at roughly the same time, he is participating in a reunion of the community acted out across the neighbourhoods, through the tower houses, and into the canyons beyond.

In fact it's an international movement. When the prayer is finished in western China lines will be bowing in Bishkek, then more lines will be bowing in Yemen, and after that in Libya and Morocco. It is a wave that follows the sun across the surface of the globe in five daily pulses that keep on pulsing, every moment of every day.

The Salafi are the most stoic and serene of the Islamic denominations. To them, an Islamic prayer is not all that different, in a physical sense, from Zen meditation. Your body is calm, and your breathing is even. You try to be present rather than absent. You still your brain. You do not agitate it. You keep your eyes open.

The liturgy acknowledges that God is the ruler of the heavens and the king of all the worlds. He has no partner. Muhammad is his messenger. 'Lead us on the straight path,' you say, and then you touch your forehead to the carpet. 'God is great,' you say. Hundreds of voices mutter along with you – allahu akbar, allahu akbar. As you lift your foreheads from the carpet hundreds of sighs rise through the air.

Praying works best if you have a bit of limberness to you. The falling to the floor is easier, and the rising from it more graceful. When you've finished the prostration, you kneel on the floor with your shins and feet tucked beneath you. Your right foot is supposed to be curled up under your haunches, its arch stretched, its toes pointing towards Mecca.

For a few days after my lesson with Said, I was more deliberate in every prayer gesture and more self-conscious. Then, knowing that this was a hindrance, I tried to forget my self-consciousness. I tried to watch the locals and when I watched them I imagined that every one of them was as I wanted them to be: a warm, woolly-bearded, sweet-tempered welcomer of Western converts to the Land of the Prophet.

One month after my first prayer lesson with Said, I happened to come early to my morning Arabic class. Instead of waiting at the classroom door, as I often did, I went down to the mosque. I stood in a patch of sunlight at the edge of our former Arab business suite carpet. A circle of young men – British talibs who had marked me out as an intruder, and therefore kept their distance – were staring at me. I performed the waist bow, the prostration, the kneeling, the second prostration and then rose. I am swimming, I told myself. My hands knew where to go. Stretch, pause, contract. Repeat. No bobbing. Never close your eyes. Concentration.

After I'd finished my two supererogatory prostrations, when I was sitting cross-legged beneath a column, reading Koran to myself as everyone does when they're waiting in a mosque, Said sneaked up behind me. He patted me on the head.

'Your prayers are becoming more correct, *mon ami*,' he said. 'With less hesitation and less nervousness. Congratulations.' He smiled.

It was the first time someone had congratulated me for performing an Islamic deed. Since the compliment came from Said, who did not suffer fools gladly, it meant something special to me.

'Keep practising,' he said. 'Don't worry if people are watching.'

Bilal, the friend from Bradford, noticed I was improving. He pulled me aside one morning in May to say, 'You're not trimming your beard any more. It looks good. And your prayers are improving. Congratulations.' Later on that month, in the middle of class, when we were reading through a textbook called *The Comportment of a Muslim*, the teacher asked me to stand up. I stood up. He smiled. 'Thabit, you're a Muslim now,' he said. 'Right?'

'Right,' I said.

'You're meant to dress like a Muslim, then. Jeans such as the ones you're wearing – where do they come from? Muslims dress as we dress here in Yemen.' He glanced at Bilal who was wearing a splendid ocean blue robe and matching cap. Muhammad himself was wearing a snowy white robe, a black and white checked headscarf, and a sturdy waist dagger. 'If you are a Muslim, you might as well start dressing like one.'

At the time, I was the only student in the Mahad Medina who didn't wear a robe. I also disdained turbans and skullcaps. The garb had seemed too strange to me at first and felt like a betrayal of my identity. But after that class my insistence on jeans and football jerseys struck me as mere self-involvement. This Western dress was a mark of pride. In what, though? Nothing. Why not just let it go?

I bought myself expensive robes and expensive smooth silken shawls to wrap around my head. At prayer on Friday of the following week, people I had barely spoken with to date, including the British Muslims, shook my hand. *'Na-eeman, na-eeman,'* they said, which literally means 'grace, grace,' but is used in everyday speech to congratulate someone who has done something small but good for himself, like cutting his hair or cleaning his body.

23

Because he had arrived in Yemen with only 300 euros, and had spent these in his first months, Said couldn't afford the Mahad Medina classes I was taking. He couldn't afford to buy his own food. He had to depend on the kindness of strangers. In Yemen, where one must be kind to strangers, provided they are Muslims, it's almost possible to live this way. When one is hungry, one stands at the entrance to a restaurant or one hovers near a table on the street. Eventually the diners look up. Eventually they wave the hungry person to their table and make him sit down and urge him to eat bits of bread or leftover scraps of stew. Said managed to get along in this way. Still, I could see in his eyes when he told me about this variety of begging that he found it humiliating.

After he lost his robe, he redoubled his efforts to find some member of his family in France willing to pay for his ticket home. His father had not wanted him to go to Yemen in the first place, and now that Said was living in Yemen, the father no longer wanted to talk to the son. When he was feeling panicked, he called up his older brother who worked for the public transit authority in Lille. Those conversations could last for as much as a quarter of an hour, but they almost always ended with Said emerging from the phone booth, grinning tightly and saying little. 'Inshallah, maybe,' he would sigh, 'maybe some little money in a little while.' On other days the conversation would be shorter, the smile at the end tighter, and when we were standing in the sun outside the phone shop, Said would sigh and say, 'He insulted me. I had to hang up on him.'

In the meantime, as he waited for money to come in from someone in France, he moped around the mosque. There really wasn't much for him to do.

He couldn't find a job or didn't want one, or both. One of the few things he could do, besides praying and eating, was to dress up in his robe and waist dagger, and visit the local tea shops. On more than one occasion, for fun, Said and I dressed in our proper clothing and rode the bus across town to the Old City. It was another world over there and it held out the possibility of interesting encounters – for instance with Parisian tourists or executives from the French oil company Total or embassy officials, hunting for trinkets. If we had bumped into one of those tourist types during our excursions, we might have laughed to ourselves at how out of place the tourist was, and how worried. Perhaps Said would have let him know somehow that he was now in territory that belonged to Muslims rather than French people. The normal roles would be reversed at that point. Said would be in charge. The French would have to defer to his customs, and show him their respect.

Sadly, such encounters never happened. They were unthinkable in our neighbourhood since there were no tourists anywhere nearby and, by bad luck, they didn't happen on our excursions to the Old City.

Instead, when we went into the Yemeni streets, we tended to bump into Yemenis. The truth is that no matter how regal and Islamic their costumes are, two foreigners in Yemeni robes speaking French in the Sana'a street will not look like proud, indomitable Muslims who have embarked, at considerable expense and personal risk, on the Straight Path. They'll just look strange to the locals. When Said and I ambled down the pavement in front of our mosque the Yemeni men we encountered stared at us with expressions of blank incomprehension.

If we were in a cafe or on a bus, a public-minded person sitting nearby would sometimes raise his voice. 'Brothers, where are you from?' he would ask. The other Yemenis would lean in and stare. Said considered himself a citizen of the *ummah*, period. More detailed discussions about national origin would have required him to explain about his Algerian-immigrant parents, his rejection of France, his embrace of Salafism, his hopes of finding a true Islamic home in Yemen, and on and on. It was none of anyone's business. Furthermore, he worried that the police might take an interest in his interest in Salafism.

So, in public, he usually scowled and said little. Curious Yemenis, however, would always persist.

Eventually, some cheerful, well-meaning Yemeni would bring a new question to the floor. It was always the same one: 'Are you Muslims?'

This ignorance rankled. Were the Yemenis really this innocent? Apparently so. Of course we were Muslims. There were times when I wanted to seize these bumpkins by the throat. 'Look, brother,' I would have said. 'When someone dresses like this, with the beard, the sandals, the waist dagger, the robe and the prayer beads, and when this person is in Yemen, it's probably a safe bet that, yes, he's a Muslim. *Although he's speaking French. Although his features are not Yemeni but North African.*' I was tempted but never did it.

Still, we were both annoyed that we had to spell things out for the slow-witted people of Yemen. Could they not read the most basic social cues? Could they not perform the most rudi-mentary of social obligations, namely welcoming their fellow Muslims to Yemen? Apparently not. Apparently the average bus passenger in Yemen felt that when people spoke French, had foreign facial features, and wore Yemeni robes, they might well be space aliens, dressed in dishdashas.

We were trying but we weren't exactly relaxing into the warm embrace of a Yemeni society.

*   *   *

Most French students arriving in Yemen head off to one of the various countryside Koran schools sooner rather than later. Their lives then have order and promise.

But Said had already spent two months in Dammaj. He felt that the place was too isolated, the valley in which the school sat too narrow and dark, and the students too desperate for money to be decent to one another. The Algerians who lived there, he said, were not above stealing money from your pockets as you slept in the mosque. They were jackals, he said, and the French brothers were not much friendlier. 'They will calumniate against you,' he declared, 'and stab you in the back.' So he returned to Sana'a where he found himself, after five months away, in a less purposeful, less certain state of mind than he had been when he lived in France.

To keep himself busy, he went to the school secretary's office every morning to enquire about his passport. He had given the passport to the school in the hope of gaining a residency permit; it had then vanished. But not entirely. As far as we could discern, it was behaving rather like a carrier pigeon. Ahmed, the secretary, had released it but he was confident that it would return some day. At first, we understood that it was resting over at the Immigration and Passport Authority, maybe taking on a new message of some kind and preparing for the return flight. It would come home in due course.

Then later on, towards the end of June, a Yemeni in our mosque whose good relations with the visa office had got him a job as a conduit between our school and the visa centre, told Said that he had sighted it in a nest of papers in the office of Sheikh Moamr. He said that he was quite sure he'd never taken Said's passport to the Immigration and Passport Authority, or anywhere else.

By the second week of July, news of the passport petered out. Maybe it had been left on a lonely ledge? Carried away by an eagle? 'It's in the hand of God,' said Ahmed. 'It will come back, by his will.' For a while, the conduit person seemed to say that he had seen it at the foreign ministry, but when we pressed him one afternoon, he shrugged his shoulders. 'You're Said from France?' he asked. 'Oh, I thought you were Abbas from London. I guess I didn't see your passport after all.'

'It's being prepared and is on its way,' said Ahmed. 'Soon, inshallah, it will be ready for you.'

It failed to turn up.

Meanwhile, Said's brother in Lille was losing patience. When Said first arrived in Yemen, he had been curious and had seemed to offer his help. But over time, the brother's mood changed and now, when Said called, he almost always got an earful.

The brother happened to be a percipient observer of Said's character. Even though they were delivered from halfway across the world, his observations cut to the quick. 'You're not becoming a student of knowledge at all,' he told Said once. 'You're just a beggar. Go ahead, then. Beg from the passers-by.'

On some days, Said took the setbacks in his stride. 'They are tests from Allah and Allah never sent anyone a test that was too strong for him,' he would say. '*C'est une épreuve d'allah, c'est sûr.*' He would suggest we visit our customary tea shop, on the avenue in front of the mosque, and when we got there, he would lean back in his chair and stare into the passing traffic and smile. 'Do you know that outside of Sana'a,' he would say, 'the *Sunnah* allows you, and it is customary to do this if you are on a pilgrimage, to eat from the fields of the farmers and to sleep in their shelters when you are tired? Of course, you cannot walk away with armloads of vegetables. You cannot stay in a farmer's house for a year, but it is the custom in the countryside to give food and shelter to pilgrims. I used to eat lettuces and carrots from the fields outside Roubaix. In France, you can be put in jail for this of course which is one of the reasons I had to leave. In Yemen, it is in the traditions of the Prophet. You are honoured, and especially so as a pilgrim.'

'Are you suggesting we *walk* to Mecca?' I would ask.

'No,' he would say. 'But we could. We could also take a bus. It costs 16 euros for a one-way ticket.'

When Said talked like this, it seemed clear to me that he liked Yemen, despite its difficulties, and that his faith was deepening from day to day. He would go to Mecca. He would commit himself, once and for all, to a life in the Arab world.

But there were other, equally eventless days, when the discouraging phone calls from France, his lack of friends in the mosque, and the unscrupulous school officials seemed to be souring him on the religious life.

On those days, he seemed resolved to confront reality, openly and without illusions. When the topic of our future movements came up, he would stare into his tea, then turn his eyes on the broken-down taxis and cow-carrying pickups passing in front of our mosque. He would look at the grease-stained turbans of drivers. The drivers would look at us with their wide, hungry eyes as if they had never once laid eyes on a foreigner.

'For the love of God,' Said would say. 'Would you look at these broken-down people? *Des vagabonds! Des clochards!*' Before the end of our discussion, inevitably, one of the trucks would break down, or a minibus would break down, or a taxi, or several of these in combination, and then the bus passengers would get out into the street and other drivers would stop to stare, and tribesmen would mill around, pushing at the dead vehicles, or just watching them. Every driver with a working horn would lean on it. Gazing into the chaos, Said would clap his palm to his forehead. 'In the name of God the merciful!' he would shriek. 'How on earth did I get here? How can I get out?'

Then he would turn to me. 'You dream of becoming like them?' he would say. 'Is that why you converted to Islam? No, my friend, we are not living in the seventh century any more. Why are you so interested in studying Islamic science, anyway? It's enough to get an honest job in an Islamic country, to pray and to fast. It's enough to work. Man must work! This is a commandment. Must you memorise the Koran? Do you need to know every ruling from every mufti in every century since the arrival of the Prophet? Don't be ridiculous, my American friend.'

*   *   *

On those mornings, his fantasies settled on workaday neighbour-hoods – outlying districts in Cairo or Amman or a mountain town in the Algerian Kabylie, where his parents had been raised. Yes, he admitted, the true Islam had not reached such places and the people there, especially in Algeria, often practised a bastard-ised, peasant's version of Islam. 'But so what? When we travel, we will bring Islamic science with us,' he would say. 'We will give them *da'wa'* – preaching – 'and show by example. It's not necessary to turn yourself into an Islamic monk with zero riyals in his pocket and a robe just to prove you're a Muslim. Where in the Koran does it say you must do that?'

The solution to Said's dilemma appeared to him one afternoon in the third week of July. We had had a difficult but not untypical day: an argument in the heat of the midday sun with a cab driver, followed by a failed attempt to recover the passport at the Passport Authority. On the way back to the mosque, we had witnessed a brutal incident in which a man in a Mercedes knocked a street sweeper to the ground with his car.

After the *asr*, or mid-afternoon, prayers, we stood in the aisle of a Western-style supermarket near our mosque as Yemeni housewives in robes and veils prodded us with their shopping carts. They wanted us out of their way and were not shy about pushing. In supermarkets, Yemeni women can be aggressive, like fiercely determined babushkas with impaired peripheral vision.

'This is not Islam,' said Said casually as we watched the women retrieving boxes of chocolate-covered maraschino cherries from a shelf high above their heads. He waved his arms at the black forms in front of us and shook his head. We watched the scene for several minutes as the shortcomings of Islam as it exists in Sana'a today flooded into his mind: the madness for Western products, the cupidity of the merchants, the beggars in the mosque hallways, the universal addiction to drugs and cigarettes, the pollution of the air, and the unaccountability of rich people – here was one long *j'accuse* that had been building in Said's head for some time. Muslims were meant to be sincere, mild, seekers of knowledge, he said. In fact Islam in Sana'a was broken. 'It's an insane asylum,' he said, 'in which the patients have thrown off their restraints and ransacked the shelves and are now crawling over one another for drugs and food and water. It's unliveable,' he concluded. *Invivable.*

He turned to me. 'You think you will learn about Islam here, in this mess? If you want to learn,' he said, 'you have no choice but to go to Dammaj. In fact, I order you to go. Do you agree?'

I agreed.

He stepped closer to me. 'Are you sure you are not an agent for the Mossad?' I assured him I was no one's agent.

He stared at me for a few moments to make sure I was on the level, and I stared back. 'I'm ready when you are,' I said.

We made our plan there in the supermarket as the Yemeni babushkas clambered after their chocolates. 'At last you will breathe the pure air of Islam,' Said said. He didn't know why we had waited this long. I felt I was waiting this long because the Dar al-Hadith was a serious academy, requiring deep knowledge of the Koran and the hadith. But I was also interested in exploring, and if this was where the currents were inclined to take me, I was inclined to go.

A van, he said, left our mosque once a week for this village in the north. Said would make my arrival in the village easy by introducing me to the sheikh of Dammaj and to the French residents. In exchange for these introductions, Said suggested, I would pay for his trip. After a month, if he wanted to go on to Mecca, I would pay for that trip, too. The total would amount to about $200. 'Are you agreed?' he asked.

'Okay,' I said. 'Certainly.'

We met the smuggler the next evening. He promised to remove our luggage from the mosque dorm the following morning at dawn. We would take our places in a second car, a van, which would be waiting outside the mosque. The smuggler needed $160 to drive us into the north. He looked me over. 'For him,' he remarked to Said, 'since I don't know him, I'll need the permission of the imam of the mosque, or a teacher. I can't take anyone off the street to Dammaj.'

I called a mosque teacher. 'Thabit's *iman* is strong and getting stronger,' said the teacher when he turned up, a few minutes later. The smuggler was satisfied. I thanked the teacher and thanked the smuggler. We agreed to meet at dawn the following morning, after the prayers.

I spent a sleepless night. There was still awkwardness in my prayers. There were thousands of *ayats*, or verses, in the Koran I knew nothing about. What if the brothers in Dammaj decided I was an imposter? What if, finding myself in over my head, I couldn't leave? Am I being set up? I wondered. I tossed and turned.

Le passeur, as Said called him, didn't turn up for the dawn prayer. He didn't turn up for the noon prayer either and in the afternoon during our customary tea-drinking hour at our tea shop, Said happened to recall that the evening before, he had had a conversation with some of the French brothers in the mosque. They were friends of a Parisian student, Qais. 'Know him?' Said asked.

'Yes,' I said.

'It seems he and his friends blocked you. They didn't want you to travel. They don't trust you. Or maybe they just don't know you. They say you should study the *ilm*' – Islamic science – 'in Sana'a for a while and that time will tell what kind of a Muslim you really are.'

24

My course in *ilm* began right away. We met at eight o'clock every morning in a classroom next to Sheikh Moamr's office. It was taught by Muhammad al-Taizi, a recent graduate of the Islamic Science department at Sana'a University. There was only one other student, Bilal, the car mechanic from Bradford.

Almost everything I learned about Islam that summer came from the conversation the three of us – Bilal, Muhammad and I – had in the mornings, as a kindergarten class chanted Koran in the mosque below us and the other students of science dozed in their dorm rooms.

Islam had come to Bilal eleven years earlier. He told us that he had led a disorderly life back then, involving dance clubs, beer and women.

At first, after his discovery of Islam, his non-Muslim wife had tolerated his new name, his friends, and his new habit of praying five times a day. But she refused to convert.

He left her eventually and she sued for divorce.

The judge in the case, a woman, struck Bilal as a classic Muslim hater. She gave custody of his daughter to the ex-wife. In late 2005, as Bilal was selling his auto repair shop and planning to leave for Yemen, he offered the daughter an opportunity to convert. She could come with him and live in Yemen. But she was only eleven years old at the time and still under the sway of her mother. She refused.

Now in Yemen, Bilal was one of the rare students in Sana'a capable of saying that the Islamic life he had dreamed of in England was happening to him, now. He had a new Muslim wife (also from Bradford), new children, stepchildren, and of course a new house. He went out of his way to be a positive, fatherly presence in the mosque. A crew of American teenagers whose parents had full-time jobs as English teachers needed supervision during the days. Instead of supervising them, Bilal befriended them, studied with them, and allowed them to fill in gaps in his knowledge of Arabic. Often, Bilal could be found in the afternoons in the mosque, surrounded by a circle of diligent, studying teenagers.

That summer Bilal was also trying to help another young man in need called Azi, who had arrived recently from Niagara Falls. Azi barely spoke Arabic and had gone to Catholic schools as a kid. Both of his parents were Yemeni immigrants to Canada, he was curious about Islam, and he was hoping that Islam would straighten out what had evidently been a troubled adolescence.

In Canada, Azi's speciality had been robbing banks. When I chatted with him, he liked to recall the exciting days when he had managed to sneak into banks, rob the tellers quietly, and get clean away. Once, he said, he had managed to net more than $40,000. He had bought himself a fast Honda and had gone on vacations with his girlfriend. Now, however, the money was gone, and the federal authorities on the Ontario–New York border were making inquiries among his friends back home.

This was another reason for his new life in Yemen. He didn't want to be napping some day in his bedroom only to have the door broken down by the Royal Canadian Mounted Police.

Azi admitted openly that he wasn't much of a walker on the Straight Path. He advocated masturbation; he openly sought Somalian girlfriends. Most of the anglophone brothers in our mosque kept away from him and the Yemenis whom he resembled physically regarded him as anathema.

Only Bilal made an effort to bring him into the fold.

The two of them used to sit together for hours in the cafes along the avenue in front of our mosque. What they talked about I don't know but I would often see them sitting together, poring over a text and sipping tea quietly. When I chatted with Azi in private, he would say of Bilal, 'Yeah, he's a good guy. He's definitely helping me. He gives me advice and stuff. He wants to help me. I can't even help myself so I don't know how he can help me.'

Bilal *was* trying. When he wanted to be tough, however, he could be very tough. Sometimes, in talking about the upside-down world of England, its female divorce judges, and the way women ran the society back home, he sounded like a man whose house had been invaded by evil spirits. They had penetrated to a deep, intimate place within him. He was angry about this violation and had come to Yemen to free himself from their power.

One morning, as we were working through a grammar exercise, he noticed me drawing a self-portrait in my notebook. It wasn't a great work of art but I was trying to make it prettier. I was almost finished when Bilal rose from his chair, strode across the classroom and snatched the notebook from beneath my pen.

He returned to his chair, pulled out his own pen, and applied a spaghetti salad of heavy blue scribbles to my artwork. Then he ripped out the offending page and shredded it. Muhammad, our teacher, was busy trying to instruct us and didn't appreciate the interruption. But Bilal didn't care. When he was done obliviating my artwork, he turned to me and said, in English, 'I did that for you, yeah. Only Allah, glory and praise upon him, has the power to create.' People who tried to usurp this power, in his opinion, were magicians who conjured with spirits and would be condemned to hell on the Day of Judgment.

He smiled tightly, then returned my exercise book to me.

Towards the end of class, his mood lightened. 'If you see an image on a bottle of dishwashing soap, or in a newspaper or what have you,' he suggested, 'just rip off the label before you bring it into your house. Understand?'

'Okay,' I said when he was finished with his speech. 'I understand. No more images.'

25

This lesson could hardly have been more explicit but that summer in Yemen representations of animate beings were everywhere. President Saleh, who was opening his re-election campaign, had had his face emblazoned across just about every possible surface in the city: it was plastered to billboards, bank facades and bus windows. It gazed down from the walls of restaurants and tea shops, and illuminated the front pages of the newspapers.

One afternoon, when I was pedalling around town, I stopped to chat with a gaggle of child campaigners. Their clothing was covered with stickers depicting President Ali Abdullah Saleh. They had stationed themselves at an intersection and were passing out stickers and posters of President Saleh to drivers who were stalled in traffic.

'Hey, foreigner! Do you love our president?' one of them asked me.

'Of course,' I said. 'Long live the president.'

The kids high-fived me and marvelled at my bike. They asked to buy it, wondered how much it cost and when I told them it cost half a million Yemeni riyals or $1,000, they burst into laughter.

As I was pedalling away, a tall, bold kid plastered a sticker of the president's face across my backpack. 'We love you!' said the legend on the sticker.

The next day, having forgotten about the kids and their stickers,

I brought my backpack into the classroom with Bilal. The sticker had collected a coating of road grime by then but the president and the slogan were still visible. 'Ali Abdullah Saleh: we love you!'

Sitting down in my normal chair, I straightened my robe and adjusted my cap. I stacked my books on a corner of my desk.

Bilal rose from his chair. He plucked the sticker from the backpack and raised it into the air, holding it away from his body as if it were a piece of toilet paper.

'Look at what Thabit has gone and done now! Would you look at this then,' he exclaimed. '*Subhan allah!* Would you look at this?'

He went on for several minutes in this vein. He brandished the incriminating evidence and condemned politicians, image makers and Western programmes that polluted the land of the Prophet with democracy.

Muhammad, our teacher, had had prior experience of Muslim enthusiasts from Europe. He had no training in teaching but he was an excellent classroom leader, who knew how to smooth ruffled feathers. He allowed Bilal to have his say and then held out his hand. 'Give the sticker to me, please,' he said in Arabic. Bilal deposited it on his desk.

Without mentioning the words 'politics' or 'magic' or uttering any other condemnation, he folded the sticker in two, ripped it into bits, and, standing over a wastebin, let the shreds fall through the air. He returned to his desk and opened a Koran he kept in readiness on top of his grammar books. He chose a simple verse, one he knew that I knew, which happened to be about earthquakes, then nodded at me: 'Recite, Thabit,' he said.

I think Bilal and I both got the message. His eloquence was in the way he detached the sticker from his hands, finger by finger, and in the way his eyes watched the shredded paper fall into the rubbish. That was quite enough. In that silence, he said that one didn't make a show of despising the president. He said that Muslims, despite the current profusion of images in the streets, did not worship pictures, or tinpot dictators and did not allow themselves to be governed by them. They washed their hands of the entire business. In the face of such a thing as politics, a good Muslim would open the Koran, then read. In this way, over time, he would discover the strength that comes to those who walk on the Straight Path of God.

26

Muhammad was an excellent teacher but he was not a worldly man. He didn't claim to be. He had grown up in Taiz, a small city to the south of Sana'a, and had moved to the capital to attend university. He mumbled in class and wasn't a talented or a natural mentor. But everyone in our mosque respected him because he was a calm, thoughtful person who kept to himself, did not speak without thinking first, and then spoke only briefly and quietly.

He hoped to take his sisters to Mecca in the autumn. If the trip came off, it would be his first trip outside Yemen.

Sometimes, when the eight o'clock *ilm* class had run its course, and we were sitting downstairs in a cafe, Muhammad talked about his dream of marrying a Western woman. 'If she is Muslim, where is the problem?' he used to say. 'There's no problem. If I marry a Western woman, I could move to France or England and teach Islamic science, there, where it is most needed. No?'

This kind of talk annoyed Bilal. Bilal felt that Muhammad had badly misunderstood what he was dreaming of when he dreamed of the West. More than once, he tried to teach our teacher a lesson: we in the West had badly screwed up our own countries, he said. Couldn't Muhammad see that?

One afternoon in late July, the three of us were sitting in the tea shop beneath our mosque. Monsoon thunderheads were coalescing in the sky to the south. We watched them expand into the highest part of the sky and felt the stiffening breeze blow through our robes. It was a good feeling and the tea was good.

'Trust me,' said Bilal addressing neither Muhammad nor me but speaking to both of us, 'neither of you want to marry a woman from the West.'

'Yes, I do. Maybe. Why not?' wondered Muhammad.

Bilal disagreed. He related a story that had been told to him by an old friend in Stoke-on-Trent. The friend had been having a drink one evening in a bar in a hotel there. He fell into conversation with a woman, one thing led to another, and within minutes, the woman had invited the man into her hotel bedroom.

'Yes,' said Muhammad. 'Go on. I understand.'

'No, she was wasn't a prostitute, not at all,' said Bilal. 'Just a normal woman. When my friend, when he got up to her bedroom, yeah, he saw there was one guy stepping out the door, right? So he says "Hello, what's this?" He steps into the room. And when he gets into the room, he sees there's another fellow in the bathroom pulling up his jeans. "Hello, what's this?" he thinks to himself. The men's faces are all flushed, and they're like smiling to themselves, like.'

What had happened, Bilal explained, was that the woman had not been satiated by the sex she'd had with these two men. She had gone down to the bar to find a third partner for the evening. 'Same room, same woman, same night, three men,' said Bilal. He turned to face Muhammad. '*Subhan allah,* this is what it's like. And you want to go there and live in that? With those animals?'

Muhammad shrugged. 'Not all of them that way,' he said in English. 'Impossible.'

Bilal shook his head and grinned. 'Yes, possible,' he said. 'Isn't that so, Thabit? The girls have a few beers. Music. Then the girls get that special feeling going in them and then . . . you know how it is. This kind of thing happens all the time, doesn't it?'

'When you put all the bars together and all the incidents and you think about it a little bit,' I said. 'Yeah, it probably does.'

'*Subhan allah,*' said Muhammad to himself. He shook his head. When Bilal had begun talking about Western women, Muhammad had listened hopefully, like a good student. Now a worried, disappointed, cold look came into his eyes.

Bilal continued. He said that he had worked as a bouncer in a bar in Stoke, and had sometimes seen the same woman leave the bar five times with five different men – in one night. 'I've seen it all,' he said. 'Woman with six guys on her. That happens, yeah?'

Muhammad sank lower in his chair. He seemed to be focusing on a bird or cloud formation or aeroplane, far away, in the distance. 'No. That can't be,' he protested. 'I know that can't be.'

'Yeah, hell it can be,' Bilal said. 'I've seen it with my own eyes, haven't I?'

'If a woman do that, she dies,' Muhammad murmured.

Bilal and I shook our heads. 'She may be tired,' we said, 'but she won't drop dead.'

'Yes, dead,' said Muhammad. 'Yes it is certain. Listen!' He gestured at the clouds on the horizon. 'Up there,' he said, indicating with his hand the highest ridge off to the west of the city, which was just then being engulfed by a plume of desert steam. 'Right up there,' he said, 'in that area, something happened recently. If you look closely, you can see a fortress on the ridge-line. Yes?' In fact, all there was to see were waves of mist rolling in from the Red Sea. A block-like form on the ridge was disappearing under scraps of coalescing mist.

'It happened near there,' said Muhammad. 'Behind.' He thought about the issue for a moment more and then said, 'Behind further. In the vicinity, in the valley beyond the mountains.'

27

'Last year,' said Muhammad. 'American soldier – training Yemeni soldiers. Up there in the mountains. See?'

As part of the training, the American officer wanted the Yemeni soldiers under his command to have sex with a girl. These soldiers, being unmarried Muslims, were virgins. The American herded them into a troop carrier and drove them to a nearby village. A house was selected. 'Any house,' Muhammad said. 'Just house. Small. Like this.' He held his hand to the height of his waist.

A door was knocked on, he said, and the door was opened. Behind it stood a girl in her black rayon robe and veil. This was her protection. 'Nothing, nothing at all,' Muhammad said – 'just tissue, a *niqab*.'

As it happened, no male member of the family was at home that afternoon. The group of soldiers and their American lieutenant entered the house. They filed into the family's only bedroom. 'Off with the clothes,' said the American. The soldiers raped the girl, one by one, over and over. As they were leaving, as the Yemeni soldiers were cleaning themselves up and putting their clothing back on and praying to God for forgiveness, the girl died.

'Died?' I asked. 'How?'

Muhammad opened his palm towards the storm clouds. He didn't know. 'From the hand of God,' he guessed. 'She just died.

Dead. AIDS?' He didn't know. That evening, the family discovered the dead girl. They wept and cursed the Americans and called the village together. The father resolved to present himself to the officers at the nearby barracks. He would demand compensation. A village delegation was formed. 'But when they got to the army camp, the officer, he say, "Go on. Away! You're Yemeni villagers. Small men. We won't pay anything." Maybe the soldiers who committed the crime were put in the prison for some days,' Muhammad continued. 'Maybe two. Three possible. I don't know.' He couldn't remember how many soldiers there were and how many days they were imprisoned. 'Some few days. Then, go. Back to work. No punishment. Nothing. The American officer is still up in the fortress. He trains new soldiers now.'

Even as Muhammad was telling it, I was pretty certain that I'd heard his story before. Sometimes, when a taxi driver told the story, the setting would be Egypt and the violated girl would not be a girl but someone's wife or mum. Sometimes, in a chicken and rice restaurant, the aggressor would be an entire squadron of Americans and the victims would be entire villages in Iraq. Sometimes, the aggressor was a single American woman. The setting was a prison. Sometimes the rapists, as in Muhammad's story, were just simple local soldiers, gone crazy with American advice. Always there was a confidence game, followed by an invasion, then sex, then death.

In theory there were Muslim armies in the land of Islam. In theory the purpose of these armies was resistance to foreign invasion. But resist they did not. The native soldiers did what they were told. What did the Americans advise? They advised them to make war through sex. That was the American sickness, the way they conquered.

And so somewhere up in the hills, somewhere close by, near a foreign military base, but where exactly no one knew, a girl whose essential innocence and connection to the land made an apt figure for the nation itself, lay dead. She had been dishonoured, murdered, as in a nightmare. She had been killed by the very people meant to defend her. Villagers had come to the scene of the crime, as they always do. They had raised their palms to the sky: Lord, who has done this? they had asked. And who will avenge us?

An hour or so later, after Muhammad had gone home and I had gone off to the Old City to visit friends, the sky had turned into a blanket of lead. From the tower house in which I was sitting, which commanded a fantastic view, I could see the water falling in thick sheets across the mountains. When the rain hit the city, it came in gusts – wall after wall of heavy raindrops washing over the mosque domes and splashing against the apartment blocks. On the outskirts of the Old City, children stood on top of the bridges that arched over a spillway. That spillway was used as a road in the dry season. Now it was a river of detergent containers, cigarette packets, qat bags, bicycle inner tubes, election posters, branches, plastic teacups, sweet wrappers and clothing.

The speed and the silence of the flood entranced the children. For fun, they hurled their bicycles into the water. Now and then a little minibus, piloted by some daring but unwise driver, tried to make its way into the river. The minibuses stalled, of course, and had to be pushed from the mud by squads of bystanders.

The children of Sana'a loved these storms. Probably they needed them. The season's rhythms of tension and release, tension and release were what the kids had instead of money and education.

On those turbulent afternoons, the rains came like a great washing away. The whole city seemed to forget its frustration for a little while and to relax in the gust and the sheets of rain. After the downpours, the mosques were filled with drenched men warming themselves, whispering into their cupped hands and thanking Allah for the rain. Everyone wanted to register his gratitude. Everyone wanted to believe that Allah planned sparkling streams and fields of waving green for Sana'a.

28

As July turned into August, the afternoon floods became more violent. Minibuses were carried away on tides of mud. Said, however, continued to be stuck. He had no passport, no money to buy a ticket out of the country, and nowhere to go. He slept on the prayer hall floor.

While he waited for his deliverance, he was, not surprisingly, bored. He called home now and then. His brother insulted him. This made him, not surprisingly, frustrated. He visited Ahmed, the school secretary who smiled at him sweetly. 'Ah yes,' said Ahmed. 'The passport? Tomorrow, by the will of God.' There wasn't much left for Said to do. He floated. His voyage of the spirit had stopped at the slough of despond.

At least when he was eating, he could relax a little bit, be with friends and put his worries aside. So on most afternoons, at around one o'clock, while the Yemenis were buying their daily bags of qat, Said and I found ourselves searching the pavements near our mosque for a suitable restaurant. Is there anywhere, we wondered, that serves something besides chicken and rice? There wasn't. Sometimes the restaurants served rice, and no chicken, followed by tea, or sometimes they served chicken and bread, followed by tea. After a while, the sameness of the food and the sameness of the restaurants made us feel as though there wasn't much left for us in the world except piles of overcooked rice. Each new pile brought on a new wave of despair.

For a brief period, in August, before he left on his hajj, a fat Parisian brother, Omar, joined us for lunch. Omar came from a family of pizzeria owners in *le 93*, Seine-Saint-Denis, on the outskirts of Paris. He missed the food of home, as many foreign students in Yemen did, and missed the fun of sitting around a clean, quiet restaurant table with pizza, Coke, air conditioning and friends.

In theory, when Omar, Said and I were together, we combined all the necessary ingredients to recreate a pleasant lunchtime experience: we had money, time and common interests.

But the kind of food everyone liked, namely pizza, was far away, in a faux European neighbourhood on the other side of Sana'a. To consort with the kind of Yemeni who ate European food and hung around with faux Europeans bothered Omar and Said, and to travel into that neighbourhood of expensive cars, cellphone boutiques and imitation Starbuck coffee shops was, for them, to separate themselves from their routine of praying and recitation.

So often, before lunch, our conversations unfolded like this:

Said: That fast-food neighborhood of Pizza Quick is strictly for unbelievers. People wearing ties and so on. We should not go over there.
Me: For heaven's sakes! There isn't an unbeliever within a million miles! This is Yemen!
Omar: Said is right. I suppose we'll have to eat the rice and chicken, Allah forgive us, that we always eat.
Me: Brothers, we don't have to. A pizza for three is $5. You want me to pay? I'll pay for both of you. I have the money. It's nothing. I don't mind. You can pay me back when you are rewarded with prosperity, okay?

Often, Omar and Said said that they could not allow me to pay, no matter how insignificant the sums involved were. They said it wasn't entirely right according to Islam. Said reminded us that the Prophet had advised against incurring debts. As soon as the Prophet was cited, everyone acquiesced and we went off to a cement shack down the street from our mosque. It served boiled hens on top of piles of rice. We sat on the floor, next to teams of Yemeni diners who screamed at the waiters. The propane stove in the back of the room roared like a jet engine. We could hardly hear ourselves think. We squabbled with the Yemeni waiters over their prices, ate, felt sick and left, disappointed.

Later, back in the mosque, Said would speak of what he hoped for from a meal: repose, clean place settings, calm and order, thoughtfully prepared food. He hoped, he said, for actual conversation with his fellow human beings. He felt that by dining as the Yemenis dined, in a rush, with people screaming and the noise of the propane stove and the chicken feathers everywhere, we violated the Prophet's instructions. As Muslims, we were supposed to eat in a clean, dignified manner.

One afternoon towards the middle of August, after we had washed, prayed, and listened to Sheikh Moamr's noontime homily, Omar and Said suggested that we make an exception to our routine by taking our lunch in the upscale neighbourhood. 'It will be good for us,' Omar said. 'We would have a change of scene. We'll see something new for a change.' As soon as the idea was proposed, I seconded it, and within the minute we had boarded a passing bus.

Soon we were sailing past the glum cafes of our neighbourhood and our mosque was receding in the distance.

We got off the bus two blocks away from Pizza Quick. In this area, the storefronts had been done up in bulging backlit plastic facades. The display windows were draped with neon signs in English. *Spicey checken*, they said and *tastie!* and *Fastfood!*

We walked in front of an international bank. We passed a billboard depicting the president casting his eyes towards a distant horizon.

Ten minutes later we were standing directly in front of the

wide, glassy but very locked doors of Pizza Quick. Omar pushed the door handle. It was definitely locked.

'*Subhan allah*,' mumbled Omar.

'Closed?' asked Said. 'Ya salaam! Have we got here too early? Is this a joke?'

We stared at the locked doors for several long seconds.

'Shall we try some of the fried chicken restaurants nearby? It won't be exactly what we wanted,' said Omar. 'But certainly better than what we're used to.'

It was true that this neighbourhood was filled with jowly men in yellow ties and business suits who imitated the West. But on this afternoon we had come down here for an air-conditioned all-male dining room, for the familiar taste of fast food, for proper service, and a reliably halal lunch. We weren't so unlike the businessmen ourselves.

Two minutes after discovering the locked door of Pizza Quick, we stood on the front steps of Spicey Buffalo Chicken. Four waiters in crisp pin-striped uniforms smiled at us. 'The blessings of Allah,' Omar called out. Said adjusted his prayer cap. Omar called out, 'Your chicken, my brothers! Is the chicken from the Yemeni countryside? Or from outside of Yemen?' *Beladi ow kharaji?*

The waiters conversed among themselves.

'*Beladi ow kharaji?*' Omar repeated.

'It is from outside of Yemen,' one of the waiters admitted. 'It has been frozen and imported but it remains delicious!'

'Thank you, my brothers!' Omar replied.

'Of course it's halal,' Said whispered. 'Why are you making a scene?'

'Are you paying?' Omar replied. 'Are you even paying for your bus fare? Maybe you should keep quiet.'

The three of us put our heads down. We walked further into the fast-food neighbourhood.

At the next restaurant, Omar wished the head waiter the blessings of Allah, then smiled, then asked again: 'Do you have the chicken of the countryside?'

'I am sorry, my brothers,' said the waiter, 'it is from outside the Yemen.'

We walked to the next restaurant and the next. At every place the answer was the same: the chicken had been frozen. It had been imported from an unknown country. It was certainly halal. But how, Omar asked, could this be proved?

At the fifth restaurant, we stood at the threshold of the dining room, frowning and wondering what to do.

'It's just very sad,' Omar said.

'Allahu akbar!' I exclaimed. I gestured at the cavernous dining hall. It was filled with boisterous Yemeni men. Their plates were covered in chicken bones. 'My brothers,' I said to Omar and Said. 'Isn't this proof enough? What more do you want? This is how Muslims eat.'

'Not so fast,' said Omar. 'Restaurants around here import the cheapest chicken. There may be a halal label attached but that means nothing. You want to be the victim of a fraud? Some chicken processor, probably in France, will make out like a king. Your food won't be halal. You'll pay a lot. That's what you want? No, I hope not. A Muslim should be vigilant.'

We walked further into the fast-food neighbourhood. When we were interviewing our final set of waiters, I knew we were no longer actually looking for lunch. Now we were proving to one another, and to anyone else who happened to see, that we were stranded in a country whose pizza restaurants closed at lunchtime, whose chicken restaurants could not do a simple thing like serving halal chicken, and whose most important food district left pious Muslims wandering through the streets like lost souls, begging for, and not finding, halal, Islam-appropriate food. Of course, we were also proving that we understood the laws of Islam and respected them. Whereas the benighted Yemenis . . .

Eventually we did find a small, ill-lit place serving frozen, reheated pizzas. When our lunch finally arrived at our table, it turned out to be a tray of weak dough on which curds of plastic floated in a sweet sauce.

We stared at one another. No one wanted to say anything. We ate in silence. A team of Yemeni waiters with ties and shaved chins stared at us.

Towards the end of lunch Said said, 'Maybe you can find better Islamic practices in Saudi Arabia? Or, who knows, maybe in Afghanistan somewhere? In Waziristan?'

'You don't even have enough money for a taxi back to our mosque,' said Omar. 'Perhaps you could shut up?'

Not at this point, nor at any other point during lunch, did any of us say what was what was most obvious: that we had come halfway across the world for an authentic experience in Islam only to find ourselves eating fake pizzas as Yemenis in make-believe European waiter costumes gazed in fascination. At least a voyage through the back lanes of Roubaix would have culminated in a hot, well-made pizza. At least there would be halal signs in the windows of the restaurants and waiters who were proud to be Muslims, wore beards, and did not slaver over people speaking French who happened to have a few riyals in their pockets.

29

When lunch was finished, we had nowhere to go, and no plans. We ambled into a tea shop around the corner from Pizza Quick. When the tea arrived, Omar relaxed into his chair, smiled to himself, and began to speak about the ideal form of Islamic government.

All the necessary rules for governing society were written in the Koran, he said, pronouncing the words loudly and carefully, as if he meant his voice to carry from table to table. Therefore there didn't need to be a government at all where true Muslims were. In a proper Islamic society there would be no president and no parliament but, instead, scholars. 'What is needed in Yemen – in every Islamic country – is respect for the Koran, period,' he said, in French. 'How can you say there is respect for the Koran here, when the leaders of the country dress like bankers in Paris and you cannot find a halal chicken anywhere?'

A portrait of the Yemeni president glared at us from the wall above the front door of the cafe. The president sat atop a horse. Omar gestured at him with his elbow. He lowered his voice.

'If there were respect for the Koran, there would be no need for an idiot knight like that,' said Omar. *Un chevalier con*. 'The Koran would govern.'

Omar shot the breeze in this way for a little while. The Koran was the word of God. Muslims did not enter into political affairs.

The very idea of politics was a departure from, or as he said, an 'innovation' on systems spelled out in the sacred writings.

The speech would have been utterly banal in our mosque, or any of the places we were used to having lunch, but here we were surrounded by people who did enter into politics – at least inasmuch as they supported the President. Omar knew perfectly that they were regime apparatchiks – their ties, suit coats and moustaches gave them away. And so he expostulated: the falling-off that had occurred since the time of the Prophet; the ever present, ever enduring Straight Path; the corruption of Islam that the modern world had wrought.

As Omar spoke, I happened to notice that one of the tea drinkers, an ugly man with a sour expression in his eyes and a long, tangled beard, was staring at him. He stared at Said, then turned to me. He opened his cellphone and tapped some numbers into it. Then he chatted with his friends a bit. Finally, he smiled at Omar, rose, stepped towards us and salaamed. We shook his hand.

He grinned. 'My friends!' he said in English. 'May I sit with you?'

'Please,' we said. 'You are our guest.'

He smiled again. 'You think we not understand,' he said after a moment, still speaking in English. His eyes sparkled. 'Some do! Yes, they do understand. You never know!'

'What?' said Omar in Arabic.

'From which city in France you are from?' said the man with the tangled beard.

'We are visiting Yemen,' replied Omar in Arabic. 'Is it your business where we're from?'

'The police,' said our new friend, still grinning. 'They listen here. Always listening. You have spoken about our religion. Do you know what you're talking about? You have talked about our president. Why? Do you have any idea what you're talking about?' He stared into our faces.

'No,' we said, quietly.

'What are you doing here?' the man persisted.

'Just visiting,' Said said.

'You have said we do not understand the Koran. Isn't that right?'

'What are you talking about?' said Omar, still speaking in Arabic. The tea drinkers in the cafe were now leaning forward on the edge of their chairs, poised, thoughtful, motionless.

'We have seen you walking in the street, visiting the restaurants,' said the bearded man. 'What are you looking for? What do you want?'

'Nothing,' said Omar.

The man opened a packet of cigarettes, and began to smoke. He smiled to himself and muttered something in Arabic to the people with whom he had been sharing his tea a few moments earlier.

Then he turned back to us. 'Be careful,' he said at last. 'You don't know where you are.'

He smiled at me. 'This young man here conducts himself properly,' he said, pointing to me. 'He does not make problems. He keeps to himself. He shuts up. Right?'

'Right,' I said.

'But you, I think,' he said, turning back to Omar, 'I think you like to make problems. Yes? Am I right? Yes?'

'Not at all,' said Omar.

'Well, be careful,' said the bearded man. 'You have been warned.' He snuffed out his cigarette. He offered to pay for our tea. We declined. He rose, smiled at the three of us one final time, and reached into the pocket of his trousers. He deposited a coin on a counter near where the cafe owner sat, salaamed, and walked into the sunshine.

A few seconds later, the old man who owned this tea shop tapped his coin on the formica counter. Omar, Said and I looked up. 'Hess,' said the old man.

'What?' we said.

'Hess, hess,' he said.

Omar and Said looked at me.

'Hess,' said the owner again and nodded vaguely at the poster of the president atop his horse. 'Hess!'

At the time I thought 'hess, hess!' might mean 'Behave yourself, young man,' or maybe, 'Asshole! You have embarrassed me in front of my customers!' Much later, when I had a deeper knowledge of Arabic, I learned that the command 'Hess!' comes from the verb *hasa*, to feel or sense, and in this context means: 'Sense your surroundings!' Or maybe: '*Feel* where you are!' Or maybe, more simply, 'Wake up!'

Out on the pavement, sunlight stabbed us in the eyes. A sound truck playing presidential election music was assaulting pedestrians.

We stumbled around for a moment, disorientated by the racket and the light. We asked a passer-by for the nearest mosque and followed him through an alley, past a nondescript ministry, and into a garage-like hall made of cinder blocks. It was evidently the mosque of a local military detachment. Soon we were standing shoulder to shoulder with a legion of mustachioed men in army fatigues and black socks. 'I seek refuge from the Shaytan, and the djinn,' the hall whispered. 'From the Outcast and his evil.'

30

Though our excursion to the fast-food district ended calmly, it must have alarmed Omar and Said. Within a day, they had quite changed their behaviour towards me. They were cold and correct. They avoided me outside the mosque. Maybe I had been too flip about our search for halal food? Maybe they thought the bearded man in the tea shop who scolded them was an undercover policeman. Did they imagine that he and I were working together? I don't know. Anyway, Said and Omar stopped talking to me.

When we shook hands in the ablution room or after prayers, they said nothing. When I sat down with them in the mosque one afternoon, they smiled to each other, waited a polite interval, then rose and left the mosque. Once, finding Said in a tea shop by himself, I asked him if he wanted to examine a pamphlet I had picked up recently: *How to Respond to the Nullifiers of Islam*.

'Ah, *l'américain*,' he sighed, not bothering to hide his boredom. 'Where have you been?'

'About,' I said. 'In the mosque.'

He sipped his tea.

'You've been seen in Hadda,' he said after a moment, referring to the faux-European neighbourhood. 'Some brothers from the mosque here have said so. Riding your bike around. Wearing Western clothes.'

It was true. I had been buying sneakers. I had been on my way to play tennis with a European friend.

'Sneakers and tennis?' he asked, shaking his head. 'I suppose that's what you want?' I left the tea shop by myself with my pamphlet.

Early the following morning, at the quietest time of day in the mosque, when the bodies of a dozen or so students were slumbering in the sunlight, and only a single circle of Yemeni grandfathers was rehearsing Koran beneath a column, Omar and Said sat down in front of me. I was involved in a grammar exercise. Omar wrapped his hand around the back of my neck. 'There he is, Brother Thabit!' he said. 'Studying still? Our American friend, always in the midst of studying.'

He smiled but the smile was forced.

'Wa alaikum a salaam,' I said.

'We'd like to talk to you for a moment, Thabit,' said Omar.

'Of course,' I said. For several long seconds, Omar and Said sat there on the carpet in front of me, smiling and examining my schoolbooks, my notebooks, my Koran and my backpack.

'Well,' I said. 'Should we have tea? Stay here?'

'May I see what you are scribbling in your notebook?' wondered Omar.

'Of course,' I said. I showed him a page of verb declensions.

'Is that all you have in your notebook?'

'No,' I said. 'I have a lot of pages of scribbling, too.'

'May I ask why you spend so much time scribbling in a notebook?'

'Because I am trying to understand Arabic grammar,' I replied. 'I am also trying to understand the religion of Islam. I am also trying to do my homework.'

'Yes, yes, that's quite normal,' Omar said. 'The funny thing is that Said and I have been noticing lately. You seem very interested in what kind of pizza we eat. And where we're from in France and who our families are and that sort of thing. But not so much in the unity of God.'

I took a deep breath. I knew where this was going.

'I am interested in the pizza you eat,' I said. 'I am interested in where you're from and what your lives are like in France.'

I could see Said's face falling. He shook his head slowly. He turned to Omar and said, 'Let me talk to him.' He put his hand on my shoulder. 'Listen, Thabit,' he said. '*Arrête tes conneries.*' Stop kidding around. 'You're very far from the point, the goal of Islam, if what you're interested in is why we've come here from France and what kind of pizza we like. You know that, don't you?'

'Why is that wrong?' I asked.

'I'll talk to him,' Omar interrupted, smiling. 'The good news is that we don't think that you're working for the CIA any more. Or the Mossad or the French police. The bad news is that we've been watching you. In fact everyone has remarked about you and everyone is wondering what you're really up to.'

'Everyone?' I asked. 'Who's everyone?'

They shrugged their shoulders.

I glanced at the circle of elderly gentlemen who were sitting beneath a column. They held Korans in their laps. Their beards were illuminated by the sun. But for the office decor, they could have been figures in a painter's fantasy of Eastern sagacity and self-contentment.

No, it wasn't them.

'Yes,' Omar continued, 'the questions you ask, the way you scribble in your notebooks, even though your Arabic grammar is not improving, is getting worse if anything, your general *façon de faire*, your attitude, even the way you dress. It has helped us understand. You're certainly up to something.'

I sighed.

'You're plotting something, yes?' said Omar. 'Spit it out. We think you're writing something. Yes?'

'All right then. Yes,' I said. 'I am writing something. Plotting – not really. But writing, okay.'

'Be serious, Thabit. Please,' Said said.

'I am serious,' I said.

'You're writing a book?' Omar asked.

I shrugged my shoulders. 'Yeah,' I said. 'A book.'

'You can't be serious,' said Omar

'You're writing some sort of crap book?' Said said. '*Stagfir Allah.*' God forgive you.

I knew I had lost the argument but I kept talking.

I said that if a book told the story of how Muslims from the West live when they come to the Middle East, it had to be true. If it was true, it might be good or bad from a literary point of view but to say that it was forbidden didn't make any sense.

'Are we ourselves impermissible?' I asked. 'What is the news with Western Muslims in Yemen now? Someone tries to answer that question and you say that's wrong? Even to try?'

The two of them stared at me. '*Subhan allah,*' Omar muttered. Good heavens.

'If this is true what you say,' said Said under his breath, 'then in the first place you are crazy to come to Yemen. In the second place, you do not have adequate learning. And do you have permission? From anyone? No. And in the third place, you have totally and completely missed the point.'

'Of what?' I said.

'Of study. Of Islam. Of the unity of God.'

We went round like this for several more minutes. Said and Omar felt I didn't know enough about Islam to write a word, never mind a book. For if a Muslim speaks to the public, especially to an unbelieving public such as in France or America, he should be informed, have years of scientific training, mastery of the Arabic language, the Koran, and the support of the *ulema*, or learned men of Islam. At that point, he should speak about the revelations of the Prophet of Allah. Period.

'I am trying to learn,' I said. 'Look.' I pointed to my backpack in which a little store of pamphlets drifted about. There were notebooks in there, too, and grammar exercise books.

Omar gaped. He shook his head. He was losing patience. He put his hand on my shoulder. 'Look,' he said, 'I'll make this very simple for you, okay? Listen closely, Thabit. Are you listening? If you have come here to denounce the religion of Islam . . .'

'Which I have not done,' I said.

'Or if you are, in your heart, or in any way, an enemy of Islam.'

I shook my head. 'I am not,' I said.

'The Yemenis will kill you,' he said.

'They will cut your throat,' Said added. 'They will consider it an honour.'

I stared at them. I stared at the old men in their circle – so calm, so focused on the Koran. 'I suppose I'm okay then,' I said. 'Because none of these circumstances are true.'

'I'm just telling you,' repeated Omar, smiling.

'I suppose I'm okay then,' I repeated.

'Yes, inshallah,' Omar said.

'Inshallah,' I agreed.

31

When I told Muhammad, my grammar teacher, about Omar and Said's warnings, he frowned, made an imperceptible flick in the air with his hand as if to say, 'what is this?' and advised me not to seek advice on Islam from Omar and Said. To Muhammad, those two were perhaps on the path of indolence or pizza or partial commitment to Islam followed by return to their comfortable lives in the West, as many students were. One thing they were not was pledged securely to the *sabeel Allah*, the Straight Path of God. 'I don't know. Perhaps because of their childhood in France, or perhaps because their Frenchness is mixed up with their Berber heritage,' said Muhammad, they had different – he meant *incorrect* – views of Islam. 'They were born Muslim, but what does this guarantee?' he asked. 'Anyway, you're not the first Muslim about whom people in our mosque gossip and you won't be the last. So concentrate on your work. Recite Koran. Remember Allah.'

In the days after my conversation with Omar and Said, I learned new suras, or chapters of the Koran. I happened to memorise, at this time, the Chapter of the Earthquake or *zilzal*. All non-native speakers in our mosque were directed to this sura early on in their education because it was easy to memorise and also because it was a kind of creed:

When the earth shall tremble with her quaking,
and the earth shall cast forth her burdens,
and man shall say, 'What aileth her?'
In that day shall mankind advance in ranks,
. that they may behold their works,
and whoever shall have wrought good of the weight of a grain
    shall behold it;
and whoever shall have wrought evil of the weight of a grain
    shall behold it.

When I was memorising, I used to sit in the back of the mosque. I used to keep an eye on a blind teenage boy, about twelve, who spent his days sitting in the sunshine in a corner of the prayer hall. He didn't use a walking stick to move around but clung to the sleeve of his little brother. He wore tattered robes and smiled at shadows. He napped during the mornings, then rose to pray, then returned to his spot in the sun. Sometimes the brother came to pick him up for lunch but often the brother didn't come, and the blind boy sat all day, grinning and waiting.

Sometimes as I was memorising, I watched a palsied four-year-old girl, the only female ever to appear in our mosque, twitching on her blanket. Her father would deposit her in a nook near the door, and would then go off to pray. The girl would lie by herself, twitching and waiting. Sometimes, in her spasms, she tried to sit up a bit and pray in synch with her dad. Usually the twitching was just too overwhelming. The faithful were supposed to give her coins. Some did. Most did not.

In the weeks to come, when I knew the earthquake chapter better, I watched military men recite it and watched the words on the lips of the sheikh himself. By then it had occurred to me that there were probably just as many victimisers in our mosque as there were victims and that not everyone here was helpless and poor.

The married men would have learned, through trial and error, how to curtail the ambitions of their wives and daughters, and how to keep them covered and quiet. The military men would have studied this practice as it relates to controlling the public sphere. Ostensibly, a Koranic verse about reversals, promising a cosmic turning of the tables, shouldn't resonate with this audience.

But it did. It was important to them, I guessed, because they knew they weren't participating in a just system, because they were aware of the suffering they inflicted on other people, and wanted to atone for it before God. Atoning for it in front of the sufferers? No, this wasn't on the agenda.

Anyway, the entire cosmos was unjust. Why were four-year-old girls punished with palsy? Why were the most ardent, faithful believers the poorest? Why was work so scarce and pay so low?

The more you focused on the Sura of the Earthquake, the more you thought that none of this mattered.

For this sura promised that the palsied girl would finally be rewarded for her attempts to pray. She would be rewarded or punished according to the purity of her heart. As would everyone else. The Day of Judgment would be a violent, terrifying day because every sin ever committed would be alive and stalking the person who committed it. Humans would straggle forth from their graves, hopeful of heaven, terrified of hell. Most of all, though, it would be a just day – and that's what the men in our mosque were waiting for: the time of reckoning, the hour of justice, the overturning of the current unhappy dispensation.

Memorising Koran is not like learning one's part in a play, for instance, or cramming for an exam. There's no deadline, no hurry, and no test. Taking Koran into your head is more like learning to row a boat across a wide lake than like learning, say, your lines in *Macbeth*. The lake is the life of this world, and rowing well is meant to give you a straight, even course. A traveller who moves across the lake stealthily, with purpose and rhythm, will not be seduced by the dark spots and will not lose his way.

The Arabic verb for memorise, *hafaza*, really means to conserve or save. One conserves the Koran in one's head. Of course memories tend to decay and so even a reciting genius must be in constant attendance on neglected memories. This shoring up is called *murajah,* or going back.

Every time I went to the mosque to memorise, I went backward over old memories first, then forward into new ones. The people around me were often doing the same thing.

Some people preferred to memorise with beads in their hands. Others held the book aloft; still others put the book in a stand, and others wrote the verses out by hand, which can improve your handwriting and is said to stabilise the memory.

Thus the book was always close by, but so were the other bodies in the mosque, and their voices and their breathing. One looked into the book. One memorised. One looked away, at the bodies of those nearby. One returned to the book.

In this way the meaning of the verses became tied up with the faces and bodies nearby – the twitching toddlers, the old shadows with their canes and misshapen backs. They had their place in the *saved* version of the text and helped to make its meaning clear.

Later on, outside the mosque, when I repeated the chapters I had learned there, the faces I was looking at as I memorised came back to me. Nowadays every time the phrase 'whoever does a mote's weight of good will see it' I think of the blind boy's brother who held out his sleeve for his sibling, and guided him through his five ablutions, his prayers, and his midday meal. If I hear the phrase 'when the victory of God comes to the people' which comes from the Sura al-Nasr, another chapter I learned early on, I think of two incredibly patient Australian Pakistani friends who helped me learn it. They sat for hours on the opposite side of my Koran stand, prompting me when I forgot lines, and smiling when I did things right.

32

When the fuss and bother over my intentions in the mosque subsided, I resumed my place at the evening homilies, in a shadowy rear section of the mosque, next to Omar and Said. Their concern about my bad faith faded away. They had their own problems. Gradually we resumed our excursions to the local chicken, rice and tea restaurants. They had to answer for gaps in the purity of their faith as well, and knowing this, and seeing that the Yemenis were not bothered by my presence, they agreed to leave me in peace.

It was the middle of August. Ramadan was approaching. The suspense about when it would arrive – this evening? tomorrow evening? the next? – was a torture for the little boys in our neighbourhood. The ones who were on the cusp of adolescence were old enough to keep the fast absolutely, to sleep during the day as their fathers did, and to perform the pre-dawn prayers in public, along with all the powerful men in the neighbourhood. When Ramadan did come, these boys would go about the alleys in the holiday finery of a man – with shawls and daggers. The girls would stare at them from behind curtained windows.

Yet when would it finally begin? In anticipation, boys would roam the streets in little packs, singing and collecting sticks for their welcoming bonfire. If they happened on a tourist or a lost

Westerner of any kind they would shriek: *There he is! Burn him! Is he a Muslim? He is not! Burn him, in the name of God!* The children would thrust balls of hay at the ankles of their victim, and hurl their firecrackers into the air. The truth was that they had no intention of burning anyone. But on those tense evenings, when only the *ulema* knew exactly when Ramadan would arrive, the kids allowed themselves to go beyond the normal, into play-acting, and then into menace. They liked threatening foreigners. Their fathers and elder brothers were too decorous, and too polite to offer to burn the tourists. But the little kids could get away with a lot, enjoyed being bold, and so took licence.

In our mosque at this time, Sheikh Moamr made a special effort to keep to the most central themes of Islam: the oneness of God and the preservation of the *iman*, or faith. He spoke in a simplified, ultra-clear Arabic so that the Western students, many of whom were spending extra time in the mosque during this period, could understand every word.

After the *Maghrib*, or sunset prayer, he would utter the normal words of welcome: 'We are gathered in the name of God. We recognise him and believe in him. We believe in his Prophet, peace be upon him and his family, and we believe in the Last Day.' Then he would turn to his audience and urge us into deeper belief. 'Believe in God and remember God,' he would say. 'Conserve the Koran in your hearts and you will conserve your faith. Only say "there is no God but God." The rest will come of its own accord.'

Sheikh Moamr must have known that these simple exhortations went down well. When he made them to the Chechens, the Nigerians and the Brixtonian imports who sat cross-legged on the carpet in front of his armchair, they raised their chins at him, and held their heads in the motionless, silent way of children watching a movie. All you could hear was the rustle of their robes, their breathing, and maybe far away, from some out-of-synch minaret across the valley, the Shia call to prayer.

*   *   *

After this first part of his speech, the sheikh would usually move on to more abstruse, technical matters. He might discuss some remark or habit of the Prophet's, or he might speak about the chain of narrators through which these habits and remarks were passed down to history. Certain remarks were passed down along this unimpeachable chain. Others were merely folk superstitions, fathered upon the Prophet by partisans and frauds.

Sometimes he would talk about some issue of contemporary importance to Muslims, such as the way Christians came to Yemen in secret, with secret medicine aimed at suppressing the growth of the world's Islamic population. Sometimes he would remind the worshippers and students in the mosque of the differences between the Islamic scripture and other sacred books. 'The Christian Bible has been doctored by Jews,' he would say, 'and the Jews have hidden away their own Torah in favour of a fraudulent text. Why? Why? Because the real Torah contains signs of the arrival of Muhammad, the final Prophet. Do not read these books, because they are lies. They are forgeries and there is only one Book of Allah, and it is our noble Koran, blessings upon its creator.'

Sometimes he discussed how exactly he knew about the population suppression programme, or the doctoring of the Bible. Certain scholars had confirmed it. He mentioned their names and the names of their disciples, or he mentioned the titles of their books.

Now and then, when the sheikh was deep into this second, more academic part of his daily speech, which was sometimes almost a list of books, I would look over to my wifeless American friend, Muhammad from Maryland or to my homeless French pal, Said. Said would be out there in the blue, just gone, almost asleep, in another world. He was all cocooned up, safe from his antagonists, more relaxed than I'd ever seen him. Yup, it's all lost on him, I would think, and the Arabic is too hard for him to understand. But sometimes I would look at him or at the row of French kids who were sitting next to him, and think: they've gone away intentionally, all of them. They can hear the sheikh better out there. 'These doctrines have been well established by sheikhs Albani, Muqbel, and many others,' the sheikh would say. 'Read their books and conserve their books in your hearts.' At moments like this, I would watch the fluttering eyelids of my fellow students and think: they may be away in spirit, okay, but out there they tune in on a finer frequency. Over time, the message will cut in deeper.

Islamic faith wasn't such an easy concept to master. Many young believers in our mosque thought they were strengthening it but they weren't. Some of the devout Yemenis were, but then the next day they would skip their prayers and spend the money they had in their pockets, meant for wife and children, on qat. Evidently, the hours they spent in our mosque hadn't done a thing for their *iman*. What were they doing wrong?

One evening in August, the sheikh gave us a lecture which showed us how *iman* really worked.

'To see what real *iman* looks like, there is a very simple thing to do,' he told us. If we took a bus to a certain mosque a few dozen kilometres to the south of Sana'a, we could see a local imam delivering an astonishing Friday speech. 'Every Friday, the entire congregation there listens to the sermon in tears. Big heavy tears roll down the faces of the tribesmen and sheikhs who come to this mosque. They emerge with their beards soaking, their hands trembling. Why do they cry like this? Why?' he asked.

'Once not long ago,' said Moamr, 'a young cleric from the neighbourhood decided to tape this imam's Friday sermons. He played the tape for himself at home, memorising everything. He returned to his own congregation the following week. When he delivered his sermon, he spoke every word the famous imam spoke, without changing a dot. He imitated the facial expressions and tone of voice.' But his audience reacted as most Friday audiences across Yemen react: they shifted a bit in their robes, coughed, wiped their brows, and napped.

'And so the following week, the young cleric returned to his mentor. "Why?" he said to the man of learning. "What happened? I spoke every letter you spoke. Where is the difference? What?"

"'Ah," replied the famous imam, "but when I speak on Fridays, I stay up the night before, reciting Koran to myself, making it pregnant within me, filling my heart with it, drinking in the sound, the feeling, and the sensations of the Koran. When the holy book is that much within you, every word you utter, even if it is about the weather, will be made of *iman*. Every silence, every breath, and every movement of your eyes. It won't matter what words come from your mouth. The people in your congregation will sense the love of the word of God. They will feel *iman*. When there is that much faith in the air, a Muslim will weep."'

'After the sheikh had made this point, he sat for a few moments in silence. He took a heavy breath, smiled to himself and then said, "So this is why you must memorise Koran. Make it pregnant within you, in every thought, every deed and in every word that comes from your mouth. And go back over your memories, day in and day out. Because *moorajah* makes the *iman* strong. So you must read every day and memorise," he said. '*Hafizu!* Please! *Hafizu!*'

As Ramadan approached, the sheikh also took time to talk about what life was like where faith was diminishing, where Islam was on the retreat.

'In Tunisia,' the sheikh told us one evening, 'Islam used to be strong. It used to be a major Islamic capital. But I have a friend who recently returned from there. He told me that Muslims are living through a time of extraordinary hardness. It is all but illegal to wear the hijab, the veil has been forbidden, and the very activity of prayer,' he said, 'makes a citizen suspect.'

There was silence in the mosque when he said this and a slow shaking of heads. 'So you see,' said Moamr, 'we have problems in Islam. Big problems.' In Tunis nowadays, he said, there were hardly any prayers offered to Allah, period. The mosques had been closed. People had to pray secretly, in their houses. Now, in public, in the streets, there was adultery everywhere and alcohol.

Moamr then folded his hands in his lap. 'Yes,' he said, 'because of the closing down of the mosques there and the abandonment of the Prophet, homosexuality has spread. It has now become a major problem in all of Tunisia. Of course God, in his throne in heaven, is watching. He is taking the measure of the situation and punishing as appropriate. You think he isn't?' He raised his right index finger into the air and let it hang there for a few dramatic seconds. 'Thirty years ago or so, in 1981 or '82 – about this time, approximately – a meteorite crashed into a village outside the capital. It was a village of homosexuals. It was destroyed like broken pottery. You see? The people do not know it but Allah is watching and will punish.'

Maybe in some other time or place, some of the students – the ones who'd studied at British universities, for instance, or the ones who had family in Tunis – would have thought: *Can this be true? Really? Or is this myth?* The young men in the audience were not suckers. They were owners of Palm Pilots and laptops. In a university lecture hall, in the lecture of some much-admired professor, they might well have dialled into Wikipedia on the campus wifi system to verify the claim. On a technical level, they were certainly capable of verifying claims.

Naturally, they did not proceed this way in Yemen. In the first place, the sheikh was not insisting on the details of his facts. Secondly, everyone understood that a different kind of truth was at hand. The students knew from their own experience that out on the perimeter of the Islamic world, far from here, but maybe not so far after all, Islam was falling into a void. Shame itself had died. Moamr added new details. Homosexuals, he said, were taking over entire villages. The surrounding country of Tunisia had all but apostatised. But God was watching. As sin compounded sin, with every passing second, God watched and prepared his punishment. The locals never bothered to examine the sky. They forgot God. They went about their business. The result was that they did not see the meteorite as it sped on its way. They were surprised when it destroyed an entire village. Moamr, however, was not. 'Allah is now killing Muslims,' he said. 'Problems. Big problems.'

Most of the Westerners in our mosque probably did not need these lectures. They recognised deep *iman* when they saw it. *Iman* was the self-discipline, seriousness and silence of those Western men who had married Yemeni women. It was the Somalians who huddled in corners in our mosque, praying and keeping to themselves. Actually, most people in our mosque knew that the two individuals with the deepest, most solemn *iman* in our mosque were the blind boy who tugged on his little brother's sleeves all day and the convulsing, four-year-old girl.

When you had faith like that, you did not wonder what contributions to your life Wikipedia, iPods and the rest of the world's gadgetry might make.

You were a child of God. You prayed. You would be rewarded for your faith when the time came.

One evening, shortly before Ramadan, the sheikh gave us a primer on the signs that would accompany the arrival of the Islamic Redeemer, or Mahdi.

'He will not necessarily come during Ramadan,' said the sheikh. 'But when he does come, we will know. Muslims should memorise the signs: the rising of the sun in the west, yes, and plagues across the globe, yes, these will be signs. And also a war in Iraq. There will be fitnas, or internal divisions, for Muslims, and temptations and jealousies. But there will not necessarily be two eclipses in the month of Ramadan. And the Redeemer himself will not necessarily appear in Damascus, but may even appear in Yemen, even among the Jews of Yemen. We do not know.' When the Redeemer finally establishes his rule on earth, he said, the *ummah* will at last feel like a family. There will no longer be divisions between the nations and the sects will unite as one.

If this speech was calculated to ease the Ramadan tension that had been building in the mosque, I think it worked well.

After the speech, in the stairwell among the beggars and the discarded sandals, the students shook hands with each other. They smiled warmly and gave alms to the beggars. Even Said gave up a few coins. Walking down the steps and out into the evening light, several of the students draped their arms over one another's shoulders.

These were reassuring moments. The Redeemer will come, the sheikh had said, and he will make things better. Scan the skies, he said, and know the signs – 'conserve the signs in your heart'.

33

The day of the Great Presidential Rally, which was held to mark the end of the first great presidential re-election campaign, dawned bright and hot. It was 26 August 2006. The rally was no regular 'get out the vote' affair but rather a national welcoming party for the arrival, at long last, of democracy in Arabia. The first real, truly certifiable presidential election in the history of the region was at hand. The president was throwing a party.

The European Union election monitors came. The international press came. The *Yemen Observer* was filled with photo spreads and banner headlines – Faris's way of expressing delight. In the pictures, the president appeared in his sunglasses, in front of crowds, in expensive suits and ties, smiling. The other Yemeni newspapers, pro- and anti-government, were also excited. So were both Yemeni TV stations. All media in Yemen were singing the same song: democracy had dawned in southern Arabia.

The sameness in the media was because the news in Yemen was fixed. The journalists knew that the president wished to see a celebration of democracy in the media. They knew that foreigners were watching. They knew what the foreigners wanted to hear. So they celebrated. *Al-Wasat* and *al-Hurria* ('the Middle' and 'Freedom', respectively), newspapers of the so-called opposition, muted their celebrations because their purpose in the Yemeni media firmament was to show that there really was an opposition. Like all newspapers in Yemen, they got their funding from the office of the president. So they were defiant, but mildly. 'We urge citizens to vote according to their conscience!' they said. And: 'Historic days for Yemen.' The rest of the press, especially the all-important satellite TV channel, Yemen TV, urged citizens to show up at the Great Presidential Rally, the first such in the history of Arabia. The President of the Republic, His Excellency Ali Abdullah Saleh, was planning to address the crowd.

At one similar rally, earlier in the campaign, twenty-eight supporters of the president had been trampled to death in Ibb, a fertile, rainy city of terraced gardens to the south of Sana'a. When the rally was finished the police heaved the bodies of the victims into the back of nearby pickup trucks. On TV, the dead looked like stacks of Yemeni tuna, pulled from the ocean and laid out in pickup beds for easy transportation.

But this was in the past. The victims had been mourned and buried. Now the citizens of Sana'a wanted to celebrate, and to exhibit their love of the president to the media of the world.

Even on the night before the rally you could feel a weird kind of euphoria descending on the streets. It was written across the faces of the country folk who had come to Sana'a to celebrate and buzzed over crowds of children as they waited to buy candy-floss on the street or fought over bags of chocolates tossed to them by big-hearted merchants.

On the avenue in front of our mosque, buses from the countryside had installed themselves in parking spaces long before midnight. The passengers bought big bouquets of candy-floss for their kids, spoke in thick hayseed accents and stood on the street corners, staring.

The Yemeni public loved its Big Man, Ali Abdullah Saleh. He was the king of southern Arabia, the hero of the unification of North and South Yemen, the scourge of the southern communists, and the defier of George H. W. Bush during the first Gulf War. He was the builder of roads and institutions. He brought satellite TV, cheap food and foreign dignitaries. On this occasion, he brought the attention of the world to Yemen.

Most at the rally and probably all the citizens of Sana'a knew his democracy didn't exist. But so what? The Yemeni public could be euphoric about the man himself. His democracy was just a system after all. No one loved a system. People loved the man.

After the dawn *athan*, or call to prayer, had come and gone, at around six in the morning, the traffic on the street in front of our mosque consisted entirely of buses and taxis arriving from the countryside. By eight o'clock, pedestrians were filling the nearby streets. Columns of marchers converged at the intersections. The minor streets were like streams emptying into tributaries, and the tributaries poured into plazas and boulevards of holidaymakers.

Here the buses, marchers, horses, sound trucks, police cars, pickup trucks, farm trucks, jeeps and battered taxis collected but did not move. Police tried to urge the traffic forward but many watching the parade were happy where they were. Apparently, they didn't want to march. They just wanted to mill around, singing and chatting.

By the time I came down the prayer hall to wake Said at nine, the avenue beneath the mosque was filling the prayer hall with an unearthly racket. Music poured from loudspeakers attached to the roofs of minibuses and the police were using the public address systems on their patrol cars to shout at the marchers.

'Haraq! Haraq!' they yelled. Move! Move!

I was amazed to find that Said was still asleep. 'Wake up, my friend,' I said to him. He turned his face to the wall. 'God knows how I am sleeping through this racket but I am,' he said. 'So leave me alone.'

I shook Said's leg again. I promised him a breakfast of fresh orange juice and Yemeni beans.

'As a Muslim I am not allowed to enter into politics,' he said. 'You're not either. Apparently you don't care.'

'For heaven's sake,' I said. 'There is no danger to your faith here. It's not a democracy! There is no democracy in Yemen. There is a fake democracy and now there will be a stage show. Why not watch it, Said? Get up. Now.'

He rubbed his eyes. He sat up and then stood up. 'I will come for breakfast,' he said. 'But only for breakfast.'

In the ablution room he put on a robe and a waist dagger. He combed his hair. He fluffed out his beard. When he returned to the prayer hall, he strode across the carpet, looking regal and healthy, like a prince in the *Arabian Nights*. 'Ça c'est la classe,' he said of his robe, but he deadpanned the line, as if his heart wasn't in it. 'A re-election rally for a tinpot dictator is not a place for a Muslim,' he said. 'I am going for breakfast, then I am coming home.'

Outside the mosque, in the blinding sunshine, we gazed up the avenue. Crowds streamed towards the parade ground. Minibuses covered in pink plastic flowers nosed through the pedestrians. I looked for an open tea shop. Seeing that there were none, I looked into the crowds for a tea cart, or a wandering kebab man, or even a child selling chips.

We started walking. We crossed a commercial thoroughfare, Zubeiri Street. After a half-hour of ambling, we were in the middle of the fast-food district. Now we were properly hungry, both of us, but every restaurant was locked up as if in expectation of a riot. We searched the side streets for signs of beans, or beet soup carts, or falafel, or bananas – or anything comestible at all. There was nothing.

The normal city buses had stopped running. All public vehicles had been commandeered to serve as shuttles, ferrying people to the old Sana'a airport, where the rally was to be held.

A couple of Sudanese diplomats who had stopped to buy cigarettes offered to give us a lift. 'A Frenchman and an American?' the driver asked. 'Here? Today?'

'They are spies,' muttered the fellow in the passenger seat. 'Are you spies?' the driver asked, turning to us with a smile.

He dropped us off a few metres from the Greenland restaurant. Above us, a squadron of helicopters flitted in front of the sun. 'Good heavens,' Said murmured.

'We'll walk just to the edge of the airport tarmac,' I said. 'Come on, brother. We'll just see the rally from a distance. We'll have a peek, then the restaurants will have opened, and then we'll go eat.'

The crowd grew zanier as we approached the Old Airport. The nation of Yemen would not be denied its euphoric moment of democracy. Several democrats walked by us with photographs of Ali Abdullah Saleh pasted on to their foreheads. One inventive Yemeni had strapped a piano synthesiser to his waist, and had somehow affixed a pair of stereo speakers to the crown of his turban. With his right hand, he banged on the piano keys and with his left he shook a tambourine. Tribesmen beat their drums. Taxi drivers hammered on their horns.

I nudged Said in the ribs. 'We'll take a short cut down this side street,' I said. 'We'll hop a fence and from there we'll have a better view.'

Now above us, on the roofs of a tall bank and the tallest apartment buildings we could see the police snipers, strolling, eyeing the crowd, cradling their rifles. We drifted down the side street. Just as we were about to turn into an alley that would have brought us to a secret hole in an iron fence, an eighteen-wheel troop carrier stuffed with blank-faced soldiers rumbled past. The soldiers sat on their benches in grim resignation, wearing helmets. Soon another such carrier passed, and then smaller police vehicles followed in its wake.

'Allahu akbar,' Said said as the fleet passed us. When the last vehicle bounced by, he stopped walking. He stared, as if he'd seen a truckload of spirits. 'I'm leaving,' he said, 'I'm going home. Now. Goodbye.' Ahead of us, in a cloud of dust, about a hundred metres away, the troops were pouring out of their trucks. Even from a distance, this outpouring made an impressive sound – a long, loud waterfall of boots and shouts and then a widening pool of helmets filling the space between the apartment buildings.

Said fled down an alley. It led backward, into the fast-food district. 'All right! Forget it!' I called out. 'Forget everything. We'll have breakfast. We'll go home.'

Jogging in my sandals, I caught up to him after a minute or so. 'I am not allowed to be here,' he muttered. 'My religion absolutely forbids this. You do what you want. This sort of thing is for your sort of people. Go.'

Unlike so many Muslims, Said had chosen sides. When it came to democracy, he was no fence-sitting, accommodationist type. He knew where he belonged. If he had kept his own counsel, he would have been fine. Instead he listened to me and, like all well-intentioned Westerners, I was a fence-sitter.

'Okay,' I said. 'Relax. We'll eat. Off we go. Food, okay?'

For a few minutes, we followed a succession of alleys. We were quite lost and then we were less lost and soon we found ourselves again on a main boulevard. We marched against the streaming crowd. At last we came to a filling station. Here the crowds of observers on the pavements had thinned. Only a sprinkling of loiterers leaned against empty cars; a lonely fellow in a tracksuit lounged against a lamp post. Out in the centre of the boulevard, a trickle of celebrants hurried towards the airport tarmac.

Generally, police protect filling stations. Filling stations might be interesting to terrorists, so the thinking goes, because Islamists like to show their control over oil and especially appreciate the satisfying black ball of smoke an attack would cause. So when there are throngs in the streets, the police in many instances go to the filling stations. This bit of wisdom was something we might have known. We did not.

As we were passing in front of the pumps, I stopped a marcher who carried a sheaf of glossy posters of the president. President Saleh was sitting at a desk, grinning officially into a camera. *With you!* said the legend in thick red letters.

'Let me have one of these, my brother,' I said to the marcher. 'Allah bless you and keep you.'

'Gladly!' He handed me two. 'A foreigner loves the president, too?'

'Of course!' I said.

Turning to Said, I murmured to him, 'For the toilet wall.' He scowled. His pace quickened. As he walked, he slipped the posters from my fingers. '*Arrête tes conneries*, Thabit,' he said. 'Leave these. *Haram*.' He took the images in both hands, ripped them once, then twice, then three times, then crumpled the bits into a ball, then deposited the ball in the filling station rubbish bin. 'No pictures, my friend,' he said. 'No politics. This is *shirk*. Do not enter into this *shirk* if you wish to remain a Muslim. *T'as compris? T'as compris?* Now let's have something to eat. I'm famished.'

From out of nowhere a wheelbarrow heaped with pomegranates like giant rubies appeared before us.

'Uncle!' I said to the seller. 'How much for two?'

He named a sum so insignificant – a palmful of Yemeni pennies – it wasn't really money.

'Too expensive,' Said muttered in French. '*C'est un bandit.* It should be half that.' But already the roundness and the juiciness of the pomegranates and the thin rind that could be peeled away with the teeth were casting their spell over him. He reached forward casually, as if he were picking from his own wheelbarrow.

'Please, you are my guest!' said the pomegranate man. He beamed at Said. He was a proud, happy fruit seller without teeth. 'Chooth, brotherth,' he said. '*Ahlayn!*' Welcome!

Now when I think back on that moment, those pomegranates which were so close to us, so cheap, so natural, and which had been nourishing Yemenis since the time of the Prophet but which we were never to eat, seem to me a symbol of the sweetness of Islam. There it was, staring us in the face. All we had to do was reach out. It would have cost us nothing. Said certainly needed the nourishment and perhaps I did too. It was not to be.

When the first soldier took hold of him, he snatched at Said's arm with such violence that Said fell halfway to the pavement. His piece of fruit bounced in the gutter. The pomegranate man pounced on it.

Another soldier seized Said by the neck. Said's hands grasped at the air. The muzzle of one of the soldiers' guns kept poking into Said's ribs. He squirmed.

This is surely dangerous, I thought.

Then more policemen, in civilian clothing, were clutching Said's hands, two to each arm, and a higher ranking policeman with a pistol and a radio but no machine gun was holding the crumpled poster of the president's face. He thrust it into Said's beard. 'Did you do this?' he yelled. 'You did do this. Why? Why?'

A plainclothes policeman took me by the arm. 'What country are you from?' he asked. 'What's your name? What's in your pockets? Why did you do this?'

Now a swarm of curious citizens descended on us. They fastened their hungry eyes on us. 'What? What happened?' they called out. '*Subhan allah!* Who are they?'

Some of the gawkers were filling station employees, and some were passers-by. Soon more policemen were surrounding us, then random taxi drivers, then the man who had been lounging against a post, and finally the man whose posters had been shredded – all of them pushed and elbowed for a better view. 'What did the foreigners do?' they shouted. 'Tore the image of the president? What have they done, in the name of God?'

Two policemen dragged Said towards a nearby military jeep. 'He's a French citizen,' I heard myself say to no one in particular. 'Tell them you're French,' I murmured. 'Tell them.' He wasn't listening.

He couldn't move his feet. The police stuffed him into the passenger seat. The door was locked. A soldier was posted by the passenger door.

With Said safely locked away, the policemen gathered around me. 'What are you doing here? Who is he?' they asked. The fellow in the tracksuit was now reaching into his tracksuit jacket for a two-way radio. The lamp-post leaners and loafers were also squawking into hand-held radios. I could see now that they were wearing pistols beneath their jackets. They were every-where, scattered across the filling station plaza, watching from inside unmarked cars, marching with the marchers. If we had searched the city for days we wouldn't have found a more carefully policed patch of cement.

'Tore up the picture of the president!' a civilian in the crowd shouted. 'Foreigners!'

'Doesn't like the president!' people said. 'Why?'

34

Until our arrest Said and I had understood that Yemen, despite its rubbish-strewn streets and its impolite, staring crowds, was somehow a better place to be a Muslim than, say, France. This was especially true of Said. He often said that France had banished all true Islamic science and that the French state controlled every mosque. But in the moments following our arrest, as the jeep sped away from the scene of the crime, and when we were interrogated in a police station, we were both of us jolted into a mood of vulnerability, and shock. We were in the perfect mood for new perceptions. They came on suddenly, as soon as we were arrested, and they kept on coming.

In the police station, from the comfort of our interrogation room we watched a Yemeni prisoner being dragged across a slab of courtyard pavement. Blood had been splattered across his T-shirt. His head bobbed on his shoulders. He looked a lot like he was asleep except that his eyes were open and one of his feet was paddling at the pavement.

All afternoon, as the interrogation progressed, as we got hungrier and hungrier, new, important truths about life in an Arab democracy forced themselves on us. I could see Said shaking his head in silence and muttering to himself and to me and drawing the conclusions I had drawn some time earlier: there are elections but there are no civil rights. The government can persecute whoever it likes. It answers to no one. When you get in trouble, you are on your own.

Since Said had committed the crime, the officers who interrogated him were angry with him, most of all. At first I thought their indignation might be an act or a pretence or a sort of fright show. But in fact they were indignant. As Said explained about the Salafi prohibition against photographs and politics, their faces flushed. 'Have you come to our country to tell us how to believe?' said the lead interrogation officer. Maybe Said wanted regime change in Yemen? Said said he didn't. He said this over and over, in Berber, in French and in shreds of Yemeni Arabic. It was fine, said the officers, that he didn't like photographs. It was fine that he didn't like politics. Then why had he come to the rally? What was he doing at the filling station? What was he doing trying to teach his American friend about Islam? Shouldn't he let someone who really knew, like a Yemeni scholar, teach? And really what was he anyway? Was he a terrorist?

'I am not a terrorist,' Said mumbled.

'The sentence for tearing a picture of the president in Yemen is three years in jail,' said the interrogator, who was dressed in a dark suit and an expensive tie. 'Three years in jail. That will give you enough time to learn what is really prohibited and what is allowed in Islam.'

'I'm sorry for what I've done,' Said said. 'I respect your president.'

'I'm sorry, too,' said the interrogator. 'You should have thought about being sorry before you tore the picture.'

Said's hands shook. His face was white. He stumbled over his words. He looked to me for the translations. He had introduced himself as a student of Islam but he could barely speak the language of the Koran, had no money, no job, no home in Yemen, and no ticket back to France. 'What kind of a Muslim conducts himself like this?' the interrogator asked.

The officers stared at him as if they were looking at a mental deficient. 'Why did you come to Yemen in the first place?' they asked. 'Is France not a nice country? Did France throw you out? You were a terrorist there?'

'I am a Muslim,' Said said.

'No you're not,' said the man in the dark suit. 'You're a terrorist.'

Maybe the object of the interrogation was humiliation. If so, the officers succeeded. After an hour or so, Said was barely speaking. To everything he said, the officers offered a mocking response or found in his words some evidence of ignorance or bad faith or both. In the end, they escorted him to a cell in the basement.

I was brought to a second interrogation room, where a pair of lower ranking officers asked me exactly the same questions I had already answered but in a friendlier tone of voice.

An hour or so into the second interrogation, I happened to mention that every now and then, I allowed myself to chew qat.

An expression of involuntary happiness and pride spread across the face of the ranking officer, a lieutenant.

'Really? What kind? Hamdani? Mattari?'

We talked about qat chewing until the topic was exhausted. Soon there wasn't much left for us to discuss except the hacky sack they had found in my backpack. A cheerful junior officer who sat by the side of the lieutenant wanted to know about the details of the sport of hacky sack. Who played? How? Why? I demonstrated. We tried to play together. They thought a bigger ball would have worked better.

At around eight in the evening, an assistant brought me tea and cookies. An hour after that, when even the secretary outside the office door had been let go, when I was ready to fall asleep because I was so hungry, we came to the heart of this second, friendlier interrogation. 'Please tell me the truth about this,' the lieutenant said. 'I suspect I know anyway. But tell the truth.'

'Okay,' I said.

'You have girlfriend?'

I wished I did. I didn't. 'Sorry,' I said.

'I don't believe you,' said the lieutenant. He winked. 'Not sometimes? Never? No foreign girls?'

'Oh, I see,' I said. 'I do have a girlfriend.'

'Good!' said the lieutenant. 'How many?'

There was only one, I said modestly. Um . . . she was German, I said. Twenty-four. But soon, I had several girlfriends. They were all non-Muslims, which, in this context, meant 'promiscuous' and lived by themselves in apartments in the Old City.

'Ah,' said the officers, smiling. 'Ah . . . But this is a shame, for you, a Muslim. Yes?'

'I know,' I said. 'A fitna. But I am only human.'

For several minutes, we sat in the interrogation room in silence, thinking about the idea of German girlfriends.

Then the lieutenant asked in a small voice, 'Can you find me one? just one? An American, please?'

'Okay, one,' I said. 'Inshallah.'

'I don't believe you,' he said. 'But think about it.'

He stretched his arms into the air, checked his cellphone, and nodded at his friend, who stood up. The two of them winked at me as if we shared a brotherly secret. In this mood of fraternal admiration, and longing for a girlfriend, they escorted me to my cell.

35

Before they ever went to jail, the American teenagers I used to teach in Vermont had imagined prison as a place of secrets, brotherhood and heightened spirituality. But in real life, as it turned out, jail wasn't nearly as interesting. It was simply a matter of angry men being locked in a cage, day in and day out, with tasteless food.

In Yemen, however, jail really was as the American teenagers imagined it would be. The underground wisdom, the brotherhood, the moral force in opposition to the world as it is – it was all alive and well in our communal cell block.

Actually, life in jail in Yemen had much in common with life in our mosque. The prisoners washed together, brushed their teeth together, prayed together and ate together. Thus, from day to day, the esprit de corps that always develops among young men living together in difficult circumstances built on itself. In jail, we sang together as well – an additional pleasure that never would have been permitted in our mosque.

As we sang, Adnan, a crazy, occasionally joyous, occasionally weepy prisoner danced. The prisoners cheered him. They laughed as he twisted his body in the sunlight and when he let himself get carried away, the prisoners sang louder so that he would lose himself in his gyrations. He giggled to himself as he danced. It was an Arabian, Janis Joplin, ain't-got-nothing-to-lose sort of dance which somehow, I think, matched the mood of his audience.

As in the mosque, each person knew how much Koran each other person could recite, how well he pronounced Koranic Arabic, how much of a reprobate he was with regard to prayer, and how circumstances, many of which were beyond his control, had led him to this point. These people were hardly the winners of the societies from which they came. I liked them more for their lack of success. The best reciters were rich in Koranic memory. They didn't want to be rich in any other way.

Of course, as in the mosque, there were problems in our jail life.

At the mosque, we were often told that the *iman* is like a bowl of milk. A believer preserved its whiteness by not thinking of sex or temptations of any kind. If a believer touched a woman, even by shaking her hand, this could bring on thoughts of sex, which would then pollute the milk.

In jail we cultivated this atmosphere of chastity. Everyone monitored everyone else. But these were young men in their twenties. They masturbated every night and sometimes during the day. I don't know what else they did with each other but, as in the mosque, you heard rumours. One evening, a lonely prisoner who used to be a barber said to me, 'I'm not gay. This is forbidden in Islam. But I do screw (*aniq*) gay people.'

None of this was permitted in Islam. Improper things did happen, though, and the gap between the law and everyday practice made everyone feel ashamed. The shameful acts made people secretive and the secrecy generated distrust. It didn't take long for our Islamic utopia to degenerate into mutual recrimination.

The bigger problem was that the young men were furious with the outside world, which had imprisoned them for arbitrary reasons. Islam doesn't offer an escape route to the frustrated, and the locked-down. 'Fast,' it says, 'and pray.' But we already were fasting and already were praying. What next?

* * *

When Ramadan came, a few days into my imprisonment, rancorous words were forbidden along with eating and dissent of any kind. Everyone stayed up in the night to pray the *taroweah*, a standing prayer that began at midnight and lasted sometimes until three or four in the morning. Everyone said then that the *iman* in the cell was very strong. But at that point it was impossible to breathe inside the jail. Everything was forbidden – eating and drinking during daylight hours, not praying, dirty words, dancing, not reading Koran, not loving your brothers. And yet the brothers stole your food as you slept and, when they thought you weren't listening, they wondered out loud if you were possibly an enemy of Islam.

In this environment, it was inevitable that talk inside the cell would circle back to the Jews. There were only 400 or so of them in all of Yemen. They were the weakest and poorest citizens but somehow they exercised magical powers over the imagination of my fellow inmates.

One prisoner, a short man in a tattered robe, told me that when he had been in Iraq, he had observed the Americans up close, had cousins in Guantanamo, and was now in possession of special information about the Jews in America.

'Did you go to Iraq to fight the Americans?' I asked.

'Yes, of course, my friend,' he said.

'All right,' I said. 'So you have secret information? I've heard it before.'

'But I do have secret information,' he said. 'You want to know the truth?'

The prisoners sitting in our circle nodded in the darkness.

'Of course,' he said. 'Were not the Towers full of Jews on that day? They were! Not Americans, Jews. The poison in America, it was in the Towers, wasn't it? Are you not better off now?' The other inmates smiled. 'The Towers were the head of a reptile,' the Iraq veteran said. 'We cut off the head of the reptile first. Above all, and before anything else, we wanted to hit the Towers. You see?' Then, as the neck bled, the tentacles were to be attacked. He smiled. What were the tentacles? The White House and the

Pentagon. 'So you see?' he said. 'You have allowed the Jews to come in among you, and you have taken money from them. You should have killed them off, my brother, long ago. But you didn't. Even now they're not dead.'

Said was locked in a cell across the corridor from mine. The prisoners there gave him bread and bits of rice and he spent the first few days napping and eating. On day three, however, as the sun was setting, he lived through a moment of panic. I was singing in the back of my cell. I could barely hear him calling for me. A criminal next to me had to poke me in the ribs.

I stood up to see Said clutching the bars fiercely. His eyes were burning. 'Call the French embassy when you get out,' he whispered, loudly. 'Call them as soon as you possibly can. Call the newspapers. Do whatever you have to do. You're a journalist!'

'I'll get you out of this, brother,' I told him. 'Just relax for a few more days.'

'Never mind whose fault it was,' he whispered. 'Just call the embassy. Tell them what has happened. Tell the brothers in the mosque. They have connections. Anything. Anything, okay?'

I was released within the week. I took a taxi to the mosque. I arrived long after the call for the afternoon prayer had come and gone. I climbed the stairs and slipped into the rearmost prayer row. Even before I had finished the final prostration, I could feel Omar, Ahmed, Bilal, Azi the bank robber, and their friends, and friends of their friends drifting over, then surrounding me, and watching me. I sat on my knees, looking into a circle of faces.

'Brother Thabit,' said Omar when I had finished. 'Come! Sit with us. Speak!'

I could tell by the tone of his voice and by the expressions of the onlookers that people knew where I had been, and approved. I had done something positive at last. The people were respectful at first, and then questions came in a flood.

How long were you in jail? Were you surprised when you were arrested? How is Said? What was the name of the jail? Were you locked up with Abdul Rahman, the American? Or Malik, the Frenchman? Did you meet two Algerians who live in a hole?

I had never before been the object of such solicitous attention in the mosque. No one had ever wanted to know my opinion about anything.

I related my story.

Ahmed from Lyon had spent six months in the political security prison. He was anxious to know what had become of his fellow prisoners. In his jail, some of the prisoners lived beneath the floors of the cells, in two-person dungeons. Had I met these brothers? Were thcy okay? Did they still have rats in their dungeons? Had I had rats?

I had to explain. Said and I were never in this prison. Yes, we did have rats. No, we did not meet any underground Algerians.

For me, as it turned out, prison was a stroke of good fortune. It won me respect and the confidence of the believers. To be arrested for being a Muslim, to be jailed, to endure it all quietly, and then to return to the mosque – this was the real testament of faith in our mosque. I had crossed a threshold.

Later on that evening, in Ahmed's living room, surrounded by his French friends and a scattering of Yemenis, I broke the Ramadan fast.

'Eat, please! More,' said Ahmed. After we had prayed and had eaten our fill, Ahmed told me: 'We weren't sure about you at first, we'll be honest with you. We didn't know who you were or why you had come. So we just watched and said nothing.'

'I know,' I said.

'We said to ourselves that time would tell what kind of a Muslim you really are – whether a fake one, an enemy of Islam, a tourist among different religions or what.'

He suggested that I might want to continue my education away from the city, in a school in thc mountains.

'It could be better for you there,' said a second Frenchman whose name I didn't know. 'There are more teachers there, there is more learning and the villagers, down to the smallest toothbrush seller and Iraqi beggar, are from the People of the Salaf.'

'We can help you in Dammaj even if we're not there,' Ahmed offered. 'We'll call the French brothers before you arrive. We'll tell them to look out for you. We'll tell them to help you find a place to live and they will introduce you to the sheikh.'

Before I left, I wanted to get Said out of jail. After a week in the police basement cell into which he and I had at first been locked, the authorities transferred him to an immigration prison on the south-eastern outskirts of Sana'a. I started to visit him there, usually at sunset, so that we could break our fasts together, chat, and discuss how to get him out of jail.

He wasn't interested, I quickly discovered, in lawyers, money, and embassy people. Instead, he wanted to talk about the great men of Islam.

'They were all of them tested for their faith,' he told me during one visit. 'Younis was imprisoned in the belly of a whale. Yusuf was imprisoned by his brothers.' A sheikh whose name he couldn't remember was asked to renounce Islam, refused, and so was tortured in jail. But the torture only strengthened him in his faith.

'I'm not being tortured,' he said, 'I'm not being asked to renounce anything.' He felt his imprisonment might have saved him from a greater danger – perhaps the anger of the crowds or a stray bullet from a soldier's gun.

One evening, to make the breaking of the fast happier, I brought him a bag of Snickers bars. The gift awakened his love of chocolate but it also awakened his instinct for *zakat*, or charity. At first he buried the bag under a pillow at the back of his cell and then seconds later, as the other prisoners watched in surprise, he retrieved the bag, and gave every prisoner a Snickers bar. There were about ten people in his cell. When he had fed all of them, he peered into the plastic bag, felt for the remaining bars, and smiled. He handed the bag back to me. 'Give it to the Somalians across the corridor,' he said. *Il faut tout donner, mon ami l'américain.* Give it all away, everything.'

On another evening Said and I stood at his cell door gossiping about the guards who ran his prison. They were lounging in a guard-room next door to his own, watching a broken television and calling their wives on their cellphones. 'They're not like us, Thabit,' Said cautioned. 'They do not pray, and do not really believe.'

When he was arrested, he said, he had been afraid of the guards. 'I was afraid of the policemen, all officials, and of the entire Yemeni government apparatus. That was a mistake. One mustn't be afraid of any human. One must be afraid of Allah, that's all. Only fear God.'

He said that if he had been afraid of Allah sufficiently in the first place, he never would have ripped up the posters of the president.

'Because I acted according to an impulse action, which did not come from Islam but from myself.' A Muslim only acts on what is within Islam, according to what is written in the hadith.'

The evening *athan* was about to sound then and the brothers in his cell were sitting in a circle around a plate of dates, waiting for the call. When it came they passed dates to me through the bars of their cell, and pressed cups of tea into my hand.

In the Old City at that hour, a wave of fast-breaking generosity was breaking over the streets. Restaurant waiters were feeding homeless men on the sidewalks. Bus passengers were passing dates to strangers. In banks, dental offices, post offices, and on mosque floors, men were squatting in circles and sharing their food.

Said lingered at the cell door. When the other prisoners had eaten, he fetched dates and tea for me.

'Eat, my brother, the American,' he said. 'Eating is a good, a sacred thing in a time like this'.

Over the next fifteen days, I made a point of making friends with the guards. Before I passed by Said's cell, I would stop to chat and offer cigarettes and qat. 'When can he be freed?' I would ask. 'What will it take?' The guards would breathe deeply and smile pained, unhappy smiles. Only God knew, they would say.

Sometimes, the head guard would reply, 'Difficult, Brother Thabit. Very difficult.' But one evening, as Ramadan was drawing to a close, the head guard did not sigh. 'Buy your friend a plane ticket,' he said. 'You'll need to make sure he has a driver to take him to the airport. The driver will be a soldier from this prison and will have to be paid. If you can pay for a ticket and a police escort tonight, he can leave tonight. Allah be with him.'

Said's idea of a desirable airplane destination was not my idea. I suggested Paris. 'Are you kidding?' he said. He said that he had never had such belief in God as now. He had never felt so full of faith, and so close to the heroes of Islam. He knew that feeling would ebb away in his French suburb. He refused to return home.

A one-way ticket to Algiers cost $350. Back at the mosque, I took up a collection, as Said had asked me to do. The brothers stiffened. Neither the French brothers nor anyone else was interested in contributing to his freedom. 'Maybe after Ramadan,' one brother said. 'We are buying gifts for our families now,' said another brother. Many brothers said that Said was impulsive, had brought shame on to our mosque, and was therefore not a good Muslim, and maybe not really a Muslim at all.

'He meant to stay out of politics,' I said. That was the whole point. He had been trying to teach me.

My argument went nowhere.

In the end, I split the cost of a ticket with Said's brother in Lille.

On the night of Said's flight, I fetched his belongings from his suitcase closet in the mosque. I fetched his passport from a French friend who had somehow retrieved it from the school secretary. At the jail, I gave the suitcase to a guard and gave Said his ticket and $50 in cash for when he landed in Algeria.

'Allah be with you, brother,' he said, pushing dates into my hand. He was looking forward to Algeria because people spoke French there and because the food was better. From Algeria, he meant to find his way to a proper seminary in Saudi Arabia.

An hour later, the guards removed Said from his prison cell. He rode away in an unmarked car.

I heard later that when he got to Algeria, the police there couldn't figure out what he had been doing in Yemen and why he had been so abruptly kicked out. Not knowing what to do with him, they put him in jail.

After that last visit with Said, I rode back to the city on a municipal bus. My fellow passengers had just watched the results of the presidential election being certified on national TV. Saleh had trounced his opponent. Now it was official. The passengers were heading downtown, into the streets of the capital, to celebrate.

Even in the outskirts of the city, the celebration was under way. Enthusiasts fired their Kalashnikovs into the air, lighting up the sky with tracer bullets.

The kid who was collecting fares on the bus smiled broadly at everyone. As the bus picked up speed, he climbed to a platform next to the driver's seat, then addressed us, his passengers. 'Tonight the bus fare will be on the house!' he called out – which in Yemen is a way of saying, 'You still have to pay, of course, but we'd like to make it free.'

He strolled down the aisle and stopped at my seat. He smiled at me. 'You're a foreigner,' he observed, taking in my light eyes and facial features. 'Are you a Muslim?'

'Of course,' I said.

He smiled to himself, then shook his head in surprise. 'A foreigner?' he wondered again.

Yes, a foreigner, I confirmed. 'Nevertheless a Muslim.'

'Not a Jew?' he said, his eyes smiling. 'Not a Christian?'

'Not at all,' I said. 'And you? Not a Christian? Not a Jew?'

The boy laughed. The bus passengers nearby laughed. 'I have a joke for you,' he said, winking at me. He strolled to the front of the bus again.

'In the name of God,' he called out to all fifteen passengers. He giggled for a moment and blinked at us. 'What are the five pillars of the Jewish religion? Does anyone know?'

'We don't know,' said an old man sitting next to me.

'They don't have five pillars,' whispered another passenger.

'What are the five pillars of the Jews?' the boy insisted.

'The pillars of the Jew are five,' he called out, laughing. 'One: cheating! Two: alcohol! Three: adultery! Four: hypocrisy!'

The bus passengers giggled. 'I can't remember the fifth!' the boy said. 'What is the fifth?'

The passengers offered suggestions. 'Drinking!' said a grandfather whose turban was decorated with sprigs of basil.

'Stealing!' said someone else.

'Murder! Killing children!' said a tribesman to my right.

No one knew the right answer. The passengers chattered among themselves. The tracer bullets arced past the windows of the bus.

My seat neighbour turned his face to me. He touched his turban helplessly with his fingertips. 'Is this true?' he wondered. 'Is this true? The pillars of the Jew are like this?'

'No,' I said. 'Don't believe them.'

'Yes,' he said, 'it is true.'

As I got off the bus, this old man turned to me with a kindly smile. He shook my hand. 'Welcome to Yemen!' he said. 'Welcome!' He stared at me as the bus pulled away. When he was almost out of earshot, he called into the night, 'Allah be with you, brother! Let him open the way forward for you!'

Walking back to the mosque, I thought about the strange election season I had just witnessed. Democracy, such as it was in Yemen, had made everyone happy. It had reinforced the status quo ante. Like so much else in Yemen, it had invited, when all was said and done, thoughts of the treachery of the Jews. But it had also made the Muslims closer to one another somehow. I knew that when I travelled into the north, as long as I travelled as a Muslim, I would be protected and kept from danger.

Ramadan, the Shariqain Mosque, Sana'a, 1427h

36

On the Night of Destiny, the father of the twitching girl brought a child I presumed to be his daughter into the mosque. The child was dead. Later on, I found out that the corpse was that of a different daughter, of the same family. At the time, I assumed it was the handicapped child to whom we, the Western students, had sometimes offered pennies. The father had wrapped the body of this unfortunate, second daughter in synthetic, pile blankets. He laid the corpse down in front of the *qibla*, the wall facing Mecca.

Three hundred worshippers from around the world stood before her. We spoke private prayers into our cupped hands. We muttered in English, Arabic, Berber, Chechen, Chinese, Urdu and French.

As soon as the prayer was finished, the father scooped up the dead child. He whisked it away with the swiftness of a thief, then skipped down the stairs and into the night.

The Night of Destiny came, as Ramadan did, in secrecy. Only the *ulema*, the learned men of Islam – committees in Saudi Arabia, Egypt and Dammaj – could speak with certainty about its arrival. And these scholars only spoke on the morning after, when occlusions in the sun's rays told them that the Night of Destiny had come and gone. Yet it was an important night. Prayer on this night was thought to be more effective than a thousand days' worth of prayer. On no other night, says Islamic tradition, do the angels of God hover so close to the surface of the earth. 'Ask God for what you most want tonight,' my French friend, Ahmed, told me. 'Ask him again and again and ask when your head is on the ground. When you are prostrating yourself, for you are never closer to God than at that point.'

The mosque was so full on that evening that it was difficult to find an empty patch of carpet. If the Night didn't arrive then, it would come the next night, and if not the next, it would certainly come on the following evening. No one wanted to miss it. The American and European teenagers had come to wait in the mosque until it was announced, officially in the newspapers, that it had come. They brought their camping gear: sleeping bags, pillows, pile blankets, flashlights, cereal, two-litre bottles of Coke, Game Boys, cellphones, iPods, grammar books, and hooded sweatshirts for ablutions and prayers in the pre-dawn chill.

Early in the evening, Ahmed removed an ID photo from his wallet that had been taken two years earlier. It depicted a beard-less face, and knowing eyes. 'I was an alcoholic then,' he said. 'I worked in a hotel in London. I drank pints in the pubs. I didn't even know what the Night of Destiny was. You see? We've all been in that place of disbelief. We've all been *kuffar*. You're not so different, you know.'

During these final Ramadan days, Ahmed had embarked on a programme of voluntary withdrawal from the world, which in Arabic is called *itikaaf*, or sequestraton. His wife brought tea and meals to the mosque. He left it only to go to the bathroom. When he wasn't praying or sleeping, he was drinking tea and chatting with friends. One evening, Ahmed and I shared his tea with a new fellow, a Nigerian, just in from Lagos.

'I will not stay in Sana'a,' he said. 'No.'

'Really, where to?' I asked.

'To the north, Dammaj,' he murmured.

He gave me the number of the driver. I called the driver.

'Peace upon you, uncle,' I said. 'I am Thabit from Beni Mattar.'
I told him that I chewed only Mattari qat and only on Fridays.
The driver giggled.

'*Mashallah*,' he said.

'I love the Yemeni people,' I said.

'Welcome, welcome,' he said. *Ahlayn, ahlayn.*

Abdul Gorfa introduced me to the other people who were going
to travel to Dammaj on the following morning: two American
brothers, a weightlifter from Birmingham, and a French teenager.
'My wife and daughters will be coming with me,' said the teenager
in fledgling Arabic

At the dawn prayer, the people smuggler did not appear. 'Go
back to bed,' the Nigerian told me. Five minutes later Abdul
Gorfa was knocking on my door. 'Hurry, Thabit!' he said. 'The
driver!' I stuffed a copy of *The Fortress of Islam* in the breast pocket
of my robe. I grabbed my prayer rug and my Koran.

In the hallway, outside my dorm room, Abdul Gorfa was in a
panic. The driver had told him that his colourful African robes
were likely to raise eyebrows on the road to Dammaj. The French
teenager had said that only housewives in Dammaj wore floral
patterns or multicoloured robes at all. Now Abdul Gorfa was
knocking on doors, trying to scare up a proper white Saudi-style
dishdasha. I found one in my luggage and watched while Abdul
Gorfa divested himself of his native costume.

We all knew we were heading into a world of Saudi stand-
ardisation and orthodoxy and that this was why we would have
to dress in white from now on. Abdul Gorfa had come halfway
around the world for this, but he seemed for a few moments to
doubt his decision. Nigerian Islam, with its regal, multi-hued
robes, and dances, and rules honoured in the breach, was finished
for him. Did he really want to let it all go? He stared at his new
white robe in the mirror in my bathroom. His face fell. Of course,
at this stage it was too late for second thoughts

He slipped down the stairs of the dorm, and walked through the mosque on his own.

Soon we were racing through the Sana'a streets at dawn. The rising sun was pouring into the driver's eyes. He flew through the intersections as if all the other cars in the world had vanished, and we alone remained to barrel down the boulevards. A clutch of policemen in front of a bank gazed at us in silence. We passed homeless men collapsed on the front steps of corner mosques. Every store was shuttered. The traffic lights blinked.

Within minutes we were passing a cavernous empty football stadium and then we came to a giant open-air marketplace on the northern edge of town which was deserted. The Ministries of Defence, Electricity, and the Interior had been abandoned. Only a handful of slumbering policemen sat on chairs in front of the ministry gates.

Early on a Ramadan morning, Sana'a is like this. It is especially devastated towards the end of Ramadan, when everyone is exhausted, and people are trying to sleep the last few hours of fasting away. On mornings like this, only the essence of the city remains: a merciless sunlight on the boulevards, tiny clutches of policemen, goats in the alleyways, and posters of the president looking down over the banks and the mosques. I didn't realise this until I was sneaking away from the city myself but the essence is also clusters of devout young men sneaking away into the countryside as the policemen sleep.

At around ten in the morning, I woke to find the van drifting through a landscape of black volcanoes. Candyfloss clouds floated over the summits. The Koran was playing on the van stereo. Certain lines leapt out: 'and we have brought this down to you the Muslims, you the Muslims. So that you may worship it.'

Later in the day, the driver dropped off the lip of the tarmac. We followed a jeep track in the desert to a village about five kilometres from the road, and here we slipped through a gate into a labyrinth of white walls and shuttered windows.

The van rocked to a stop in front of a one-room mosque. Three old men in robes and caps sat on the carpet inside. They smiled at us but did not rise. Outside, sheep nibbled in a court-yard. When we had finished praying, one of the old men told us that the government soldiers had passed through the village a week earlier but had not been seen since.

'Praise God,' said the driver.

'Yes, praise God,' the villagers agreed.

On stepping out of the mosque, we saw that two new drivers had materialised along with two olive green army jeeps. We retrieved our baggage from the van. The jeeps set out into the trackless desert. On the horizon, a line of low-lying tabletop mountains glinted in the sunshine.

Around four in the afternoon, I woke up to find our jeep creeping along a knife-blade ridge. We were high in the air, and a cloud of steam was washing over the ridge. Rivulets of moisture trickled down the windows. We couldn't see a thing. Then quite suddenly the cloud dissipated. We peered down, over the knife-blade ridge into a perfectly square, immaculate white city: whitewashed houses, white mosque dome, white cemetery.

From a single gateway at the foot of the city, jeep tracks spiralled into the surrounding steppe.

Abdul Gorfa pressed his nose against the window of the jeep. 'What do the sheep eat here?' he wondered. 'No green, is there?' No one said anything. 'We are having an adventure,' he concluded absently.

'Yes,' I said at last.

'I didn't know it was going to be like this,' he murmured. 'Very dry and white. Red dirt. What do the people eat in this country?'

'There's more green in Nigeria, isn't there?' I said.

'Yes,' he said. 'But *mashallah*, there is no knowledge in Nigeria.'

For the next two hours, we passed village after village like this: desiccated, silent and white. Old stone watchtowers, once used to guard the crops, had been left to rot in the sun. Sometimes toothless old men sat beneath acacia trees, watching us and keeping perfectly still. Goat carcasses lay half buried in the sand at their feet.

In fact most of the smaller towns in northern Yemen have this ghost town appearance. Much of the region was abandoned in the 1970s, when oil money began to spread across the countryside. The old economy of sheep, beans and potatoes died because it was easier and cheaper to buy mass-produced, imported goods. Young people who had been scraping a living from plots of lumpy topsoil learned to live from low-skilled jobs in Saudi Arabia and low-wage jobs in southern Yemen.

With no agriculture to stop it, the desert swept through these villages like a slow-motion flood. It poured down the main streets, and filtered into the dooryard gardens. Nowadays, sand waves lap at the ground floor windows of the houses. The people who remain in these former villages tend to be elderly, rough-hewn survivor types. They harvest their firewood by hacking at the limbs of acacia trees and drink a muddy, brackish water which they pull from wells with buckets attached to strings. To drive through these villages is to feel that the environmental catastrophe everyone else is waiting for has already come to this part of the world and left it. The survivors are evidently unperturbed; the women cluster at the wells in their black cloaks. The men doze in the shade of acacia trees. Their sheep, goats and camels are now mostly carcasses. Bones and hooves lie in piles beyond the wells and now and then a camel skull pokes out of a drift beside the jeep track.

After two hours of trekking through the mountains, we rejoined a government tarmacked road. Soon we joined a line of cars waiting at the checkpoint on the outskirts of the city of Sa'ada. Because Sa'ada is the headquarters of the Shia insurgency in Yemen and because it is also a smuggling hub in which Saudi entrepreneurs load up on guns, qat and Djibouti alcohol, this checkpoint was meant to look forbidding. Behind the barrier, barbed wire had been strung across the road, guns poked from behind sandbagged machine-gun emplacements, and pickup trucks, mounted with light anti-aircraft guns, sat in the sunshine, pointing their guns at the oncoming traffic.

Our driver had stashed Yemeni-camouflage gear beneath the seats. Abdul Gorfa, an American named Malik and I slipped into dinner jackets. The driver tucked his Kalashnikov under his seat. It felt a little like we were preparing ourselves for a wedding, and a little like we were on the verge of a commando assault on the government sentries.

'Sleeb,' urged the driver, 'sleebing now.' We fell on to the floor of the jeep. We buried our heads among the duffel bags. Lying on the floor of the van, we waited for the dialogue we had heard a half-dozen times that day.

Driver: Officer! Evening of the light to you.
Officer: Evening of the rose. How is the world of this life with you?
Driver: We praise God. Peace unto you.
Officer: And unto you. Off you go!

Soon we were winding our way up a back road. Twenty minutes later, the jeeps had stopped on a windswept promontory. All ten of us stepped out into the red dirt. 'This is the Dar al Hadith,' said the driver, sweeping his hand over the valley at our feet. 'Welcome. The Shia live there and there –' he said, angling his beard towards the southern end of the fields beneath us: 'and they live beyond the mountains there and there, but beneath us, here, in these vineyards, this is our place of study. Welcome.'

37

From up here, about 500 feet in the air, we could take in the sweep of the landscape: beneath us lay a steep-walled valley whose floor was covered in vineyards, and rows of corn. It was about five miles long and one mile wide. At the northern end of the valley, near where we stood, a village of mud houses and corrugated tin roofs was spreading into the fields. Further away, towards the southern end of the valley, a scattering of cobblestone watchtowers and smaller, more decrepit huts huddled under a band of cliffs.

The northern end of the valley was by far the more prosperous, fertile spot: a winding river bed, now dry, was lined with deep green orchards and plots of grapes. The houses had backyard gardens in which fruit trees and corn stalks shimmered in the last of the evening light.

At the middle of this settlement, a cement warehouse, not unlike a suburban mall, rose from the sand. Its most prominent feature was the garden of satellite dishes, speakers and antennae on its roof, which made it look as though it was listening to the surrounding cliffs and the sky.

This building, said our driver, was Sheikh Muqbel's *marqiz*, or centre; here we would study, pray and eat.

For several minutes the ten of us stood in the wind, gazing out over the white box and the surrounding valley. After four hours of desiccated villages and brown landscape, the agriculture at our feet had a mirage-like quality. It took a moment for our eyes to adjust.

I happened to be standing next to the Americans and the French father. I watched them snapping pictures with their cellphone cameras and listened to them exchanging expressions of awe: 'subhan allah,' they murmured, and 'ya, salaam!' and 'mashallah!'

My travelling companions may have been right – the will of God may have been at work – but in a more immediate sense what we were looking at was the will of the Saudis. This was how the Saudis proselytised: to the centre of a valley that had belonged to the Shia for a thousand years or longer, the Saudis brought construction equipment, cinder blocks and white paint. They brought loudspeakers and satellite dishes. They also brought well-digging equipment which is often illegal in Yemen but evidently has a salutary effect on the landscape.

The result of this influx was a seventh-century scene of agriculture and cobblestone towers into which a fortress had been dropped. The fortress was occupied by a corps of Sunni whose mission it was to pacify, then convert the natives.

Evidently, the Saudi-sponsored mosque had not entirely succeeded. From above, the lines of the current entrenchment could be discerned in the landscape itself: the Saudi-backed Sunni had the white cement, the satellite dishes, the well-digging equipment and the proliferating huts.

The indigenous Shia held the mud houses at the furthest end of the valley, their own vineyards, and the surrounding valleys. The watchtowers that rose near their end of the valley were tall and formidable; in a time of need, they could probably have functioned as snipers' nests. From a strictly military point of view, however, it would have been better to hold the Salafi mosque, which was reinforced by heavy concrete walls and probably could have doubled as a bunker.

The Shia were further disadvantaged by the fact that they were losing the battle of the demographics. In Yemen, they were a minority of a million, among twenty million Sunnis. In the

Muslim world at large, they were about 175 million among 1.5 billion Sunnis.

Now, every day, a trickle of foreigners from this larger Sunni world was filtering into the Saudi-sponsored colony. Even from high above the village of Dammaj, on a sandstone bluff, it was easy to see how this immigration was likely to upset the already fragile local ecology.

38

About ten days after my arrival in Dammaj, I was hanging around on a bench in the village square. I was thumbing through a Koran and watching the tall cedars overhead bend in the breeze.

The noontime prayers were about to begin. A parade of religious students from across the world drifted into the Great Mosque. Every now and then, some former resident of Anaheim, California or Aubervilliers or Dortmund would address me in formal, classical Arabic: 'Salaam alaikum, brother of mine,' the person would say. 'See you inside? Is everything fine?'

'Of course, brother,' I would say. 'Inshallah, I'll be inside in a moment.'

This was a typical late morning in Dammaj. The village guards hung about the entrance to the mosque, clutching their machine guns. The merchants locked their shops in preparation for the noontime prayer. The students trekked through the dust in their robes and slippers. An Iraqi who sold sports jackets from a clothes rack at the foot of the mosque stairs pulled a plastic tarp over his rack. He pushed it into a corner, climbed the mosque stairs, and slipped off his shoes.

Just then, a teenager in a white robe and white silken scarf emerged from the village internet cafe. He loitered in front of the cafe, kicking at piles of sand with his sandals and frowning. Then he sat on the stoop of the cafe and unwound his headscarf. His schoolbooks fell into the sand. He made no effort to retrieve them. Instead he folded his headscarf into a perfect triangle, then folded it again into a band, then carefully spiralled the band around his forehead. Having accomplished this upgrade in his dress, he did not blend himself into the procession that was moving into the mosque. Instead he loitered.

I ambled over to the steps of the internet cafe, and sat down. 'Where are you from, my brother?' I asked him in Arabic.

'You know, brother. Around,' he replied in English.

In the conversation that followed, I discovered that this young man had been having some behaviour problems at home in Islington, that these involved court orders, counsellors and a succession of schools, and that his parents, who were at their wits' end, had sent him to Yemen. They hoped that a few years in a Koran school would straighten out his life.

At fourteen the young man, Jowad, was now the youngest English student of knowledge in Dammaj.

'It's certainly a test from God,' he said, 'but me, I can get used to anything. Anyway, if something's been written for you, it's the only thing that's going to happen to you.'

The procession of students had dwindled to a trickle. The square in front of us was nearly empty. Only a pair of guards on the mosque steps was watching us.

'We had better pray,' I said.

In this mood of resignation, we strolled into the mosque. We joined the last of the rows, in the back of the hall. The front of the room was already on its knees. We looked out over a little sea of humped backs, towards Mecca. It was only a few hundred miles away, and it seemed much closer. 'Lead us on the Straight Path,' we mumbled, 'the path of those thou hast blessed, not those with whom thou art angry or those thou hast cursed.'

39

In the days that followed, Jowad introduced me to his favourite internet game, PimpWar.com. We chatted more about London and he told me more about his life of juvenile crime.

I understood the details of Jowad's story only from his side, and he was not beyond bending the truth a bit for the sake of a good yarn, so perhaps the particulars were off, but this is what I gathered. He had misbehaved and had got into trouble at school and with the police. There had been conferences with the police and with the school authorities. And then, one day, he and his stepfather had decided on an approach that would circumvent the English educational system altogether.

Now on the ground in Yemen, Jowad had pennies to live on. He wanted to buy shoes, sweets and internet time. He wanted to call his mum in Islington. But the merchants of Dammaj had already extended him all the credit they were likely to extend, and the phones did not work unless you paid in advance. Jowad, however, was taking things in his stride. He had a phlegmatic side to his personality that allowed him to relax where other kids might have panicked.

'It's just a boring life here,' he liked to say, 'the most boringest in the world.'

★   ★   ★

One Friday, we spent an afternoon wandering through the vineyards around the mosque in Dammaj, discussing his options. He hoped to go to Aden because there was a mall there. But he knew no one. He hoped to go to Sana'a to live on his own and to teach English, as some of the English brothers in Dammaj did.

'But you're only fourteen,' I said. 'That's ridiculous.'

At one point in our discussion, he paused at a bend in the path and looked out, over a field of grapevines. 'What I really ought to do,' he said quietly, 'is to hang around here for a while and finish memorising the Koran.'

We kept on walking. He had already been in Dammaj for four months and in that time had memorised only the easiest, shortest suras.

Later on, as the sun was going down, we sat around on the bench in front of the internet cafe, waiting his for his mum to call. But she didn't call. He had been expecting to hear from her for four days, and she had neither emailed nor left messages with the cafe clerk. 'I just wish she would be honest with me,' he muttered to no one in particular as we dug our toes into the sand. 'Ever since I hit puberty she hasn't wanted me in the house.'

The longer we sat on the bench, the more the reality of the situation crept up on us. Jowad really had caused everyone trouble in London. He was now banished to Dammaj. Because Dammaj was surrounded by a thousand miles of Arabian desert, and Jowad had no money, and no way to get out, that banishment was likely to continue – perhaps for several years. Meanwhile, the stepfather was in the house of his childhood, living with his mum.

'The last time I talked to her,' he said, sighing, 'she said she would send me some football boots. She didn't send nothing.'

The sun was sinking quickly behind a band of cliffs that towered over the mosque. We watched more brothers treading into the prayer hall. For a long time neither of us said a word. 'I don't mind living on my own,' murmured a small voice next to me. 'I've done it in the past. I can get used to anything.'

40

From where I was sitting, I could see the opening of a winding, sandy pathway. The path led away from the mosque to a bluff that gave a view over a lake of millet and grapes. Only two hurried talibs were visible on that path – and they were rushing towards the mosque. Behind them was emptiness. Privacy. To me, the path beckoned.

I had in mind a speech I might give to Jowad. I meant to wind the clock back about twenty-six years to when there was no Saudi-sponsored mosque rising over these vineyards, and no Koran students shuffling through the sand. I was going to tell him about the siege of the Masjid al-Haram in Mecca in 1979, how the Islamic apocalypse was supposed to take place that year, and how, when it didn't take place, Sheikh Muqbel had established his academy here in Dammaj. In the succeeding years, it had become known to the Western intelligence agencies for its skilful, highly dedicated graduates.

'Look, Jowad,' I was going to say, when I had finished the lecture. 'I know that in this mosque you have many good British brothers looking after you. I know that your mum and dad think this place has the power to straighten out your life. I know that we focus here exclusively on the ways of the Prophet, peace be upon him.'

'Nevertheless,' I might have said, 'the people who are in charge of our village have the will to do something frightening at home. You might know this?'

I could then have said, 'Jowad, brother, I just don't think it's right that a kid like you, a seventh-grade dropout, should be left to finish out his education here.' He would have stared at me. I could have added, in his silence, 'So let's find a way to get you out.'

Personally, I liked my speech okay. But on that Friday afternoon, as I contemplated my speech to Jowad, I was worried for myself. It wasn't proper for a newcomer like me to take so much interest in someone already under the care of the sheikh, nor was it proper for me to be chatting while everyone else was praying. Also: I didn't think I could really accomplish anything anyway. Instead of acting, I started thinking. That was the end of it.

'You wanna walk around a bit?' I asked.

'What's your problem?' he said. 'Where to?'

In Dammaj, there really is nowhere to go. You can't walk far because no matter where you go, you're liable to run into Shia. It's quite dangerous to walk through their part of the valley.

There were still a few stragglers rushing into the vastness of the Great Mosque. We trickled in among them. Inside, in the back of the mosque, we stood next to each other – hands across our chests, little toes touching – in line, with 400 other heavily committed Muslims. Jowad and I cinched our shoulders together tightly, as one always does, so that no Shaytan or whisperer might, at this vulnerable moment, insinuate himself in among us. It was the *Maghrib* prayer. We made the *Maghrib* number of prostrations – three, always three – in front of our sheikh.

The current sheikh, Yahya al-Hajoori keeps a militia in order to defend the village from the Shia and whatever other enemies – American spies, devils – might be lurking in the hills. His militiamen, who are called *haras*, or guards, study, pray and eat with the students and so the mosque is, in a way, their headquarters, too.

When the guards want to memorise Koran, they sit cross-legged in front of their Koran stands with their guns in their laps, or they discard them on the carpet nearby, where they collect in little piles. When they want to pray, they lay their Kalashnikovs on the carpet between their legs. It makes for a strange sight: the barrels of the guns pointing towards Mecca, the heads bowing and bobbing over them. And then the guards rise, sling their weapons over their shoulders and walk away, more or less as if they've been practising at a firing range.

From an architectural point of view, the Great Mosque in Dammaj is a nonentity. It has been designed on the parking garage model, with sturdy, efficient cheapness as the guiding principle.

There are no mirrors, gateways, vaulted ceilings, patios, domes, inscriptions on the walls, pools or marble sitting rooms, and of course there is no minaret. There are heavy, square columns, and there are bookshelves. The footprint of the building covers about two acres or about enough space to accommodate 5,000 worshippers.

In theory, this radical simplicity repudiates the 'innovations' or false traditions which, from century to century, have accrued to the edifice of Islam.

The first mosque in the first city of Islam, namely Medina, is thought to have had no minarets or domes, nor any walls at all, but only a thatched roof to protect the faithful from the sun. So, in theory, the mosque in Dammaj brings worshippers back to the carpet-on-the-desert-floor plainness of this time.

This is the theory. But everyone in Dammaj knows that the greatest falsifiers of Islam came recently. Everyone knows that a certain family of petrocrat neighbours to the north is now pouring layers of gold and marble over the holy sites of Islam. Their mosques are simply piles of chandeliers, carpets, crenellations, friezes, mirrors, domes and minarets lit up like Christmas trees.

In Dammaj, to criticise these people too much is a game that comes dangerously close to biting the hand that feeds you, and so one tends to see the criticism more than one hears it. It is in the strenuous simplicity of Muqbel's mosque, and in the way the students walk to class in bare feet. It is in the way they eat rice and beans five days a week and fast the other two, in the barrenness of their huts, and in the *mahar*, or bride price they pay for their wives, which is often little more than a Koran.

41

The Dar al-Hadith has no website and produces no promotional literature; nor are there recruiters or guides who will meet students at the airport to bring them into the mountains. Nevertheless, the village square there has an international Islamic elan, like an airport in the Gulf during the hajj. If you look through the crowd carefully, you'll eventually find people who come from your part of the world.

At first, however, it takes a moment to get one's bearings. The people with the russet beards and light eyes could be from Chechnya, Dagestan, Sarajevo, Albania or anywhere else where light-skinned Muslims predominate, or they could be converts. It's hard to know in what language to speak to them, and harder still to know who is approachable and who not. Generally speaking, if you speak to everyone in classical Arabic and ask no questions beyond 'how is your health and the health of your family', you can make no mistakes. You might not learn very much, but at least no one will take you for a spy.

Perhaps the best description of what the Dar al-Hadith actually does for the communities that send these young men can be found in an essay posted at SalafiTalk.net. When Sheikh Muqbel began to build his mosque in Dammaj, says the author, a Canadian convert and long-time village resident named

Abdullah MacPhee, Islam in Yemen was in a state of disarray. It was he said, 'plagued by tashayyu [Shiism] in the north, tasawwuf [Sufism] in the south and hizbiyyah [sectarianism]' in general.

Then, says MacPhee, destiny, in the person of Sheikh Muqbel, asserted itself. 'The Sheikh set up an institute of knowledge that by Allaah's will has changed the face of Yemen.'

> The Institute started as a small masjid [mosque] made out of mud, then as the students numbers grew a bigger masjid was built adjacent to the Sheikh's house then later a bigger masjid was built which is today the library then an even bigger masjid was built and now that masjid has just been expanded. The latest masjid is very big and is active day and night with classes and students memorizing Qur'aan . . .

Now at this bustling centre, says the essay, students new and old are served two (simple but free) meals a day: 'usually beans and bread in the morning and evening and rice for lunch.'

Single students, MacPhee says, usually live in rooms made of mud bricks, many of which have bathrooms attached. As for families, 'a small family can easily get by on a $100 a month', provided the head of household is not profligate. 'A student of knowledge should spend his money wisely so he can focus more on studying,' he cautions.

The curriculum itself is described simply because it is simple: 'classes are opened in all sciences and go all year round only stopping for Ramadaan when most people focus on reviewing Qur'aan . . .'

MacPhee wants the newcomers to like the place and at the end of the essay makes a special plea for tolerance:

> Many westerners when they first arrive complain of the trash scattered around and the smell of a sewage system

that has been blocked up and things like this . . . I advise the brothers and sisters that they read the history of our Prophet, may the peace and praise of Allaah be upon him, and the history of our Salaf As-Saalih [righteous ancestors]. We are all on a journey to our Lord . . . Our Prophet, may the peace and praise of Allaah be upon him has said: Be in this life as if you are a stranger or a traveler.

As a student, MacPhee himself was in no position to give *naseeha*, religious advice, to the strangers and travellers of cyberspace. But the genius of social networking sites allowed the residents of Anaheim and Englewood who were asking the questions at SalafiTalk.nct to address the sheikhs on the ground in Yemen directly. Those dialogues have also been uploaded to SalafiTalk.net – for instance, as follows:

the Imaam Rabee' ibn Hadee was asked on the 23rd of Ramadhaan 1424:

'What is your opinion of going to study at Daarul Hadith in Dammaj, Yemen, knowing that I am a new student?

The Imaam answered by saying 'Indeed it is befitting that you journey to this strong hold from the strong holds of Islaam, to this light house from the light houses of Islaam. Indeed journey should be made to it and the knowledge should be sought there. By Allah, we urge studying at this abode . . . in this time period in which innovations have accumulated and trials have evolved.'

Perhaps the most illuminating words I read about Dammaj before I knew much about the place turned out to be the ones spoken by the founder himself, Sheikh Muqbel, in an interview he gave to a pair of reporters from the *Yemen Times* in 2000. Dammaj, he announced, was the beneficiary of an international trend among young, well-heeled but spiritually empty Westerners:

> They have shifted from a luxurious life in their homelands where they were uncertain what they were living for to a humble life but with faith and deep knowledge inside that there is life after death. They want to know what life is for, why they are living. What is beyond life? What is death? A start or an end?

How many of these seekers had actually studied in Dammaj? the reporters asked.

'There have been over 100,000 students studying in our institution in Dammaj,' he replied, 'and they all know how peaceful the Sunni movement is because it calls for a return to the Holy Koran and to the prophet Muhammad, peace and blessing upon him.'

At first, when I had only walked along a few of the pathways and had prayed only a half-dozen times in the Great Mosque, I doubted Muqbel's numbers. To accumulate a total enrolment of 100,000 students the school would have had to bring 5,000 new people to campus every year for each of its twenty years of existence. Was that possible? His school was located in a war zone in a remote canyon in a no man's land in northern Yemen. It didn't seem likely.

Yet something unlikely was clearly under way here. Hundreds of students were camping on the mosque floor when I arrived. Hundreds of huts were being built by hand in the talus fields beneath the cliffs. Everyone had a friend lodging with him and it was common to hear of families and siblings on their way.

Meanwhile, in an adjacent settlement known as the *mizra*, or farm, modern life was coming to Dammaj: the huts had running water, upstairs bedrooms, and electricity several hours a day. There was a sewer system, and a local telephone network.

Closer to the mosque, Indonesian bachelor students had erected a residential area made entirely from mud-brick cells. It was less like a suburb than like a giant ant colony. Those who didn't have enough money for a cell erected one-man sleeping chambers on the roofs of pre-existing cells. Those who wished to expand their cells into houses added vestibules and tin-roofed sheds which spilled outward, beyond the perimeter of the settlement and into the desert.

To enter this village was to slip into a labyrinth of tracks, adobe staircases and tiny dark windows, like eyes. Often the tracks led round and round, under laundry lines, past doorways made from hanging towels, and into dead ends, which were the execution grounds for the local poultry and filled with chicken feet. Other tracks led on to the roofscape of the settlement. From up here one could take in a view of hundreds of beehive-shaped hovels, and in the distance, across a span of desert, a range of dark brown mountains in southern Saudi Arabia that wavered in the heat.

I never would have been able to guess at the population of Dammaj by wandering past these shacks and earthen huts, but a decent opportunity to gauge the total number of inhabitants came on the morning of the Eid al-Fitr, which is a high holiday in Yemen and the only moment in the year when the men, women and children of a community pray as one. We prayed outdoors that morning, beneath a band of cliffs lit up in the pink light of dawn. I arrived a bit late, but not too late to miss the thousands of black figures who were kneeling in the desert.

Further away, on the far side of the black forms, hundreds of rows of men in white were humped over in the sand. The light had turned their robes to pink and the entire assembly – row after row, receding more than two kilometres into the desert – glowed softly.

It was a stunning, unique and, as it happened, eminently countable display.

Here were 10,000 men, women and children, give or take 500. Two dozen militiamen watched over them like shepherds. The sheikh stood in the bed of a pickup truck, surrounded by guards, clutching a microphone and speaking softly.

After that day, Muqbel's 100,000 estimate did not seem like the exaggeration I took it for at first. In any case, by 2006 the numbers were adding up. If 100,000 students had not come through the village by then, the figure, it seemed to me, would be reached soon enough.

Muqbel's *Yemen Times* interview turned out to be a useful guide in one other respect: he knew the character of his students well. 'We have students from the UK, the USA, Germany, France, and many other countries, seeking to know more about Islam.'

> They have come of their own will to realize their goal of knowing their religion which they either converted to or knew little about. We accommodate them in simpler rooms with a sociable environment which is less of luxury than what they used to live in. These students don't want to be comforted in luxury. They keep on praying in the long nights. They suffer hunger sometimes but resist as they have powerful faith.

In my first evenings in the village, I would sit on the mosque terrace as the moon rose over the grape arbours. Because it was Ramadan, we were all suffering (or anyway enduring) hunger and performing the *tarroweah*, or night-time prayer, into the early morning hours. Sometimes, I would sit in a circle of Somalians. They would smile at me and push clumps of dates into my palm. The voices of Americans, French and English brothers would rise from the circles nearby. Everyone was famished. No one wanted to leave and we would linger under the moon, sipping tea and speaking to one another in the formal Arabic which has died out elsewhere in the world.

Yes, I would think to myself, it is all exactly as Muqbel advertised it to be: the hunger, the camaraderie, the students who've been called to return to the holy Koran and the repair of Islam. It was all true and happening before my eyes.

42

I found these scenes persuasive but I also knew that an alternative story, illuminating a second, less apparent purpose of Dammaj was circulating through the Western embassies in Sana'a.

This was more a military story than a tale of the revival of the *Sunnah*, and it did not begin in Dammaj but in Afghanistan in the early 1980s.

According to this narrative, the Arabs who came from Yemen and Saudi Arabia to fight the Soviets were dismayed by what they saw on the ground: Muslims communicating in a welter of languages, employing a hodgepodge of strategies, responding to several chains of command rather than one, and, in the end, throwing themselves into the breach without purpose or result. From the point of view of these Arab believers, the gravest problem in Afghanistan was that the social and doctrinal fragmentation which afflicted the rest of contemporary Islam was now taking a lethal form, as chaos on the battlefield.

In 1983, a philosopher of the Afghan jihad, Sheikh Abdullah al-Azzam, issued an appeal to believers everywhere in which he all but denounced the current generation of jihadis for hindering more than they helped. 'We do not deny,' his message said,

> that a large number of arrivals [in Afghanistan], with
> simple thinking, shallow Islamic juristic knowledge

drawn from diverse founts and different pedagogic schools, and disparity in levels of age and knowledge, has brought about a kind of catastrophe . . . It has cast a great burden upon our shoulders. But what could we possibly do when so few mature people are coming?

According to this second history of Dammaj, Osama bin Laden, himself a former student of Sheikh Muqbel, felt that only the jihadists who had had religious training in Saudi Arabia and Yemen understood what Islamic warfare actually was. The other soldiers might have been well-meaning but when they spoke no Arabic, prayed according to the traditions of their Uzbek grandfathers or their Kandahari uncles, and recited Koran without understanding what they were saying, they were missing the point: the point was to work in synch with the will of God. The point was to behave according to the battlefield traditions set down in the hadith and the biographies of the Prophet. In the absence of such an ethic, the armies of Islam were not much better than any other kind of ignorant army. They might win or they might not but their victories would be meaningless. Their soldiers would not necessarily be martyrs, and no truly Islamic nation could be founded on territory which they had won. When armies win by chance, chance, they believed, would surely sweep away their gains.

According to this theory, the success of the Afghan jihad settled into the minds of the Arabs who fought there as an object lesson. In the wake of that victory, they developed a new theory of warfare. These Arabs were offered an opportunity to put the new theory to the test in 1994, in their own backyard. In that year, the last of Yemen's communists – the former rulers of the People's Democratic Republic of Yemen – made an ill-fated attempt to secede from President Saleh's federation of north and south Yemen.

For the most part, Saleh fought these secessionists with conventional soldiers and employed conventional army strategies, but it seems he also called on the veterans of the Afghan campaign for support. These veterans brought a new style of warfare to the battlefield. They sent soldiers out in cells of three or four, rather than in platoons, and the cells were led by people who had memorised the Koran, had studied proper Koranic pronunciation, often for years, and knew how to pray in the ultra-calm, unified, trance-like style of the Salafis. The cell leaders were generals made in the image of Muhammad himself: they preached to their fellows as much as they fought the enemy. On the battlefield, of course, they were competent. But they were competent in every realm. They knew how to behave in the mosque, at the dinner table, in the bathroom, and what words to say in the presence of the poor, the sick, the powerful and the deceitful. This self-confidence, which came from having accomplished a complete interiorisation of the Koran and the Hadith, happened to make the soldiers into good teachers. They conquered territory, and at the same time they conquered hearts and minds.

According to this second story about Muqbel's soldiers, the Yemeni president, Ali Abdullah Saleh, understood how vital this new fighting force was. He believed it had made important contributions to bringing about the death of the Soviet regime in Afghanistan and knew that these believers had helped defeat the communist remnants in Yemen's south. In recognition of this accomplishment he promised Muqbel permanent political and military protection. His valley in the north – and his school and his pupils – were to remain forever his.

Perhaps President Saleh had the cultivation of a secret, pro-Saleh fighting force in mind. It would stand in reserve, and would quarter itself in the hills along the Saudi border. Perhaps he simply meant to leave the seminarians to their own devices. In any case, in the wake of the victory over the southern communists, Muqbel's academy entered its own golden age: money flowed in from Saudi Salafis and occasionally from the Yemeni president himself. Meanwhile, the students drifted in from the big Yemeni cities, southern Saudi Arabia, North Africa, and occasionally from the West.

Some time in the mid-1990s, it seems, Osama bin Laden turned his sights on a new target: the United States. According to this second narrative, by the time bin Laden got around to drawing up a plan of action, Muqbel's school in northern Yemen was producing talibs unlike any others on the face of the earth: they were travellers, good at slipping into foreign countries, and sleeping there, perhaps for years. They had been taught well and were themselves good teachers. Because they lived in a war zone amid hostile Shia, they were skilled at lying low and avoiding trouble. Because they were steeped in the teachings of the Salafi, they believed that Allah had called on them to perform three essential tasks: to purify Islam; to reveal the true teachings of the Koran to the world; and to take the fight to the unbelievers.

According to this second understanding of Dammaj, bin Laden had precisely these goals in mind as he planned his new, twenty-first-century jihad. He didn't need many soldier scholars, but he did need them to be calm, and so confident in their faith that they could, for instance, take over aeroplanes in mid-flight, slitting the throats of the stewardesses, while not forgetting to utter the correct invocations for entering into battle. In this way, the aeroplanes would be guided by God, rather than by half-baked, multi-ethnic, non-Arabic-speaking, adolescent adventurers.

In Dammaj, I found that almost every student knew this theory, or some version of it, and hated it. The students disliked the thought that to the outside world their years of praying and memorising amounted to so much preparation for murder.

But they didn't repudiate the theory totally. Many students told me that in the late nineties bin Laden had indeed made a visit to Dammaj and that he had come then with a single goal in mind: to recruit for a new campaign, which would be based in Florida.

I heard one version of the story from a Canadian student, Shakr al-Canadi who told it to me in order to emphasise his ending: Muqbel had turned bin Laden away. There were no jihad preparations under way in Dammaj and there never had been, he insisted. 'Muqbel,' said Shakr, 'told bin Laden, "your jihad is wrong, you will have no students from Dammaj, and you cannot establish a training camp at all. Go!"'

When I arrived in Dammaj I found it hard to believe that the school was producing anything specific at all, and harder to believe that it was now or ever had been guided by a single purpose. The current sheikh of Dammaj, Yahya al-Hajoori, screams a lot in his lectures. Up close, he comes across as frazzled and outraged, like someone who's been shouting at his unruly children for hours, knows he'll be shouting again soon, and cannot bear the disorder of it all. He recalls an absent-minded professor more than a military genius.

As for his school, it didn't seem modelled on a military plan or even on a university but rather on the principle of constructive chaos, as many institutions in Yemen are.

Classes were taught by students or former students, most of whom had no university degrees, no training as teachers, and were not paid. The classes met on the mosque floor or under acacia trees on the edge of the desert or in private houses. There were no rosters, no grades and no exams. When a student felt that he had mastered a particular topic, he moved on to another study group sitting in a different corner of the mosque, or he established his own group to teach the topic he had just finished studying. The mosque loudspeaker announced the schedule of classes in the morning, and there was a bulletin board in the mosque terrace covered in handwritten notices which functioned as a kind of course syllabus. By reading the syllabus, one could see that courses were offered in all the Islamic disciplines: *fiqh* (jurisprudence), *tajweed* (koranic reading), *tafsir* (exegesis), *sharia*, and *hadith*, as well as Arabic grammar. But the syllabus often left out crucial information: were there synopses of the courses? How many weeks did they last? At what times of the day did they meet and were they meeting now, at the end of Ramadan, or had they been cancelled for the following month as well? Sometimes the teachers were away on a pilgrimage to Mecca. Sometimes they were in residence in the village but sick, and available for private instruction at their bedsides.

There might have been a single intelligence guiding the working of the Dar al-Hadith, it seemed to me, but if so it was more like the collective intelligence that guides smart mobs and Wikipedia. It brought students from across the world to Dammaj, though the place was unadvertised and dangerous to get to. It cultivated the grapes, fed the students, accomplished the five daily prayers and divided the community day by day into cell-like classes.

One thing it was not doing while I was in Dammaj was training for jihad in the West. There were rumours that Sheikh Hajoori had permitted the Somalian students to leave for jihad in Somalia, and other rumours that certain Iraqis had been given leave to fight in their homeland. These rumours spoke of people leaving for jihad in ones and twos. My feeling was that if there was an organised programme for sending fighters to the front, it was a well-hidden one. In three and half weeks of eating and sleeping in and around the Dammaji mosque, I never saw it. Instead I saw students building more mud huts and more cement shacks. They studied and memorised. The wider trend in Dammaj was not to take off for the territory ahead. Instead, it was to find a Yemeni wife, or to import a wife from Europe, and then to settle in.

43

The settlers were certainly busy. They rose at 4.30 in the morning to the sound of the sheikh's voice inviting them to prayer. During Ramadan, the students ate breakfast by candlelight, before the prayer, in the privacy of their huts. Those who slept in the mosque had their breakfast on the prayer-hall floor. They were usually in a hurry because dawn was coming, and the communal prostration was at hand.

Shortly after I arrived in Dammaj, a former bike mechanic from Kensington invited me to stay with him in a hut that had been built in the talus fields, high off the valley floor. In the mornings, we hurried through our ablutions together, sharing the cold water. Then we ate a plate of oranges and stumbled out into the darkness.

Lines of flashlights and illuminated cellphones were trickling through the boulders. No one spoke, but the village dogs were barking, candles in some of the houses had been lit, and the smell of wood fires rose from their kitchens.

Those October mornings were clear, and filled with stars. They were also freezing. We trundled into a satellite mosque a kilometre or so distant from the main prayer hall, which had no electricity and no heating. We lined up in the candlelight. Everyone shivered but the Europeans shivered less because they wore North Face parkas, cold-weather cycling jackets, and fancy fleece sweaters over their robes. The Yemenis stood in the prayer rows in their woollen dinner jackets and turbans. On those mornings, the congregation looked like an expedition into the Himalayas: we, the Westerners, were dressed to the nines, the locals were dressed in charity shop dinner jackets and everyone was huddling together for warmth.

After the dawn prayer, most of the students went back to bed. A handful of the most pious ones went off to the Great Mosque, where there was electric light, and warmth from the bodies who slept there. Already, at a few minutes past five, the most pious of the students were inside, forming their study circles.

Later, around 6.30 a.m., the village square came to life. About a dozen merchants, some from Somalia, some from Sana'a and some from England, came to unlock their cement shacks. An Iraqi entrepreneur sold sports jackets and used robes from a clothing rack at the foot of the mosque staircase The grocers sold fig bars, cola, vanilla wafers, tins of tuna fish, and hot sauce. Farmers sold spinach, coriander, onions, parsley and tomatoes. In addition, there was an internet cafe, a barber, a clothing store, a hut for eggs, a hut for school supplies, and a man with a cart full of uncooked potatoes. This was downtown Dammaj.

The central event in every twenty-four hours in Dammaj was the evening hadith recitation. In these moments the entire community spoke from the same page at the same time, in response to the sheikh's explicit commands. At no other time were we as close to the sheikh, or for that matter as close to the Prophet of God.

Often the hadiths we recited detailed the domestic economy of Muhammad's household: in these hadiths he spoke about his bedtime rituals, his favourite foods (cucumbers, dates, pumpkins), his ambivalence about garlic (not to be eaten when eminent guests were expected) and his feelings about sex and marriage. His wives and friends spoke.

Typically, an evening of hadith recitation in Dammaj unfolded like this: about 3,000 students sat on the prayer-hall floor. The sheikh entered, usually from the rear of the mosque. A hush fell over the hall. He processed through the columns inside an envelope of bodyguards. When he arrived at his armchair, he adjusted his microphone, then seated himself. 'Where were we?' he would mumble. 'At what point did we stop last?' Then he would open a volume of hadith he had brought with him, then cough, then gesture with his right hand at the western wing of the prayer hall. 'All those in that section, recite,' he would say. Five hundred young men in the west would rise. They would recite from memory and the recitation would come out as an extended drone. This would last about three minutes, or as long as it took to recite two pages of text.

When the students in the west had completed their recitation, the sheikh would wave his hand at the students in the east. 'Students there, rise,' he would say. 'Recite.' On some evenings he divided the congregation into new ad hoc denominations: 'rise all those from France,' he would say, or 'all those from Hodeidah!' or, 'all those whose names begin with the letter A!' Always there was the slow lifting of the sheikh's right hand followed by the slow rising of the students from the prayer-hall floor. Always the students droned. The militiamen sat at the feet of the sheikh, and looked south into the student body. The students looked north, past the militiamen and the sheikh, into the *qibla* or Mecca-facing wall.

These recitation sessions lasted about forty-five minutes. When the sheikh spoke, his commands were lifted from the roof of the mosque by loudspeaker; they rose into the cliffs and bounced across the vineyards into the mud huts of the village. Here the wives and daughters of the students were, in theory, reciting in their turn.

These recitations occur every night of the year, regardless of holidays. Attendance is mandatory.

After ten days in Dammaj, I had my own theory about why the sheikh required every male student to attend every night.

Yes, the sayings of the Prophet were spreading through the

minds of the students. They were certainly mastering their hadith, and certainly doing their best to bring the time of the Prophet alive. Meanwhile, the sheikh was mastering the students. Who inched closer to the master of ceremonies? Who inched away? Every evening, just after the *Maghrib* prayer, the sheikh waved his right hand at the students and watched them. Over time, some retreated into the columns at the back of the mosque. But those who liked the exercise gathered in concentric circles at the feet of the sheikh's chair. They spoke loudly and raised their chins at him as they recited. They had memorised well and wanted the sheikh to know.

No one was coerced. Everyone volunteered. It was an entirely voluntary, self-selecting system of submission. Anyone who didn't like the staring of the militiamen or the scrutiny of the sheikh or the pressure to memorise was free to abstain.

But they were not exactly free to go. Some students were too young to leave on their own, or too poor, or didn't know what they would do when they left, or didn't like the idea of turning their back on their friends. Some were simply too passive to get their act together, and a few were all of these things at once. For this group, it was much easier to fall in line, and to allow the prostrations and the memorisation to work whatever effect nature and God wished them to work.

44

My first friend in Dammaj was a clerk at the internet cafe, an eighteen-year-old from Gays Mills, Wisconsin called Mujahid. In an earlier life, he had been a farm boy on the prairie and his mum and dad had been Lutherans, like all their Wisconsin neighbours.

Mujahid and I struck up a conversation one morning when the electricity in the cafe had failed.

Did he miss the prairie at all? I wondered. Did he still have feelings for Gays Mills? He cast an amused eye at the dead computers in the cafe, then grinned. 'Not really,' he said. 'What is there to miss?' He thought for a moment longer, then said, 'I miss hunting in the winters with my father. I miss the snow.' He hoped his father would send him the first two volumes of the *Lord of the Rings* trilogy.

Mujahid (formerly Tim) had come to Dammaj six years earlier in the company of his mother, two siblings and a stepfather. At that time, his mother was a new convert recently divorced from his Lutheran father. It had taken him a while to adjust but now, six years later, Mujahid felt that the adjustments were bringing rewards.

In his six years in Yemen, he had memorised the Koran, hundreds of hadith, and had acquired a remarkable, idiomatic command of Yemeni Arabic. He had studied so much in fact that he had almost got bored with his subject.

One morning as we chatted in the internet cafe, he asked me if I would be willing to give him French lessons. 'Of course,' I said. We agreed to meet that evening in the mosque, before the prayers. In the meantime, I would find a suitable lesson somewhere on the internet and download it.

Later in the day, as I searched through French poetry websites, Mujahid sat at his clerk's desk, reciting Koran. His voice filled the cafe. At first, not seeing where the voice came from, I thought I was listening to a tape or a live TV feed from one of the Saudi stations. His voice had that much confidence, and he had the fluidity of a native speaker.

'*Mashallah*,' I said to him when he came to a pause in the text. I wondered how long it had taken him to get to this level – six years, he said – and why exactly he was reciting.

This was *murajah*, he said, or review. He did it for two or three hours every day, because he enjoyed it and because it allowed him to pass the time in a profitable way.

In fact, *murajah* does have a specific purpose. People who have memorised the entire Koran as Mujahid had are like the owners of a vast, ancient property that has been built out of friable bricks, on unstable ground.

Every hour, forgetfulness attacks a distant crenellation. *Murajah* is the activity which sweeps across the grounds, patrols the parapets and mans the turrets in defence. It enters rooms, uses the disused furniture, walks the floorboards and then throws open the windows. Everything should be in its place, precisely where Allah put it.

Without *murajah* the furniture can rearrange itself. Rooms can swap places with other rooms, dismantling the larger order of things. Over time wings and towers can fall away into the abyss. A derelict property like this, as imams often remind students, is one in which alien presences – words, ideas, false memories – take up residence. If the memoriser isn't vigilant, he'll assume that the words he recites at prayer are the correct, orthodox ones when in fact they are just a disorderly melange of personal memories and guessed-at phrases.

* * *

When he was finished with his *murajah* I asked Mujahid what he liked to read. He said he enjoyed Tony Hillerman novels (about detectives on a Navajo Indian reservation), though he had long since finished all the books he had on hand. Now he spent his free time tracking down facts about Tolkien on the internet and reading the Google News page.

We couldn't do our French lesson that evening because Mujahid's mother called him to her hut, and the following evening he was sick. Our first lesson occurred a week later, in a shady, quiet section at the back of the mosque.

The poem I picked out for him was an eighteen-line vignette called 'Le Cancre', or 'The Dunce', by Jacques Prévert. It tells the story of a boy who is called on to recite his lessons in a French classroom. Some rebellious element in his soul, we learn, a fifth column of the heart, refuses to cooperate with the teacher. He stands but he will not speak. His classmates snigger. Meanwhile, his misbehaving brain attacks the entire programme of schoolboy information which the boy has committed to memory. His mind erases everything:

> Les chiffres et les mots
> Les dates et les noms
> Les phrases et les pièges
>
> The words and figures
> Names and dates
> Sentences and snares

Mujahid and I translated the poem together. When it was clear to both of us what was described in the poem, I asked Mujahid to reflect on why the boy forgets. 'What do you think is really going on?' I said. 'Is it a good thing to forget or a bad thing?'

He stared at me. 'I don't know,' he said. 'What?'

'Yeah,' I said. 'I mean, here's the schoolmaster with his history lesson. But I don't think much of it. Do you?'

'Maybe,' he said. 'I don't know.'

'What do you think of the schoolmaster?' I asked.

'I dunno.'

'Do you like him?'

'Yeah.'

'Why?'

'I dunno.'

'Look, Mujahid,' I said. 'This attack of memorylessness, in the context of this poem, it's a good thing. Right?' He stared at me. 'It's a good thing,' I repeated. 'Why?'

Mujahid shook his head. His lips moved but no sound came out. His eyes scanned the mosque which was now filling with people preparing for the sunset prayer. 'Subhan allah,' he shrugged. 'I don't know.'

In the poem's final lines, the child strides up to the blackboard to mark out his schoolboy declaration of independence:

> Et malgré les menaces du maître
> Sous les huées des enfants prodiges
> Avec les craies de toutes les couleurs
> Sur le tableau noir du malheur
> Il dessine le visage du bonheur.
> [And despite the teacher's threats
> And and the leers of the infant prodigies
> With chalk of every colour
> On the blackboard of misfortune
> He draws the face of happiness.]

'You see?' I said to Mujahid, when we had finished examining these lines. 'This is a poem about the triumph of the human spirit. There is something irrepressible in the kid. It will have its day. In this case, having his day means *tout effacer* – forgetting everything. It means saying, "Teacher, classmates: I will be me."'

Mujahid smiled faintly. His face searched the forest of mosque columns. He'd been fasting that day, though by this time the mandatory fasts of Ramadan had passed.

'Okay,' he said at last. 'The boy wants to do his own thing?'

'Look,' I said. 'This is a poem about how the soul of the boy is stronger than the soul of the teacher. The teacher's soul is made up of dry facts and figures. The souls of the other kids can only mock.'

'Yeah,' he said.

'The kid's a bright kid, isn't he?' I suggested.

'Yeah.'

'But bad in school. He's bright like Holden Caulfield, right?'

'What?' he said.

Mujahid had left America when he was twelve. Perhaps this had been a bit young for *The Catcher in the Rye*. I mentioned other works of art I thought he might know. Did he remember Elliott in *E.T.*? Did he ever see *The Shining*? I wanted him to notice that the boy in the poem was an archetype, and that our American culture was full of such creations. They were emblems of America itself: an illuminated child; yes, naïve – but a defier of the adult world, who sees his way through to independence. 'You know who Huckleberry Finn is, right?' I asked.

'I think so,' he said. 'Well, not exactly. But I get the idea.'

'Do you really?'

He looked into his lap. He sniffled. 'No.' He made a weak smile. 'I guess I don't.'

I spent an hour trying to help him understand. I couldn't get the message through. In the end, I don't think it was Mujahid's fault. It wasn't really mine.

But there were problems. For one thing, during my explanation I kept referring to people and ideas generally known to American teenagers, like Holden Caulfield and *a rebellious soul*. I did this the way teachers do – in order to leverage a store of extant knowledge. There was some extant knowledge in Mujahid. There was Tony Hillerman, Tolkien and scraps of information from Wikipedia and the Google News page. There were certainly memories of Wisconsin. But this amounted to a trickle of memories. It wasn't substantial enough to allow him to understand what the child in the poem might be thinking. The world of that boy was too far from Dammaj and too alien. In Dammaj, rebellious kids could not be admirable. Schoolmasters could not be pettifoggers. Going one's own way could not be good.

My tutorial suffered from another problem, which was that I was arguing on behalf of memorylessness. Mujahid could not, or would not accept the premise of such an argument. Memorylessness in Dammaj was distance from God, failure in the mosque, loss of face before the other students, and shame. To forget God or the Koran was to live in ignorance, like unbelievers. The whole purpose of life in Dammaj was to avoid that fate. To avoid that fate, one had to memorise.

Perhaps our lesson's biggest problem was that Mujahid had been fasting for more than a month, had grown sick, and had now embarked on a new regime of fasting for the Six Days of Shawwal. He had trouble concentrating. Though the temperatures were in the 30s, he shivered inside a plaid woollen Wisconsin deer-hunting shirt.

As soon as the first note of the call to prayer crackled on the loudspeakers, we were jerked out of the French classroom. We were back in Islamic time. We hurried on to the mosque terrace. We knelt and thrust our hands into plates of sticky dates. They were delicious. We poured tea down our throats. As we washed ourselves at the ablution faucets, I think we were both relieved. We spoke tentatively about a second class but made no plans.

Only one person, Qais, a French student I had met in Sana'a, made an effort to discover what I was really up to there. The last time we had spoken, I had made a poor impression. Back then, eight months earlier on the pavement in Sana'a, I had told him that I was an American, working at the local government newspaper. When he asked if I believed in God, I temporised. Later in the conversation, he told me he couldn't play football with unbelievers like me because their presence weakened his faith. 'If I am talking to you at all,' he had told me, 'it is for the purpose of bringing you to Islam, and for no other reason.'

Now, standing on the stoop of a vegetable shack, he squinted into the sun. 'What are you doing here, my friend the American?' he said, speaking under his breath. 'I assume you've stopped your journalism?'

'Yeah, I never really was a journalist,' I said.

'But that newspaper in Sana'a?'

'Yes, I did leave it behind.'

'You sure?' he said. 'We'll find out if not.'

'Search all you like,' I said. 'I'm here, not there.'

'You're not going back there?' he asked.

'Of course not,' I said.

'You sure?' he said.

'Yes, sure.'

'You are here to mind your own business?'

'Of course,' I said.

'To keep to yourself and to study on your own account?'

'Yes.'

'If this is true,' he said, 'you are welcome here.'

'Good,' I said.

'Good,' smiled Qais. 'It's much better for you that way. In any case, Allah – he knows everything. Time will tell.' He winked.

'Yes, time will tell,' I agreed.

45

During the following two weeks, I minded my own business. I never missed a prayer, never skipped a lecture, and sat in the shadows of the mosque a lot, memorising and writing in my journal. It was an innocuous routine that raised no eyebrows. Every day I talked to European talibs who'd been living this way for years. They didn't know what month it was back home or did know but had had so little contact with home over the years that they didn't much care. The weather was always pleasant in Dammaj. The altitude – about 1,000 metres – made the air temperate, with rain during the summer monsoon season and breezes in the winter. Because it was never too hot outside and never too cold, there really wasn't much need to watch the months roll by on a calendar. I spoke to several students who were not sure if George Bush was still president of the United States.

In Dammaj students who let the outside world slip away like this were admired. It was supposed to slip. Incoming students who let it go without a thought, with no homesickness, no complaints and no regrets, were said to be strong in their *iman*; they were *mookhlis* (sincere) and their *aqeedah* (creed) was correct.

One morning, about two weeks into my stay in Dammaj, Jowad, that rare variety of student in Dammaj who insisted on clinging to the present, and I were chatting on the front steps of the internet cafe. I noticed him examining my headscarf, which was tied in a sloppy, indifferent way. His eyes smiled.

'You remind me of my solicitor,' he observed. 'No, my mentor.' Actually, he couldn't remember who I reminded him of. In any case, I reminded him of some figure in the structure of secular authority in Islington to whom he had recently been referred by the English court system.

As we sat a procession of talibs and teachers was filing into the Great Mosque. 'Aren't you a little young to have a solicitor?' I asked after a while. 'Are you some kind of a troublemaker or something?'

He said that he was fourteen and that he wasn't at all too young to have a solicitor or to make trouble. 'I got in trouble with girls, mostly,' he remarked in a matter-of-fact tone of voice, as if this was not a startling admission in Dammaj. 'Italian girls, they're my biggest fitna. They like romantic, and I used to be quite romantic.' He sighed.

In an earlier life, apparently, he had gone to nightclubs, had had girlfriends, and had drunk wine. When he was poor, he said, he robbed grocery stores and rode away from the police on his BMX bike. 'Slowest bastards ever,' he recalled, under his breath.

As we chatted, two separate groups of English talibs stopped by the steps on which we were sitting to shake our hands and to invite us into the mosque. We salaamed them and told them we would be along in a moment.

At one point, an American brother noticed us and shuffled over to recite a hadith, the burden of which was that the Prophet had said that Muslims who prayed on time would enter heaven. 'We're waiting for someone in the internet cafe,' I said. 'We'll be along in a second.'

When the American had ambled away, Jowad stretched his arms to the sky and yawned. 'I've had a difficult childhood for sure,' he mused. He had been thrown out of schools, beaten by his stepfather, and arrested by the police. 'There was some lonely, lonely times,' he said. 'But it's what I always say. You can't judge a child by his childhood.'

Recently, he had read a biography of Clint Eastwood. Now, sitting in front of the internet cafe, the moral of that story came back to him. 'Clint Eastwood, he had a terrible childhood and look at him now. He has his own gun named after him. Every year he gets in a beautiful movie.'

'True, *mashallah*,' I said.

'Yeah,' he said, '*mashallah*.'

Mujahid was now locking up the internet cafe. He salaamed us, then hurried across the village square.

When he first arrived in Dammaj, Jowad had lived with Abbas al-Britani, the oldest and most respected of the British talibs. But after a month he tired of living in Abbas's hut and moved, on his own, into the mosque. Now, four months into his new life, he slept on a mattress in the north-eastern corner of the prayer hall. He had no plans to go back to England. His parents had no plan to visit him here. Only Allah knew when he would leave or where he would go.

'It's just a boring life here,' he mused, 'but this is my life now. If it's *maktoub*' – written – 'it's the only thing that's ever going to happen to you.'

Jowad was clearly a bright kid who had devoted some thinking to the question of how much control individuals exercise over their destinies. Clint Eastwood, it seemed, had suggested to him that even those who begin life in difficult circumstances can exercise considerable control. It is never too late to turn things around, he felt, and even impossible destinies, like becoming a movie star, could and did happen.

On the other hand, this particular fourteen-year-old happened to be living in an environment designed to bring about one destiny only. No one in Dammaj wanted reversals of fortune. The students and teachers had come to drift backwards, away from the world, into the mythological time of early Islam. Now Jowad's parents were far away. They had cut him off from England and from his earlier life. Now he apparently had little to do. To me, he seemed to be drifting.

As he talked about his new life in Dammaj, it occurred to me that the advice of a solicitor or mentor or some other benevolent figure in the local government of Islington could possibly have made a difference to Jowad. A person of this sort might at least have offered a different perspective on things. Jowad had evidently met with some such figure once. But those days were over. For better or for worse, he was now on his own.

Jowad, of course, was not asking for advice. He wasn't even hinting. On this occasion, I chatted with him for as long as was reasonable, and when the prayer could be postponed no longer, I prodded him off the steps. We walked together into the mosque. When we took our places in the prayer row, the hall was already on its knees. As we said, 'God is great' it was rolling forward through the first of the four noontime prostrations, and as we bowed it was already moving into the second. We had to hurry to catch up.

For reasons I did not understand – extra fasting? fatigue from fasting? – classes over the following three days were cancelled. This left the students with time on their hands.

Jowad and I spent the first morning of our vacation carrying out an errand his former guardian, Abbas, had asked him to perform. We were to retrieve a set of pots and pans that had been left in a hut far from the mosque, on the edge of a millet field. To get there, we had to wander through the back alleys to the south of the mosque, and then along a berm at the side of a leaky cesspool. Its contents were draining into the adjacent millet.

The house itself, a single floor adobe hut with a tin roof and an interior courtyard, had a pretty setting on a bluff of red dirt, with a view across the valley, into a row of Yosemite-like cliffs.

When Jowad and I visited, the owner of the house had been called back to London, and the other British Muslims, who used the house as a feasting spot, were memorising in the mosque or sleeping. Turning the lock in the front door, we stepped into a ghost house. Animals scurried away from a stack of dishes that had been left to moulder in the sink. A thin film of dust lay over the kitchen floor, the prayer rugs and the ablution basins in the bathroom. The community which feasted here was evidently a pious crowd but one given to drifting. The owner of the house had left the keys with Jowad and had invited him to stay there during his absence. There was however nothing in the deal for Jowad: no adults, no food, no company, nothing to play with and no reasonable way for him to pass the time. The whole purpose of sending a teenager to live in Dammaj, as I understood it, was to provide him with a community of ethically minded elders: the village would guide and ground the wayward kid. This was the theory. In practice of course the parents were busy performing their religious rites, or they were busy flying off to the UK, or they were busy being arrested by the Yemeni police. The wayward kid was certainly surrounded by ethically minded elder brothers. And yet he was very much on his own.

The two of us tiptoed through the remains of the holiday feasting. We retrieved Abbas's set of pots from the sink and hurried away.

The pots belonged in a hut a kilometre or so away, across the millet fields. Abbas's front door was a black curtain behind which a woman spoke to us in rudimentary, English-accented Arabic. We passed the pots one by one into a black-gloved hand that emerged from the curtain. We didn't say hello and we didn't say goodbye. It was an odd interaction, all in all, especially since it seemed pretty obvious that she was from the UK. I would have liked to have spoken with this woman more. Was she happy with her lot? Sad? Did she want to go home? It would have been unthinkable to ask her these questions of course. I had the opportunity to see her hand, and to listen to a fragment of conversation between her and Jowad. When she withdrew her hand, Jowad and I walked away in silence.

At the time, Jowad's default recreation was a multi-player internet game called PimpWar.com. Having finished with the morning chores, we were now free to pursue an afternoon of leisure. As soon as we arrived in the internet cafe, Jowad dialled up a website that depicted an American inner city in ruins. The law of this particular jungle stated that whichever pimp accumulated the most thugs, guns and whores won. 'This game is NOT for whiners,' said the website. 'PimpWar players have 5000 ways to call you a bitch ass.'

As Jowad toured the streets of his virtual ruin, he giggled. The website streamed a jazzy pimp music tune into the computer speakers which trickled out into the cafe, but not loudly enough for the other students to object.

They were busy clattering on their keyboards. One of them was trying to communicate with his relatives in France via Skype. With only a dial-up connection shared by six other computers, the student's conversation was going nowhere. 'Salaam alaikum!' he yelled into the computer. *'Te's là? T'es là?'*

Jowad and I spent an hour or so relaxing in the cafe in this way. Soon it was time to pray. Mujahid shooed us from the computers, locked the cafe and the three of us walked together into the mosque.

46

Jowad was an especially good companion during the sheikh's speeches, which could be long disjointed affairs, more like a tour through the mind of a rural Arab chieftain than instruction in Islam. Usually the two of us sat against a side wall of the mosque and listened while the sheikh followed his stream of consciousness. Now and then, a funny or surprising or otherwise noteworthy idea would strike Jowad and he would turn to me to whisper his commentary.

One evening, the sheikh's speech took him on a detour through the sexual habits of Westerners. He said the normal things that are said when rural chieftains in Yemen address this issue: that AIDs is spreading through the West because the people know no sexual restraint, that apes and monkeys are more civilised than contemporary Christians and Jews, and that despite all the coupling that goes on in Europe, they are having fewer and fewer babies, while the Islamic world is having more and more. 'Is this not a sign from the hand of God?' he said, grinning.

Most of the students nodded sleepily. We had all heard versions of this speech before, and most people, I think, were inclined to assent. For Jowad, however, the ironies of the situation were too rich to ignore

'Hell!' he whispered. 'There are kids right here in this mosque selling their booties. Why is he so worried about what people do back home?' Older, wealthier students paid for sex and the younger boys – usually local kids – were happy to sell. There were covert couples, and assignations and break-ups. 'It's a regular soap opera in here,' he said.

'That can't be true,' I murmured. 'Wouldn't they at least leave the House of God to do all that?'

'No,' he said, shrugging, 'not really.'

I did not witness this amatory aspect of prayer-hall life myself, but as Jowad whispered and the sheikh wagged his finger into his microphone, I did see a certain logic to the arrangement.

One hundred young men, for whom masturbation was forbidden and contact with the opposite sex unthinkable, lying in the darkness together over a period of months probably would, I thought, from time to time fall into each other's arms. A lot of those kids were lonely. Probably some wanted companionship. Probably some wanted cash.

'Yup, they sell their booties at night and in the daytime, they read Koran. What's that all about?' Jowad asked, shaking his head and smiling.

Other conversations I had with other talibs later on suggested to me that there was really only one inviolable taboo concerning sexual contact in Dammaj: girls mustn't be involved. Everyone accepted this taboo and no talib I knew or heard of tried to break it.

But homosexual relations – provided the partners turned up at prayer every morning, provided everyone shut up about what was going on – were tolerated. Silence, it seemed, kept the village on an even keel.

On another occasion in the mosque, Jowad pointed to a short, chubby Yemeni sitting on the carpet a few rows away from us. 'All the English brothers,' he said, 'first thing they want when they get here is a gun.' It was against school rules to assemble an arsenal but there was no one to enforce such a rule and there was a regional arms market, just south of the Saudi border, 20 kilometres away. Since Jowad spoke excellent Yemeni Arabic and

English and knew all the English and American brothers, he had helped the man on the carpet distribute his weapons. Jowad had been cut in on a percentage of the sales and for several weeks, until the Yemeni found another, older broker, had lived well.

Sometimes, when Jowad was gossiping in this way, the logic of Yemeni life, which was the only logic on hand, took over. Tribesmen in northern Yemen had been living with the Koran in one hand and the Kalashnikov in the other for generations. The Western talibs wanted this for themselves. Well, why not? Were we not living in the Wild East, beyond the last jurisdiction of the last gun law? We were. At least the young men were doing their gunslinging in the desert wastes; it was better that they do it here than in a subway train at home.

There were other times when the logic of life in the West took over. I looked at the blank-faced talibs cradling their Korans on the mosque floor, and imagined the arsenals that were growing inside their huts. In Yemen, you can buy grenades for $5, anti-tank mines for $100, and shoulder-launched missiles for less than the cost of a good microwave. With their beards, their memorised verses and their weaponry, it seemed to me they were turning themselves into a league of hut-based warlords. The only reason such people would want women and children in their lives, I thought, was so that they could reign and decree, like domestic deities.

I could see their pride in themselves taking root, and being in the presence of so much emergent self-confidence reminded me of my former students in Vermont. Those young men had also descended into a period of self-mythologising and gun acquisition. In America, those periods tended to end on the front page of the local newspaper.

At times like this, I would think: this is clearly no environment for a fourteen-year-old. Someone should do *something*. But I was in no position to do anything. Nor was Jowad. Nor did he want to do anything.

Instead of actually going anywhere, we spent a lot of time wandering through the vineyards. If we passed a village guard as we strolled along the pathways, Jowad would tell me if the guard was strict or amenable, and if we passed a group of kids playing football, he would tell me which ones belonged to the sheikh (dozens), which ones belonged to Abbas (only a few) and which ones were Yemeni kids sent from Sana'a and Aden to live on the Straight Path of God. Then we would hang around for a bit in the vicinity of Jowad's home, at the back of the great mosque. He had kitted out his mattress as a champion visitor to PimpWar.com should. He owned the plushest pillows in the prayer hall and the most velvety duvet. At the head of his bed, next to the pillows, he displayed a magnificent unused, unusable (in Dammaj) pair of basketball shoes. When we were done with this tour of his bedroom we would drink tea on the mosque terrace with the Somalians, or wander a bit more along the paths, or return to the internet cafe for another round of PimpWar. com. This was his life. It was calm, and there was no drinking, clubbing, or robbing of convenience stores involved.

Stable as this routine was, there were times when the loneliness and boredom of life in Dammaj got to Jowad. Usually this happened when he had just finished a phone conversation with his mum, for instance, or when he was waiting to have one and she did not call and was sending no email messages indicating when she might call. At times like this, Jowad's mind wandered back to his mother's house.

He didn't have a perfect understanding of what was going on at home but as he talked more about his mother, I for one began to discern the outlines of a familiar family drama unfolding on the other side of the world, in Islington.

Jowad's mother, a Yemeni, had arrived in London in 1998 in the company of her only son. She had applied for and received some form of asylum. Now, in 2006, she had learned English, met a new husband, and was settled into an apartment near the Holloway Road.

This couple had recently had two daughters – twins, as it

happened. Jowad's mum pushed them along the Holloway Road in a twin stroller. The stepfather, Adel, also a Yemeni immigrant, worked in a successful travel agency on the South Bank. His reputation for piety, fluency in recitation, and for the beauty of his voice was now on the rise at his mosque, in Wembley Park. The story, in short, had a happy denouement for everyone but the teenager in the household.

'Ever since I hit puberty, my mum hasn't wanted me in the house,' Jowad told me one afternoon as we sat on the steps of the internet cafe. 'I know that's the truth. I just wish she would say it, flat out. Then I could make up my own mind. I could go wherever I want to go and be free.'

When Jowad talked about this subject, he tended to lower his voice. He would shake his head slowly, as if he couldn't believe what was going on. Sometimes, he would just sit on the cafe stoop with his head in his hands. His mother was clearly busy. That much he understood. But why this business should involve her expelling him from his own house, not calling him, and installing a self-regarding travel agent named Adel in his place Jowad could not (or maybe did not want to) understand.

Jowad's biological father had died when Jowad was young. But how? Where? Under what circumstances? Jowad didn't know. His mother gave him various, contradictory stories. So now in Jowad's head there existed a vague, vanished father, and a time when everyone had been together as one in Yemen.

During Jowad's darkest moods, when his uncommunicative mum and dead father were weighing on his mind, I would sometimes look at him and think, some day and perhaps not too many days from now, the clouds that are hanging over this kid will break. When that hour comes, he will give himself permission to do things he's only been daydreaming about. I didn't have any idea what sorts of things were on his mind. Probably he didn't either, but it seemed likely that whatever they were, they would be imbued with the emotional logic of the places in which he was spending his time. He was spending a lot of time with the nihilist gang of street warriors at PimpWar.com. He was spending the rest of his time with the soldier scholars in our mosque.

In actual life, Jowad did not crack. He was much steadier than I gave him credit for being. Every time the clouds above coalesced, he pulled himself together. He would pick up a stone and fling it into the sand, or kick his shoe, or readjust his turban. He would stand up, eventually, and smile. 'Let's go pray,' I would say and soon we would be standing indoors, facing Mecca. The voice of the sheikh, which was soft and paternal, even as he recited the most ominous prophecies, fell across the prayer rows. 'Straighten your rows,' he would murmur through the loudspeakers. 'Straighten them, straighten them,' he would say again and then he would sing familiar verses in a familiar tone of voice over the microphone. Jowad and I and our prayer-row neighbours would touch our toes together. We would straighten our rows. Soon the entire mosque would be linked together at the feet and shoulders. As we bowed, three thousand sighs would spread through the mosque.

Jowad was much better at praying than I was. He lost himself quickly in these prayers. I worried about the placement of my hands or the pronunciation of the verses but next to me, in a separate world, Jowad's body would be rising and falling over the carpet like a little wave.

One evening, about two weeks after our first meeting, when we were hanging out beneath the cedars, and Jowad was again talking about being cut off from home, and the time for the prayer was closing in, he refused to get up off the stairs. His mother had not called in days. 'Why not?' he said without curiosity. 'I'll tell you why not. She wants me to stay here. For ever.' He kicked the sand. After a few moments of silence, a small voice on the steps next to me said, 'I know this is a test from God, but I should just go to Aden. They have a mall there.'

'That's impossible,' I said. 'Aden is 800 kilometres away.'

He sighed. His eyes seemed to dart around beneath a glassy sheen of tears. 'I'm stuck,' he murmured.

Suddenly, I knew exactly what to do. Four years earlier I had come up with a plan to overcome exactly this conundrum: the teenager in the act of giving up on life, resigning himself, allowing the walls to close in. Back then, sitting in my locked-down classroom in Vermont, I had daydreamed about meeting free teenagers, on the road somewhere, anywhere, in the mountains of a believing country.

I planned to come across them early in their voyage, at a rise in the trail, perhaps, just as they were sizing up the territory ahead. Some adult should make it his business to stand at that place, I had said to myself.

From jail, it had seemed like a simple idea: go to an interesting spot, make friends, say sensible things, be of use. It had also seemed a vital, important idea because I knew that each of my jail students had arrived at his critical juncture alone, and lonely. They had taken what counsel they could. Usually it came from weird peers who were not all that stable themselves. Sometimes it came from internet role-playing games, and other times from DVD movies about adventurers who lived well by killing well.

More than anything else in the world, I had thought, such teenagers were in need of decent company. They needed a sensible, sympathetic, older-brother figure in their life who was interested and wanted to listen. In jail, of course, I did listen, but by then it was much too late.

Back in Vermont, when these ideas were filling my head, my schedule was empty. So I bought a ticket for Yemen. As it turned out, on the ground, in the presence of three-dimensional human beings and an actual Arab society, the plan collapsed.

Now, listening to Jowad fumble about, the idea of standing at the rise in the road came back to me. It occurred to me that I had been waiting for an opportunity like this for some time, for three and three-quarter years, to be precise, and that it had died several times along the way. Now my dead plan was staring me in the face. It was alive.

⋆ ⋆ ⋆

In the event, I didn't say more than a word or two. As I was thinking about carrying out my rescue mission, I was aware that he and I were visible through the mosque windows. We had been visible in this way for almost two weeks now. I was also aware that my presence in the village had awakened suspicions, especially among the French students. Within seconds, I was thinking of the ambient anxiety in Dammaj concerning whisperers, spies, infiltrators and Jews.

On that occasion, on the bench in front of the internet cafe, I flinched. I said nothing. I'll lay it all out for him later tonight, I told myself. Or tomorrow or the next day.

47

Before I left Dammaj, I did deliver a kind of hortatory speech to Jowad. It came out less like a lecture and more like a conversation. In fact, I had no solutions for him. Going home would not guarantee him an easy adolescence, nor were his parents inviting him home.

'Nothing has been decided or written or predetermined for you,' I told him, hoping to make the best of a complicated situation. 'You can leave today if you want.' We were drinking tea on the front porch of a house, by the edge of the desert. I nodded at a pickup truck that was rolling away into the dunes. 'I can give that guy, or some guy like him some money. He'll drop you in Sana'a. What do you say?'

He shrugged.

'You want me to call your parents?' I asked. Maybe he or I or both of us could persuade them to fetch him. 'I'll pay. You want to call them yourself?'

'I'll be fine,' he said. 'Don't worry.'

'Three weeks in Dammaj is long enough for me,' I said. 'I'm sorry but I'm finished with this place.' In fact, I was beginning to worry a bit for my own safety. I gave him my phone number and told him to call me in Sana'a.

'Okay,' he said glumly. 'Thanks.'

We sat in silence for several minutes, eyeing the pickup truck.

It hovered on the crests of the dunes, vanished, then reappeared a little further away, in a smaller cloud of dust.

Evidently our conversation was over. Evidently our friendship was over.

We both knew what had happened. I had turned up in his life, and had invited him to take control of his future. I had hinted to him in a hundred small but telling ways and in other, bolder ways that freedom was his to take. Just as he was warming to the idea of independence, I had pulled the plug.

He looked away into the desert. He unwrapped his headscarf, examined it closely, and reapplied it to his forehead. 'Go,' he said, smoothing the headband. 'See ya later.'

He nodded sleepily. The truck that had been bobbing up and down in the distance was now gone – vanished somewhere behind a dune. Jowad and I were alone with our teas.

At the time, I had little faith in him. I thought I might see him again in a year or five years or never.

48

The internet cafe in Dammaj was our village post office. It had its routines and its local characters like village post offices everywhere. In the afternoons, before prayer, an English convert, Abu Dawud from Manchester used to sit in a corner, typing out notes to friends and family back home. He was fifty-nine years old and had been passing through cults on various continents since the seventies.

'They do not write back,' he would say of his brothers and sisters. 'Do you see what the family has become in England?'

Bilal from Nantes would be searching for girlfriends on the internet and Mujahid would be reciting Koran.

On Fridays, late in the afternoon, Western women would sometimes come to the internet cafe to call home. Yemeni custom dictates that women venturing out of the house should be accompanied by a *mahram* or guardian. In theory, the *mahram* protects the woman from insults, while guiding her through the hustle and bustle of everyday life. But in Dammaj, there was no hustle or bustle, and no one who might have insulted the dignity of a woman. When these silent husbands, who were also from Europe and America, entered the cafe in the presence of a woman, the students there cast their eyes on the ground. We did not salaam and stopped talking to one another. The woman would enclose herself in her phone booth and the *mahram* would likewise keep his eyes on the ground.

A few seconds of silence would pass and then a high-pitched frantic shouting would issue from the cabin: 'Hello, Mummie? Mummie? Salaam alaikum!' Perhaps a second of quiet would follow and then a new round of shouting would ring out: 'al-hamdulillah! And how are you? Jizak allah u khair, Mummie! We got the money, al-hamdulillah!' Or: 'We haven't got the money, NO! It hasn't come!'

And so on.

The *mahram* would lean on the wall next door to the phone booth, his eyes on his sandals, his hand in his beard. When the woman was through with her phone call, she would open the phone-booth door and tiptoe towards the exit. She would say nothing to anyone and look at no one. Her shouts would still be echoing from the cinderblock walls but the flesh and blood human with the money issues and the Mummie back home would be gone. In the space she had occupied would be a silent, doll-like figure wrapped up in folds of black nylon.

In those moments, it was easy to imagine that a ritual of occult communication had just taken place. A medium had been awakened, conducted to a booth, and made to contact the spirit realm. There had been screaming and worry. Now the disturbance had passed. Now the medium would be conducted back to her cave. As the couple glided out of the computer room, the *mahram* would deposit a small stack of coins in Mujahid's hand.

Such was the rhythm of life in our post office. The nearby Shia lived by their own rhythm, which we could hear but not see: their prayer call sounded from their minarets a few minutes earlier than ours did, and their prayers were slightly different, consisting of different supplications, spoken at odd times of the day, and directed to actual people (Hussein and Ali) whom we felt unworthy of attention. We directed our prayers only to God.

The Shia were also strange in that they chewed qat in the afternoons – unthinkable in our section of the valley, and – so rumour had it – practised the *zawaj muta*, or 'pleasure marriage'. The *zawaj muta* was an arrangement in which Shia men paid women – or their families or friends – for a marriage that both parties agreed would expire after a certain period. The periods could be absurdly brief: a month, a week, even an evening. These marriage contracts were blessed by the Shia authorities; sometimes the authorities themselves took a percentage of the value of the contract.

By our lights, prostitution was bad enough. But to make out that Islam condoned such a thing, as the Shia did, with their 'expires at midnight contracts' and stealthy sex, was to parody Islam. It was real-life PimpWar.com. The students and the sheikh felt that the Shia did this to poke a stick in the eye of their more powerful neighbours, the Sunni. Likewise they felt that the Shia habit of extolling their *ruh-allahs* and *ayat-allahs* ('spirit of God' and 'sign of God' respectively) from their minarets was a betrayal of the most fundamental principle of Islam, namely monotheism. From our point of view, these incarnations of God – Rafsanjani, Muqtada al-Sadr, Hassan Nasrallah and so forth – were simply religious hucksters.

'How can these people call themselves Muslims?' our sheikh would thunder from the rooftop of our mosque, 'when they worship men? Men! Muslims must worship none but Allah! Allah alone! He is one! One!'

'If you continue to insult our leaders,' the Shia minarets would reply, 'we will send a missile into your mosque.'

One evening shortly before I left, a rumour passed through our mosque that war with the Shia had begun. The Shia had taken over the two roads leading from Dammaj to the outside world; we were cut off. We would have to fight our way out. No news came from the mosque loudspeaker but older, more experienced students who'd been around during previous wars with the Shia whispered about what would happen next. The women would not emerge from their huts, not even to attend the daytime prayers in the upstairs foyer of the mosque. Every man would have a war job. The married men would look after their wives. Others would defend the fields and the wells. The sheikh's militia would defend his person and the mosque. Still other militiamen would do long-range reconnaissance patrols, monitoring the hills above the village, looking for Shia squadrons.

Unknown persons who succeeded in entering our mosque would be watched for suspicious behaviour. If they did something wrong, or even if they didn't do anything wrong but merely looked wrong, they could be shot on sight.

49

At the height of this tension, my old friend Qais invited me to dinner. By Dammaji standards, his house was a palace. We sat on the floor of his dining room beneath a big TV and a shelf of religious books as his wife, a Yemeni, prepared pizza in her kitchen. His daughter padded around on the carpet in a frilly pink dress. She was three years old and the owner of many fluffy stuffed animals. Beyond the mosquito screen of his front porch, a 1,000-acre vineyard rippled away to the base of distant cliffs. But for the call to prayer, we could have been in California or Provence.

Few students in Dammaj lived in this luxury. Qais, however, was exceptional. He had exceptional talents. Four years earlier he had been one among hundreds of Western religious pioneers in Yemen. He had turned up with his suitcase and a certificate of conversion from an imam in France.

Now, at twenty-six, he owned one of the three Dammaji internet shops, had married a daughter of the land, and was a confidant of the sheikh.

If war with the Shia ever did break out, all the talibs knew that the thousand-strong community of Westerners in Dammaj would look to him for guidance. Should they fight? Lie low? Leave? The students in Dammaj counted on him to strike the right attitude – it would be defiant, passionate and measured. This was Qais.

When I had dinner with him in October of 2006, he and his closest friend, Hamza, a Moroccan French student, originally from Lyon, did not show a hint of worry or interest in the doings of the Shia. The two of them lounged on the floor like happy pashas. 'We will defend our religion,' Qais said, smiling broadly, when I asked him what he would do in the event of a Shia attack. He was in the prime of his life then, with property, a business, and friends.

'Are you sure you want to fight?' I asked.

'We have no choice,' he replied, hardly paying attention. 'Our religion demands it.'

As we waited for our pizza, Qais and Hamza tried to discover if I really had come to Dammaj in order to spy. But they were curious and amused rather than aggressive. How exactly had I arrived in Dammaj? By taxi? By jeep? By CIA helicopter? I explained, fully.

What about my conversion? asked Hamza. I spoke about my stalemate at the newspaper, and my interest in Islam. They had me recite a few verses from the Koran and a hadith or two. They chose easy passages that were so simple and so short it would have been impossible not to have memorised them.

Soon we were on to other topics. Evidently, Qais and Hamza took me as an emissary from the world of universities, newspapers and contemporary knowledge. Once my bona-fides as a Muslim had been established, they asked me to address questions to which their curiosity had turned over the years.

Had there really been thirteen Jewish popes? Did I know that *les frères maçons* had founded America? What about the *Protocols of the Elders of Zion*? Did I know that the Jews planned out every war in the twentieth century one hundred years in advance? The book is a forgery, I said. They disagreed but did not insist.

All such discussions eventually end up at 9/11. How could I be sure that Bush hadn't done it himself? Hamza wanted to know. I spoke about the pilots, Atta, Jarrah, al-Shehhi and Hanjour, their education in Europe, Jarrah's Turkish girlfriend, Atta's work as an urban planner in Hamburg, and their trips back and forth between Germany and Afghanistan. The everyday details of motels in Florida and rental cars were new to Hamza and Qais.

The two of them must have liked listening to me because soon we were talking about my future in the village. I should stay, Qais said. My things could be brought from Sana'a in the next van coming north. The sheikh didn't like people hurrying away. Neither, for that matter, did the talibs.

'Yes, but I just want to go,' I told them. They did not insist.

Towards the end of the evening, when Qais's daughter had toddled off to the kitchen and we were drinking tea, we returned to the topic of war with the Shia.

'Isn't this is a 1,400-year-old squabble?' I said. In my opinion it belonged only to this high-altitude steppe and these two tribes of feuding brothers. 'You, however, do not,' I said. 'If you wanted to, you could learn about the topics that interest you at university in France. You could introduce your wives to Europe.'

Qais smiled. He was long past wondering where his loyalties lay. He hardly bothered to respond in words but let me know how he was feeling by grinning to himself as I talked.

'Allah,' he said when I had finished, 'has given me this house, this wife, and this child. Are you mad? I shouldn't defend this?'

Eventually the discussion tailed off into an academic dispute. I maintained that there were hadith prohibiting Muslims from killing other Muslims. He adduced hadith and Koranic passages to prove that the greatest thing an able-bodied Muslim could do was to defend the religion, the next greatest thing was the defence of the family, and the next greatest thing the defence of the self. In fighting the Shia, he was fulfilling all of these obligations at once.

'You're crazy,' I said.

'You don't understand Islam, my friend,' he said.

The argument of course was merely silly. Qais wanted to participate in a war. His wife supported him. His friends admired him for his boldness. He had passages from the Koran and the hadiths on his side. It wasn't clear that the sheikh was going to allow foreigners to fight, but it wasn't clear that the sheikh would or could stop them, either.

Perhaps success had made Qais a bit bored with his life. Perhaps he felt he had accomplished as much as could be accomplished in this far-flung hamlet. Anyway, his fortunes among the talibs had been rising for some time. He would continue to rise, if Allah willed it, and no amount of friendly talk was going to dissuade him.

Of course, a war with the Shia finally broke out. We knew that it would come some time. It had always come before. I was back in Sana'a by that point and heard about what happened to Qais from a Swedish convert who happened to have been in Dammaj as the war began.

One evening in the winter, Qais volunteered to undertake a long-range reconnaissance patrol with an Algerian friend. He was killed in the dark, without so much as a warning word beforehand or time to say a prayer. His Algerian friend was shot in the leg and managed to escape. Qais took a bullet in the head. By the time I heard about his death, Qais was buried, the war was over, and the wife was preparing to marry one of Qais's friends. To marry the wife of a martyr was an honour for the friend. The sheikh would look after her and her child for ever. It was the will of God, the Swede concluded, and Qais, God's mercy upon him, was in paradise.

50

On the night before I left Dammaj, the sheikh's evening lecture happened to discuss just retribution. The hadith he examined told of an incident early in the life of the first Islamic polity, when a handful of Muslims lived surrounded by the Jews of Medina: 'A Jew crushed the head of a girl between two stones,' said the sheikh into his microphone. He held a gold-embossed volume of hadiths in his lap but recited the text more than he actually read it.

> It was said to her. 'Who has done this to you – such-and-such person? such-and-such person?' When the name of the Jew was mentioned, she nodded with her head, agreeing. So the Jew was brought and he confessed. The Prophet ordered that his head be crushed with the stones.

The purpose of the lecture, as I understood it, was not to fire up the audience with Jew-hatred but to describe the slow, Prophet-like use of retributive violence. It should never be angry. It should be proportionate to the crime. It should crush the enemy the way snakes are crushed.

But perhaps there was another, subtler purpose behind the lecture. They were certainly out there, the sheikh was telling us. These were sick, demented people, inclined to crush little girls' skulls. Perhaps the enemies were Jews; perhaps not. For our part, we were to stick to the *Sunnah*, to the words of our Prophet. We were to wash and fast. We were to stand by one another.

As the sheikh recited and the 3,000 talibs followed along in their gold-embossed volumes, anyone who was thinking about leaving this community of brothers would have felt like a criminal. A person like this would care only for himself. If he left, it was probably because he hoped to desert his brothers, and probably because he meant to make common cause with the demented, sick people of the world.

The farmer who volunteered to drive me back to Sana'a told me to meet him in a lane, on the periphery of the village, just after the morning prayer.

A streak of pale-blue light wavered over the peaks in the east as I emerged from the mosque. He and I and his wife piled into the pickup truck in silence.

In the desert, beyond the last house of the village, the truck floated through thick powdery sand like a sleigh. We fishtailed round the turns and sank through to the desert floor wherever the sand was soft. When the blue streak in the sky opened up a crack, we watched as new light leaked out over the huts, the sand and the grapes.

It was a beautiful, even a holy time to be awake. Under her breath, the driver's wife recited the Sura of the Dawn over and over. It's one of the short, poetical suras. Every convert learns it in his first weeks as a Muslim:

> I seek refuge in the Lord of the Dawn.
> From the mischief of created things;
> From the mischief of Darkness as it overspreads;
> From the mischief of those who practise secret arts.

We drove for a long time on tracks in the desert. Once near a Shia village we ran out of petrol and had to ask the locals to supply us which they did, generously. We passed giant dunes rising like fins out of the desert and abandoned villages. We passed stone hovels from which men emerged who sprinted across the steppe like gazelles, flagged us down and climbed into the bed of the pickup. They wore ragged robes, and wild cavemen beards. I didn't remember having passed this particular clan. Were we going further back into the past? So it seemed. It took us a solid hour of desert driving to regain the government tarmacked road.

We drove further into the south. When we were stopped at a construction site in a small city on the plains, the driver lifted his finger. He pointed to a figure standing on a mound of construction debris, directing a digger.

'See the Jew?' said the driver. He pointed to a shrouded person looking up from the foot of the mound. 'See his woman?' he said.

The town was called Amran, and was the last city in Arabia in which Jews live. About 400 of them out of a population that numbered as many as 60,000 in 1948, still cling to the land here. They chew qat, veil their women, and practise polygamy as Yemenis do. Israel is willing to take them but they believe that the Messiah will only come if they remain in Yemen.

After so many months of discussing Jews in the mosques, I half expected that a real one might be equipped with a cape or shining eyes or some other sign of sinister powers.

In fact, those who remain are digging in. This particular Jew was busy directing a digger which was making repairs to a drainage ditch at the side of his house. These people clearly love the land, manage to get along with some of their neighbours, and do not want to leave.

To Yemenis who do not live in Amran, however, they are performers who stage their desperation in order to wheedle money out of the office of the president. Worse, they consort with foreign powers. My driver felt that the Jews of Yemen cooperated with Christians who came to Yemen equipped with special medicine designed to suppress the reproductive capacity of Muslim women. He believed that the same thing might be happening to Muslims in America. 'Are there very many Jews there?' he wondered quietly, as we stared at the Yemeni Jew and his wife.

'Yes,' I said. He pondered this information. A few minutes later, another question came to him: 'America and Israel are very close?'

'Yes,' I said.

He shook his head slowly. 'They control you,' he murmured. 'The Jews are very powerful, and you do not know it.'

'The Jews of Yemen – do they not impress you with their courage?' I replied. 'With the power of their faith?'

'They are faithful,' he replied, 'but they are from among the enemies of God.'

Arriving in Sana'a, we slipped into a different world. Lines of taxis beeped their horns at the stop lights and qat markets spilled into the highways. Unemployed men sat in battalions on the street corners, staring at the passing traffic. The Ali Abdullah Saleh presidential mosque, which was then only half complete, towered over the city with its four sky-piercing minarets, sixteen domes, aeroplane warning lights, and soaring crenellations.

The driver deposited me at the entrance to the humbler Shariqain mosque. The beggar women in the hallway lifted their hands to me as I passed. Inside, three rows of talibs, or about twenty worshippers, were going through their afternoon prayers. What kind of mosque is this? I thought as I entered the hall. Where was the bustle, the crowd, and where were the 3,000 talibs with their dripping beards and their shining foreheads? Not a single shopkeeper nearby had shuttered a single stall. In Dammaj at this time, not so much as a child could be found stirring outside the mosque and a merchant who kept his stall open was subject to expulsion or worse.

Sana'a clearly belonged to a separate world. A strange abdication of Islam was under way here. Women felt free to sit in public hallways. Shopkeepers didn't pray. Even the talibs at the Shariqain mosque, of whom there were certainly more than twenty, felt free to skip the afternoon prayer.

Really, of course, you can do what you like in Sana'a. No one wonders what you're up to. You can be a reporter, scholar, drunk, student, athlete, woman-chaser or all of these things at once. Like many cities in the Islamic world, it is divided into zones. If you want to live in the anything-goes zone, off you'll go. You're free.

It took me a little while to remember this fact but when I did remember it, I was relieved. I had not given up my apartment in the Old City, and intended to return there as soon as I could gather my things from my dorm room.

Later in the day, praying in a line of new students, recently arrived from Nantes and destined for Dammaj, I wanted to yank on their robes. I wanted to herd them into a corner and shout at them: 'For heaven's sake! Here in Sana'a you have more freedom than you'll find in any religious institution in the countryside. Are you sure you want to leave it?'

These young men, however, were excited about Dammaj.

Had my trip been safe? they wanted to know, and had it cost much?

Life in Dammaj had been almost free. It could have been free but for the internet time I bought and the toothpaste.

'Was there a war on?' someone asked.

'Sort of,' I said. 'Maybe soon.'

The more I talked, the less they listened. They had obviously been planning this voyage for months, if not years. Now they were poised on the cusp of the golden time. They were in no mood to turn back.

Three weeks later Jowad called me. Did I have a room to spare? he asked. Could he stay with me? He would be arriving in Sana'a that afternoon. Could I meet him?

When I brought him home, he found an unused television set in a corner of my apartment and dragged it into the spare bedroom. He hooked it to a satellite dish on the roof, and scattered his clothing across the floor. Within a matter of hours, he had erected a teenage paradise of empty soda cans, half-eaten bags of potato crisps and cheap cologne. Here, he made it known, adults were not permitted. In the mornings, at eleven when I woke him up, the sound on the TV had been turned down but not entirely off. In the two weeks he stayed with me, I'm not sure he ever turned it off, or even, for that matter, switched it from MTV.

As an elder brother I was much too indulgent. But I had never had a younger brother before and had a hard time saying no. I bought him a football jersey and shoes and cheap Chinese sunglasses. He wore a robe on his first day in the city but after that the robes and headscarves vanished. So did the sandals. In the ensuing days, he wore jeans, a leather jacket, and the enormous basketball sneakers that had decorated his mattress-bedroom at the back of the Dammaji mosque. He spoke to taxi drivers and street pedlars in a thick London accent, like a tourist. If anyone mistook him for a Yemeni teenager, he quickly set the person straight: he was an English traveller, passing through. He didn't think much of Yemen, he wanted the cab drivers to know. He had better places to be.

One afternoon, I took him to play football at an international school, in Sana'a. The kit he wore on the field involved his leather jacket, the mirrored aviator glasses, his basketball shoes, and a generous spritzing of sampler perfume we had picked up from a street pedlar. It wasn't an efficient football-playing outfit exactly but it did unfurl a new and unmistakable personal identity, plus cologne. The other players scarcely knew what to make of him. He was an efficient if rusty midfielder, however, who had picked up some useful tricks in London. Once the game got under way, his mixture of teenage fashion and football skill made him stand out as a distinguished addition to the hodgepodge of locals, expat kids and street kids with whom we played.

After two weeks of TV paradise in the Old City, I brought him to the British embassy. They called his mother in London, who promptly made arrangements for his cousins in Sana'a to fetch him. The cousins sent him along to his grandmother in Addis Ababa.

Hem, France, June 2007

51

All morning long, Said and I watched TV bulletins broadcast from someone else's country, *la République française*. Nicolas Sarkozy was about to trounce Ségolène Royal in a landmark election, thus ushering in a government many Muslims in France feared. Said wasn't interested. Anyway, politics were forbidden to him. Football highlights came on later and towards noon women appeared in a TV living room in sparkling dresses.

We did not know who the women were and the scores of the football games meant nothing to either of us. We kept the sound low.

Outside, curtains of rain swept in from Tourcoing and Waterloo. It had been a rainy spring. Now the grass on the lawn in front of Said's mother's house was knee deep. A disused, padlocked chapel at the far end of the lawn was being set upon by a jungle of saplings. If it hadn't been for the police car circling the streets of Said's housing development, it would have been easy to imagine that humans had abandoned the area and that the luxuriant flora of northern France now had the upper hand.

Such was Hem, Said's Algerian enclave outside Roubaix, in early summer, 2007. Hem was empty, with rain showers splashing through the plane trees.

In the afternoon on my first day there, the sun burned through an opening in the clouds. Said and I walked out to a recreational lake nearby to hunt ducks. It had been six months since Said's return from his excursion through the jails of Yemen and Algeria. In that time, he had not looked for a job, and had found no place to live other than his childhood bedroom in his mother's house. She was vacationing in Algeria for the summer.

He had, however, developed a scheme to take advantage of what he felt he was entitled to as a Muslim and a citizen of the French Republic. His plan, which he had already implemented in part, was to live off the fat of the land. He would harvest ducks and potatoes as necessary, while visiting the French super-markets only for staples such as coffee and sugar. Meanwhile, he would construct a proper Islamic course of study for himself from the diversity of options available in Roubaix – the mosques, the study groups, a branch of the Institut du Monde Arabe, the internet – many of which wouldn't cost a penny. Therefore, he would not need to work.

Our first order of business that afternoon was to pursue ducks. 'You sure those things are halal?' I wondered, as he stood in the shallows of the recreational lake, eyeing a family of mallards.

'"Lawful to you is the pursuit of water game, and its use for food." Sura Ma'ida, Ayat ninety-six,' he replied, without moving a muscle.

Evidently he was finished with his search for a true Islamic life in Yemen?

'Of course,' he said.

'And finished with Algeria, too?'

Of course. He had spent two weeks in his mother's Algerian village after his release from the Yemeni jail. The people there had disappointed him: he had found no religious enthusiasm and there had been no formal instruction in the Koran or the hadith in that village or anywhere nearby. As soon as he had adequate cash in hand, he left for France.

Waiting for the mallards to paddle closer to the edge of the lake, Said mused about his experience in Arabia.

'The entire Arab world is a catastrophe,' he said. 'On the level of their economies, their governments, their hospitals, their legal system – every individual thing – and the totality of it is,' he said, '*une catastrophe énorme*.'

France had its problems, I countered. The teenagers in his neighbourhood sold marijuana in broad daylight and at night they torched cars for the sheer pleasure of it. They drank themselves silly, I said, and smashed the city bus shelters, so that in the morning nurses waiting for buses had to stand in pools of shattered glass, like war victims.

'Yes?' he said. 'And so?'

At least there was food enough to live by and if you sought it out at the right mosques, in certain corners of the internet and among knowing friends, the possibility of a proper education. 'You can lead a proper Muslim life here,' he said. 'You have to be very discerning, and very careful to avoid the false doctrines.' He inched towards the ducks. 'It's not complicated,' he whispered. 'Read carefully and believe in Allah. *Voilá, c'est tout.*'

The ducks knew what he was up to. As Said held out his arms, a mother duck went scudding away into the blue depths. Soon the whole family was speeding towards the centre of the lake, where French windsurfers were zipping around in glistening wetsuits.

On that afternoon, Said only managed to catch a tiny crayfish. 'Some Shia forbid the eating of shellfish,' he said as he cradled it in his palm. 'But there is no textual basis for it. We permit it.' We, however, would have had to catch dozens of those crayfish to have had enough for lunch. We ended up eating at Quick Burger.

During this visit to Hem, my arrangement with Said was that I would stay in his father's apartment, which was near his mother's house but in a separate building. Said's father, like his mother, was away in Algeria for the summer. He had given Said the keys to the apartment and had asked him to keep an eye on things. Now this bachelor flat was my home in Hem.

* * *

It contained a heavy TV set, heavy curtains, a single bed, an armchair, a kitchen chair, and place settings for one. On the wall in the kitchen hung a bank calendar which showed the proper prayer times for Muslims living in France. The months of April and May had careful check marks. In the kitchen pantry, I discovered several varieties of tea and a row of half-empty honey-pots. Beyond these hints of personal identity, the apartment was as barren and as anonymous as a hotel room.

After the hunting expedition, Said and I sat at his father's kitchen table, drinking tea and chatting.

'What was the reason behind your parents' divorce?' I asked. He shrugged. It had happened a long time ago.

I knew that his mother and father had arrived in France from Algeria in 1981, and that the father had worked in a textile mill in nearby Roubaix. He had raised three children in Hem, had acquired the large TV, the bachelor flat, and the divorce.

Other than this, the father seemed to have lived out his sojourn in France the way the Koran says humans pass through the world of this life: like a shadow.

I was curious: how, in Said's opinion, had these twenty-six years changed his father? Was he pleased with his sojourn in France or did he regret it? What kind of a person was he, anyway? A dreamer? Angry? Forgiving? Pious? I wanted to know what Said stood to inherit from his father's life. To judge from the apartment itself, he wasn't going to inherit much in the way of things. Maybe the father hoped to pass on an understanding of Islam? or of the French? or of French–Algerian relations?

I tried to ferret out the answers to these questions. They baffled Said. Soon, they were annoying him. 'Why are you so curious?' he wondered when I asked about his father's view of his career in France. 'Why aren't we discussing the unity of God? In any case, as you can see, my father is gone.'

It was true. Both Said's mother and father had retreated to Algeria for an indefinite period. Which left Said by himself in Hem with his plans for an Islamic Emirate of the suburbs. Until I turned up to visit him, he was the only citizen in his emirate. The good thing about my arrival was that it satisfied his need for a subject. Now there was someone to govern, to guide, and to teach.

We spent the next few days wandering through the back alleys of Roubaix, looking for places where we might undertake two weeks of profitable Islamic study. When we were too wet, we ducked into cafes to drink hot Belgian chocolate and to chat with Said's friends, who were, like him, unemployed French Algerian men.

One afternoon, we sat in the car of an ex-distributor of pharmaceutical products as Said told the story of his search for the time of the Prophet in Yemen. The friend listened for several minutes, then interrupted.

'Look, my young friend,' he said, annoyed. 'What to you is the essence of Islam?'

Said stared back at him: there were the five pillars, he said. There were the six articles of the faith.

'Nonsense,' said the friend. 'We don't pray and we don't go to Mecca, yet we are Muslims. No, the essence is respecting your mother and father. The rest is optional. Go tell that to your imams in Yemen.'

Thus ended our conversation. We stepped out of the car into a rain shower.

Later that afternoon, we passed the Da'wa Mosque but declined to go inside. The people there were too finicky and too doctrinaire, Said said. *'Ils haramment tout.'* We passed the Institut du Monde Arabe – too governmental – and a storefront Arabic language institute into which we poked our heads. Classes had been suspended for the summer.

'Come back in September,' said a secretary.

'Merci, madame,' we said.

In the middle of an especially violent downpour we took shelter in the cellphone shop of a Salafi brother. We considered buying a cellphone equipped with an electronic muezzin but the cost was out of reach for both of us. The shop owner, a friend from Said's estate, invited us to pray in the stockroom.

He locked the door of the shop and we stood on chilly tiles in our soaking clothing as a computer file made the call to prayer.

On our way back to Said's house, we encountered an acquaintance, Tarek, strolling across a lawn. It was possible to study the true Islam in France via the internet, Tarek suggested, but not in the French mosques. He wore a long beard, slacks and carried a baguette, which was destined, apparently, for a wife and child in a nearby apartment.

'Before 9/11, the government used to let in preachers from Algeria, from Yemen, from everywhere,' he said. 'You could live here and at the same time really study Islam. But now they've blocked it all at the borders. If you really want to study,' he advised, 'you've got to go abroad.' He nodded at his baguette: 'I have a child and a wife here. I have my obligations.'

Later that evening, we dropped by the mosque around the corner from Said's mother's house. In the early sixties, when the housing development was young, the mosque had been a supermarket. Now the freezers and shelves had been replaced by wall-to-wall carpeting.

As we stepped inside, the call to prayer tinkled through the public-address system. It was so faint that it might have been an echo of the vanished shopping music.

Said and I washed in the sinks that had once been used by butchers and supermarket fishmongers, then prostrated ourselves in a row of elderly Algerians. It was a quick, mechanical prayer performed without an imam. When we were finished, the retired men with whom we were praying shuffled away from the rows in silence, with their eyes on the ground, as if they were embarrassed by what they had done.

Since Said and I had nowhere to go afterwards, we spent the remainder of the evening sitting outside, on the plaza of the former supermarket. A local figure named Rachid gave audiences there in the evening. On this occasion, he happened to be holding forth on the education he had received in Saudi Arabia. A cluster of curious onlookers in tracksuits listened as he described the discipline of his life there, the heat, and the not always sincere Saudi practice of Islam.

During the discussion, one of the tracksuits asked Rachid to comment on Said's practice: what about his programme of living on the bounty of the French countryside? 'Those are French ducks,' Rachid scolded, 'and that is a French lake for windsurfers.' He turned a cold eye on Said: 'You are stealing from the municipality if you eat those ducks,' he said. 'This is one of the major sins and wrongs in Islam.'

'They are the ducks of Allah,' Said protested.

A squabble ensued. At least Said had a programme and a plan for living an Islamic life in France, said Said. Whereas Rachid, in Said's view, had no job, no plans for a job, and spent his free time hanging out on the mosque terrace, blowing hot air.

Rachid's face darkened. He accused Said of blabbering about Islam when in fact he knew very little. He accused Said of bringing me, a person who might possibly be an American spy and who was certainly an outsider, to the neighbourhood mosque. 'You told Thabit that I spent five years in Saudi Arabia. Why?' he demanded. 'Why?'

Said apologised.

'I don't like it when people speak about me at all, period,' Rachid announced. He stood up from the wall on which we were sitting, shook hands in silence, and walked away, alone.

In Rachid's absence, the role of ranking Islamic authority on the mosque plaza reverted to Said. The half-dozen young men in tracksuits knew he was no academic expert but they were interested in his adventures. They knew he had been in jail, and knew that Yemen was a dangerous, even an extreme place in which to be a Muslim. They wanted to hear more.

At first Said and I chatted with them, dropping hints but revealing little. We watched the sun set, and looked down the street to where the teenage drug dealers of Hem were assembling for an evening of friendship and commerce.

Eventually Said warmed to his topic. His diffidence about the Arab world fell away. He did have some knowledge to share, after all, it turned out. It wasn't knowledge of the Jews such as we had gained in Yemen nor was it exactly knowledge of the time of the Prophet. He skipped over the qat addiction and the decrepit state of the bureaucracy, aspects of life which had tortured him when he was in Sana'a.

Instead, he spoke about the 5,000 brothers who stood at one's shoulders as one prayed in Dammaj, and the way any student could become fluent in the ancient Arabic of the Koran just by going about his daily life in the streets of Sana'a. He also spoke at length about the Yemeni-Salafi style of prayer, derived from the hadiths In his view, this was exactly how the Prophet had prayed, and it had been preserved in Yemen as nowhere else on earth.

The six young men on the mosque plaza did not argue or fidget or challenge. Perhaps they didn't believe everything Said said but they were clearly prepared to listen to any tale involving a departure from Hem.

So for a little while, as the drug dealers swooped around on their BMX bikes, and a new trickle of Algerian pensioners shuffled into the supermarket, Said owned the mosque plaza. He expatiated. No other authority, religious or otherwise, was vying for the souls of his audience, as far as I could tell, except perhaps for the drug dealers who were, for the time being, otherwise occupied.

So Said talked on, like someone who had come into his own at last, after a long period of pennilessness. 'Are you Muslims?' he said. 'Well, take what's yours then. They don't sell knowledge in the Arabic world; it belongs to us all. It is free.'

Everything he said was true. It wasn't the entire truth exactly but it did establish that something exciting was happening in Yemen, and it communicated how open and welcoming the Straight Path in Yemen was. In fact Said had developed a skill in the mosques of Sana'a and Dammaj: he had become an effective communicator of the *da'wa* – the invitation to Islam.

Now he was working with powerful subject matter – the simple beauty of life on the Straight Path – and on this evening, the combination was more than enough to keep his audience from wandering away.